Does Community Development Work?

Praise for this book

'The beauty of the book is its eloquence in demonstrating the possibilities of a decolonized, emancipatory community development, not just in theory but in practice. The authors demonstrate that creating transformative knowledge and practice, unfettered by what one already knows or assumes, requires radical thinking, co-inquiry engagement, and a reflexivity of discomfort about our own subjectivities and power. It is a must read for all those interested in the praxis of decolonization.'

Professor Stella M. Nkomo, University of Pretoria

'The authors successfully introduce the importance of a community-led integrated micro-macro level community development framework, together with the four most applicable approaches available to practitioners.

This book provides a timely introduction for students, practitioners and citizens into the history, context and suggested future framework for community development in South Africa, aligned with the contemporary global context of decolonization.

The richly described case studies, and the authors' convincing argument for self-reflective practice, will appeal to community development practitioners at all levels.'

Cornel Hart, University of the Western Cape

'One of the greatest challenges of our contemporary world is inequality. It is leading to a more polarized world and we cannot address this challenge unless we come together as a community. This is as much a question of practice as a question of policy and government intervention. But such practice is unlikely to be effective unless we deliberate on the science of community development. This book is facilitative of this deliberation on the science of community development practice, reflecting deeply on the philosophy, methodology and case studies of community development. Authored by academics who have long been immersed in this community of practice, the book is a necessary read for all those interested in inclusive development and social cohesion.'

Adam Habib, Vice-Chancellor and Principal of the University of the Witwatersrand

'This book is a must read for community development workers at this critical moment in our global history. Traditional development work has often subjugated communities to comply with the status quo – fitting into what exists now. The critical questions – with whom are we aligned, who benefits from economic policies and structures, and do communities have a say in their own destiny – are deeply discussed in this book. Protests globally indicate that there needs to be a reconstruction of development, and this book provides insights, progressive analysis, and some pragmatic ways forward.'

Sally Timmel, co-author of Training for Transformation, Vol. 1-4, and founder or co-founder of seven non-profit organisations in South Africa post-apartheid

'This is a book that rings bells and switches on lights. It is fresh and rooted in real life experiences, contemporary, visionary, practical and accessible, working with accounts of deep practice, with insights to stimulate the thinking and guidance that can support us through the obscure messiness and paradoxes of social change. Rigorous academically and grounded in reality.'

Doug Reeler, Development Practitioner, Tamarind Tree Associates and the Barefoot Guide Connection

Does Community Development Work?

Stories and practice for reconstructed community development in South Africa

Peter Westoby and Lucius Botes

Practical Action Publishing Ltd
27a, Albert Street, Rugby, Warwickshire, CV21 2SG, UK
www.practicalactionpublishing.com

© Peter Westoby and Lucius Botes (2020)

The moral right of the editors to be identified as editors of the work and the contributors to be identified as contributors of this work have been asserted under sections 77 and 78 of the Copyright Design and Patents Act 1988.

All rights reserved. No part of this publication may be reprinted or reproduced or utilized in any form or by any electronic, mechanical, or other means, now known or hereafter invented, including photocopying and recording, or in any information storage or retrieval system, without the written permission of the publishers.

Product or corporate names may be trademarks or registered trademarks, and are used only for identification and explanation without intent to infringe.

A catalogue record for this book is available from the British Library.

A catalogue record for this book has been requested from the Library of Congress.

ISBN 978-1-788531-29-0 Paperback
ISBN 978-1-788531-30-6 Hardback
ISBN 978-1-788531-31-3 Epub
ISBN 978-1-788531-32-0 PDF

Citation: Westoby, P., Botes, L., (2020) *Does Community Development Work?: Stories and practice for reconstructed community development in South Africa*, Rugby, UK: Practical Action Publishing < http://dx.doi.org/10.3362/9781788531320 >.

Since 1974, Practical Action Publishing has published and disseminated books and information in support of international development work throughout the world. Practical Action Publishing is a trading name of Practical Action Publishing Ltd (Company Reg. No. 1159018), the wholly owned publishing company of Practical Action. Practical Action Publishing trades only in support of its parent charity objectives and any profits are covenanted back to Practical Action (Charity Reg. No. 247257, Group VAT Registration No. 880 9924 76).

The views and opinions in this publication are those of the author and do not represent those of Practical Action Publishing Ltd or its parent charity Practical Action.

Reasonable efforts have been made to publish reliable data and information, but the authors and publisher cannot assume responsibility for the validity of all materials or for the consequences of their use.

Cover credit: Practical Action Publishing
Printed on demand

Contents

Tables, figures, boxes, and maps — vii
Abbreviations — ix
Acknowledgements — xi
About the authors — xiii
Foreword — xv
Peer review declaration — xvi

1. Introduction — 1

PART I: CONTEXT AND PERSPECTIVES

2. The South African context: The double story — 17
3. Where we are coming from — 29
4. Community development effectiveness – how do we know what we know? — 47

PART II: INTENTIONS AND IDEAS

5. Reaching for a social reconstruction tradition — 61
6. Reconstructing frameworks for practice — 77

PART III: AN ASSEMBLAGE OF STORIES AND POSSIBILITIES

7. Accompanying, horizontal learning, and structuring: Political practice and the Southern Cape Land Committee — 92
8. Action learning and research, food security and Abalimi Bezekhaya — 107
9. Staged place-based community development and the Hantam Community Education Trust — 119
10. From marginalization to destiny: Anger, violence, and community protest in South Africa — 135
11. Informal housing and community development: A historical and human rights approach — 153

http://dx.doi.org/10.3362/9781788531320.000

12. 'Seeing like a state' and neo-colonial cooperative
    development within South Africa   169
13. Interlude: In dialogue with Es'kia – the decolonial turn   183
14. In conclusion: Promissory reflections   193

Index   201

Tables, figures, boxes, and maps

Tables

9.1	The five stages of place-based work	122
9.2	Levels of maturity of people's organizations	125
11.1	Key national programmes in housing provision and creating sustainable settlements	161
12.1	Relationship between community development and cooperative formation	172

Figures

6.1	The colonizing-decolonizing cycle	87
8.1	The farmer development chain for organic farming projects	114
10.1	Major service-delivery protests, by year (2004–2018)	138
10.2	Service-delivery protests by province, 2018	138

Box

6.1	Stages of professional development	78

Map

7.1	Locational map of the Republic of South Africa with markers for the stories and case studies	92

Abbreviations

ABCD	asset-based community development
AIDS	acquired immunodeficiency syndrome
ANC	African National Congress
APF	Anti-Privatization Forum
BCM	Black Consciousness Movement
BEE	Black Economic Empowerment
BLARF	Baviaans Land and Agrarian Reform Forum
BRICS	Brazil, Russia, India, China, and South Africa
CBO	community-based organization
CBP	community-based planning
CDE	Centre for Development and Enterprise
CDP	community development practitioner
CDRA	Community Development Resource Association
CDW	community development worker
CDS	Centre for Development Support
CDPP	Community Development Practitioner Programme
CDWP	Community Development Worker Programme
COPAC	Cooperative and Policy Alternative Centre
CSA	community-supported agriculture
DFID	Department for International Development
DSD	Department of Social Development
DTI	Department of Trade and Industry
ECD	early childhood development
FEDUP	Federation of Urban Poor
GEAR	Growth, Employment And Redistribution
HoH	Harvest of Hope
HDI	Human Development Index
INGO	international non-government organization
Khanya-aicdd	Khanya-African Institute for Community-Driven Development
LED	local economic development
MIT	Massachusetts Institute of Technology
NGO	non-government organization
NPO	non-profit organization
NQF	National Qualification Framework
PHP	People's Housing-Project
PLAAS	Institute for Poverty, Land and Agrarian Studies

PO	people's organization
RDP	Reconstruction and Development Programme
SAQA	South African Qualification Authority
SCAR	Southern Cape Against Removals
SCLC	Southern Cape Land Committee
SDGs	Sustainable Development Goals
SDI	Shack Dwellers International
SEDA	Small Enterprise Development Agency
SLA	sustainable livelihoods approach
SMSE	small and medium-sized enterprise
TfT	Training for Transformation
UK	United Kingdom
UN	United Nations
URP	Urban Renewal Programme
USA	United States of America

Acknowledgements

Peter and Lucius

This book is a product of a 14-year friendship between Peter and Lucius. It shares with its authors a deep respect for the challenges of community development practice but it also holds vivid impressions of the importance of community resilience and the possibilities within community development.

This work would not have been possible without the support of staff and colleagues at the University of the Free State (particularly those within the Centre for Development Support – special thanks to Willem Ellis, Lochner Marais, and Anita Harmse) and North-West University (the Faculty of Economic and Management Sciences), South Africa. Specific thanks to Cecile van Zyl of North-West University for the language editing, Adeline Ngie for developing the case-study map of South Africa, Martie Esterhuizen for the literature searches, Herman van der Merwe, Babs Surujlal, and Angelica van Rensburg (North-West University) for their support, and Belinda Eslick of Queensland University of Technology for editing and uploading the manuscript. Thanks also to Queensland University of Technology, Brisbane, Australia, and North-West University, South Africa, for their support in our research endeavours.

Special and specific thanks go to many people for generously giving us their time – accounted as stories within this book. They include:

- Rob Small of the Abalimi Home and Community Garden Movement.
- Angela Conway, Phumi Booysen, Patrick Sambo, Amos Dyasi, Nettly Maarman, Chriszanne, Oom Elias Rens, Oom Arrie, Oom Jaffie, and members of Baviaans Land and Agrarian Reform Forum (BLARF) of Southern Cape Land Committee.
- Rubert van Blerk and Nomvula Dlamini at CDRA.
- Sam Chimbuya from Khanya-aicdd.
- Lesley Osler and so many other un-named staff of the Hantam Community Education Trust.
- Thabo Masukela and Mahlomola Mahloba, Public Participation Officers at the Department of Cooperative Governance and Traditional Affairs.
- Members of Dillo Disabled Primary Cooperative, Makawe Financial Services Coop, Halala Basadi Primary Cooperative, Thaba Blinds Cooperative, and Mamello Support Group.

To the many people of the Department of Social Development who were constantly gracious within the partnership we developed. Particular thanks to Sadi Luka, Mpontseng Kumeke, Mbulaheni Mulaudzi, Lindiwe Mahlangu, Harry Diamond, Makhetha Thabana, and Lucy Xaba.

Last but not least, our sincere appreciation to the Es'kia Mphahlele Foundation (in particular Puso Mphahlele and Pascal Mphahlele) for their support and permission to include the texts from the work of Es'kia, their grandfather.

Peter

To a fellow sojourner in the mysteries of a soul-life, Verne Harris, what can I say? This book would not have been possible without those many weekends in the mountains, endless email dialogues, and Melville conversations.

Also, thanks for the hospitality, friendships, and engaged conversation of so many South Africans – but special thanks go to Allan Kaplan and Sue Davidoff, Sipho Sokhela, Angela Conway, Sue Soal, Holle Wolkas, and Rubert van Blerk. Without each significant contribution it wouldn't have been possible. Finally, thanks to Emily McConochie for giving significant input to the text, space for dialogue, and accompanying over many years.

Lucius

Special thanks to Zachi (Sethulego) Matebesi, who was my student and colleague and now my fellow sociologist and lifelong friend. From you I learned a lot about community dynamics and civil strife in the townships of South Africa.

Also to Lochner Marais and Johannes Wessels who introduced me to many of South Africa's housing challenges and the importance of human and humane settlements.

About the authors

Peter Westoby works, teaches, and researches on the borderlands between community development and other disciplines and fields of practice, from phenomenology, dialogue, depth psychology, peace and conflict, and forced migration. He has worked accompanying youth, community, and organization for 30 years, from places as far afield as South Africa, Uganda, Vanuatu, Papua New Guinea, Nepal, Philippines, Brazil, and Australia. He is an associate professor in social science and community development at the School of Public Health & Social Work at Queensland University of Technology; a visiting professor at the Centre for Development Support, University of the Free State, South Africa; and a director with Community Praxis Cooperative.

Lucius Botes is a scholar in the fields of development studies, sociology of developing societies, development economics, and community development. He is a professor in development studies and the director of research development in the Faculty of Economic and Management Sciences, at North-West University (South Africa) and a director of the Karoo Development Foundation. His research and teaching work include the domains of development studies, participatory development, socio-economic research, affordable housing research, local economic development, sustainable livelihood analysis, municipal cost recovery, community protests and service-delivery protests, survey research, and methodologies. His work predominantly covers South Africa, Namibia, Zambia, and Zimbabwe. He acts as a development and research consultant to international and national organizations, government departments and companies, and is a director/trustee of various NGOs.

Foreword

Despite increasing calls for decolonizing knowledge and practice in Africa, there is much less specificity about how to transform what has been designated as universal and hegemonic. As a scholar grappling with decoloniszing management and organization knowledge, I welcome this book. The beauty of *Does Community Development Work? Stories and practice for reconstructed community development in South Africa* is its eloquence in demonstrating the possibilities of a decolonized, emancipatory community development for the country, not just in theory but in practice. The authors demonstrate that creating transformative knowledge and practice, unfettered by what one already knows or assumes, requires radical thinking, co-inquiry engagement, and a reflexivity of discomfort about our own subjectivities and power. It is a must read for all those interested in the praxis of decolonization.

Professor Stella M. Nkomo, University of Pretoria, South Africa;
co-author of the critically acclaimed Harvard Business School
Press book, *Our Separate Ways: Black and White Women
and the Struggle for Professional Identity* (2003)

Peer review declaration

The Publisher endorses the South African 'National Scholarly Book Publishers Forum Best Practice for Peer Review of Scholarly Books'. The manuscript was subjected to a rigorous blind peer review prior to publication. The three reviewers were independent of the publisher and/or authors in question. The reviewers commented positively on the scholarly merits of the manuscript and recommended that the manuscript be published. Where the reviewers recommended revision and/or improvements to the manuscript, the authors responded adequately to such recommendations.

CHAPTER 1
Introduction

Abstract

Chapter 1 provides a brief overview of the authors' perspectives on community development, and the goals of the book. Three analytical frameworks are discussed: (1) The seeing and making sense of community development; (2) A decolonial perspective; (3) Does community development work?

Keywords: perspectives, analytical frameworks, community development

Not so long ago, a dear colleague of ours, Dr Lynda Shevellar, was participating in an international conference on 'the politics of evidence'. On stage were some academically credentialled presenters being questioned about community development. One of the presenters, a Massachusetts Institute of Technology (MIT) global policy leader and researcher, stated, without blinking an eyelid, 'The research shows that community development does not work'. Our colleague was incredulous, and came back home with a renewed determination to strengthen the theory and practice of community development.

With this in mind, one of our goals has been to write a book and examine community development in a way that such an ignorant statement by an MIT professor is shown to be patently untrue. As will be shown, such a statement can only be untrue when the utterer fails to take into account the *unambiguous* history of people working together in their communities to make a better life.

However, let us not conflate two aspects. Communities, or people working together *as a community*, have made a better life. But, how about the 'practice' of community development, deployed by *practitioners, workers, professionals, civic organizations, NGOs, states* and, increasingly, *private-sector commercial enterprises*? And by 'practice', we mean a clear set of practices with a clear intention, supported by an infrastructure of journals, workshops, conferences, and so forth. That is, a 'practice' as a profession. So, *how well is professional community development doing?* Perhaps it is not as unambiguous in terms of effectiveness.

From our combined rich experience, community development is certainly not perfect, not revolutionary, not solving the endemic structural problems of power, powerlessness, and poverty; perhaps community development is even marginal to the big picture of society – yet it is making *some* people's lives a little better. And obviously, to the kind of statement the MIT professor made, a reply would be: 'What kind of community development are you talking

http://dx.doi.org/10.3362/9781788531320.001

about?', and, 'Considering all the community-led or community-based initiatives around the world – even those supported by professional practitioners – that continue to impact profoundly for good on people's lives, in what way does it not work?'

With this in mind, we state clearly and unequivocally that there is no such 'thing' as community development in the Platonic sense that a pure version of anything exists. Instead, while community development has a reasonably clear 'in order to' – in the sense of function and hoped-for intention and effect – which is about group or collective forms of social change where 'community' is both the site and vehicle of social change – there are then various kinds of community development praxis depending on the theory and practice drawn upon. In stating this, we acknowledge and position ourselves as coming from post-structural, deconstructive, and decolonizing perspectives. We briefly explain these here, but readers should jump to Chapter 2 for a more extensive discussion.

Briefly, our perspectives

Although we talk about being **post-structural**, disrupting essentialist perspectives, we do not subscribe to a rigid theory of community development. Instead, we have looked at the field of community development through multiple sets of practices and disciplines; we have paid attention to what is conceivable to be imagined as community development; we have engaged in multiple dialogical and relational encounters to understand practice in South Africa; we have subjected our own logic to a rigorous scrutiny; we have looked historically at the practice; looked critically at community development; and have also examined its effects or impacts. In doing this, we have then come to a *best possible account* of what community development might be (in this point in time). The 'best possible account' is the post-structural imperative.

The added **deconstructive angle** is to recognize that, again, while community development has historical roots – originary concepts (to do with collective efforts, working 'with' communities; working 'for' social justice; and yet also tainted with problematic elements of colonial thinking – entangled in the globalizing idea of 'development', and doing things 'for' communities) – there are also inherent tensions, contradictions, and fissures. In light of this, again, there is no 'true' community development. Instead, there are many kinds, and yet there is also – as per Jacques Derrida's philosophy, always the hauntology of justice – the call to justice. A deconstructive angle is therefore *a call to renewal*, ensuring that community development theory and practice do not get stuck. New issues and contexts constantly insist on reform in the programme or discourse of community development. We hope this book will contribute to this reform, or reconstruction, as per the subtitle.

To frame community development in this post-structural and deconstructive way is to also start a **decolonizing process** *within the project of community development* itself. If the deconstructive element insists on renewal, then surely the most urgent renewal is that of rethinking community development in light of big issues such as growing inequalities, human-induced climate change, and recent events such as the global pandemic of COVID-19, but also – and this is the reconstruction we mostly aim for – the 'decolonial turn'. Such a renewal in turn is an intervention into one of the 'epic intellectual struggles' of the day – between subjugated knowledge, stolen lands, epistemologies, stories, praxis, and that which is dominant. This is a vexed and complex question in Africa generally and South Africa particularly, for the land question foregrounds both the social justice questions of land and the 1913 Land Act – linked to current land reform endeavours – and also the more direct and difficult question of returning lands to particular Indigenous owners of land, discussed as the Khoi-San in the Human Rights Commission report 'National Hearing Relating to the Human Rights Situation of the Khoi-San ...' (Human Rights Commission, 2016). Struggles to reclaim stolen land – for all Africans, and also the Khoi-San – represent parallel and yet different struggles, hence the need for specific human rights hearings for the latter. In saying this, like the report cited above, we recognize that, 'While all Africans may rightly be considered indigenous to Africa, recognition must be given to the fact that some groups are structurally more marginalized and vulnerable than others' (ibid: 17). Hence we are using the term 'Indigenous' both in the generic meaning of Africans generally, and also in reference to particular groups that are systematically discriminated against, such as the Khoi-San.

The question, 'does community development work?' occurs within this historical context of a decolonial turn and epic struggle, and we endeavour to signpost a decolonizing perspective. In light of this, we were tempted to put 'decolonizing' where we have put 'reconstructed' in the subtitle. Feel free to insert 'decolonizing' as well.

So, in a nutshell, we are for a renewed community development that aims to decolonize the minds, imaginations, and praxis of professional practitioners and people (through dialogue, critical thinking, healing, accountability, and concrete action), and also for transforming practices and institutions that are infused with 'dominator culture' (hooks, 2010). Like Chela Sandoval's *Methodology of the Oppressed* (2000), community development that is in dialogue with, or responsive to, this decolonial turn is reaching for a 'set of processes, procedures, and technologies for decolonizing the imagination' (Sandoval, 2000: 68). Community development, in decolonizing renewal, aims to expand people's 'imaginative literacy' and 'epistemological curiosity' (Freire, 1997: 100), seeking – as Subcommander Marcos of the Zapatista puts it – 'a world in which there is room for many worlds'. Yet, decolonizing requires work that is beyond just the imaginary and epistemological. As Tuck and Yang (2012) remind us, 'decolonisation is not a metaphor' – it is also a set of practices that disrupt settler perspectives and often foreground the core issue of land (or stolen land during colonization).

Such a renewal in no way means anyone can make the certain claim of what 'must definitely' be done, certainly not two white male practitioners, scholars, activists. People and practitioners can only make a case – a best interpretation of 'what they think community development is, and what should happen' – which is what we will be doing. However, we can weigh up arguments and make some claims in light of the perspectives we have outlined and expand on in Chapter 3. Anyone craving certainty or a simple 'how to do' manual might want to toss this book aside about now.

While coming from such post-structural, deconstructive, and decolonizing perspectives, we do, however, want to demonstrate – through an assemblage of stories and possibilities, emergent from many relational and dialogical encounters and inquiries over several years – how community development *can work*. In many ways, the answer lives somewhat in discovering afresh what the qualities of the practitioner are, what 'the practice' is, and what the practices are that make for effective community development that is responsive to reconstruction and the decolonial turn.

The second goal of this book is to concretize the vision and hopes articulated by the (late) South African scholar-activist-humanitarian-revolutionary Neville Alexander, who argued that:

> besides the ongoing political and economic class struggles in which we are willy-nilly involved, and by means of which we attempt to create and consolidate more democratic space in the short to medium term, we have to go back to the community development tasks that the [Black Consciousness Movement (BCM)] initiated so successfully, if not always sustainably owing to the ravages of the apartheid system (Alexander, 2013: 199).

He goes on to argue that:

> we have to rebuild our communities and our neighbourhoods by means of establishing, as far as possible on a voluntary basis, all manner of community projects that bring visible short-term benefit to the people and that initiate at the same time the trajectories of fundamental social transformation. ... These could range from relatively simple programmes such as keeping the streets and public toilets clean, preferably in liaison with the local authority, whether or not it is 'delivering' at this level, to more complex programmes such as bulk-buying clubs, community reading clubs, enrichment programmes for students preparing for exams, teachers' resource groups at the local level and, of course, sports and cultural activities on a more convivial basis (Alexander, 2013: 200).

This is a strong vision, but one grounded in what our research indicates is happening in *some* South African spaces. There is a huge amount of community-based and community-led work occurring within South Africa, and there are numerous networks linking or converging – as Alexander puts it – into a vibrant socio-political space where alternative worlds are being imagined and created. From a decolonizing angle, this is the work of undoing or creating alternatives to the dominator culture. The point is, they do exist, however fragile or vibrant – and Alexander's vision is being made true, and the MIT professor's analysis is found to be banal and false.

Community and micro-macro articulation

While coming from post-structural, deconstructive, and decolonizing perspectives on community development, we also recognize that 'community' has a key role, both as site (a place) and vehicle (method) in social change. We do this because 'community' is the 'mezzanine floor between the small and large' (Kelly and Westoby, 2018: 9). In this sense, 'community' reaches to the very personal and private domain of the everyday lives of South Africans – individual, family, household – and yet reaches for the larger world of the public sphere – the spaces of statecraft, society, and market. The links between the small and micro – and large and public – are what Chilean economist Manfred Max-Neef (1991) refers to as 'micro-macro' articulation. By this, he is referring to the linkages between community-level transformational work and larger system changes. Such linkages are expressed in Alexander's vision of community development 'that initiate[s] at the same time the trajectories of fundamental social transformation' (Alexander, 2013: 200). As we will discover, effective community development 'should' be cognizant of such micro-macro-institutional issues.

The possibilities – our vision as practitioners

Another goal is to probe or provoke community development workers to not only think about their practice, but also to think about their vision of society. In this sense, we are interested in what sociologist Erik Olin Wright has called 'emancipatory social science' (Wright, 2010). We argue that while community development workers may have a clear *practice*, working *with communities*, they also need to have a clear *vision* – or, in Wright's language, a 'real utopia' for society. It is not enough to work with communities based on *only their vision* of what they want. It is important for community development practitioners to bring to communities, in a spirit of dialogue and accompanying, a desirable, viable, and achievable vision of society. Such a vision should be emancipatory if the practice is to be informed by a decolonizing perspective. Alexander's quote above indicates that he had a vision, and we are also going to argue that community development practitioners need to be able to articulate a renewed vision for society.

For example, it is not enough to work with a community that wants to get rid of so-called illegal migrants or refugees, or annoying young people, because this could contravene a community development worker's vision of global and local social justice. Furthermore, it is probably not emancipatory if the community development vision is of 'everyone in society becoming an entrepreneur'. In turn, community development is certainly not taking decolonization seriously if it's ignoring the central issue of needing to return stolen land and be accountable to those who lost their land. Community development workers then need to not only think *pragmatically* and *ethically* about what will work – that is, how to get done what a community wants – but also *normatively*, with a clear vision of social, cultural, environmental, political, and economic justice, along with decolonization imperatives. Such a vision cuts through those traces or trajectories of dominator culture manifest in discrimination due to class, race, gender, disa/ability, and even ageism. However, within a particular South African context, as per any African country still embroiled in the epic struggle between colonization and decolonization, this justice vision must be expanded to include an epistemological and ontological struggle; that is, a vision of how Indigenous and African *epistemology* and *philosophy* might also inform community development praxis.

Our inquiry in focus

With these goals and thoughts in mind, the inquiry informing this book involved constantly asking, 'Does community development work?', or, more accurately, because any half-baked researcher will suggest that a closed question is not a good one, 'What makes for effective community development?' – where the effect includes a decolonizing dimension that accounts for the reconstructed community development required.

Three analytical frameworks for community development

In responding to our research inquiry, three analytical frameworks have been developed: the first is to do with how we 'see and make sense of community development'; the second is to do with what the renewal of a decolonizing perspective means; and the third is to do with the question of 'does it work, or what makes it effective?'

Analytical framework (1) The seeing and making sense of community development

This first analytical framework provides interpretive clarity to understanding how people are organizing themselves, or are being accompanied in organizing, using 'community' approaches to social change. Within this analytical approach, we draw on a framework with four dimensions.[1]

Firstly, we examine what is occurring within the field of actual community development practice, that is, taking a look at what *is* going on, but we do this searching for stories of renewed community development, dealing with some of the difficult issues of the day – from land to education, housing to livelihoods. In this sense, the book is a series of essays reflecting on *what we interpret as going on* in light of our post-structural, deconstructive, and decolonizing perspectives.

Secondly, the framework draws on multi-, inter-, and trans-disciplinary approaches. Recognizing that community development is not only a political or social activity, but also an economic, cultural, environmental, and even spiritual and emotional practice, requires engagement with different disciplines (multi), integrating different knowledge (inter), and also working for new frameworks emerging from working with people-in-communities (the trans). Our analytical frame provides the conceptual space to engage with any or all of these dimensions of community development practice as encountered. Importantly, as per the decolonizing perspective, the framework also acknowledges the importance of epistemological, linguistic, philosophical, and material violence, and foregrounds some of the issues to do with knowledge, language, philosophy, and materiality, such as land.

Thirdly, the framework is comparative, arguing that how the poor are organizing themselves, or at times being supported or accompanied in organizing, within South Africa, should be recognizable and comparable with what is taking place in other parts of the world. South Africa, like anywhere, shapes the practice, but there is no 'special case' or exceptionalism – something we have often encountered, with commentators suggesting, 'Peter and Lucius, what you must understand is that the South African situation is unique'. It is not.

Finally, while not supporting any exceptionalism, the framework is historical and contextual, recognizing that community development does have a *particular history* within South Africa.

Analytical framework (2) A decolonial perspective

We have suggested that the urgent deconstructive renewal of community development requires, among other things, a recognition of, and reshaping by, the 'decolonial turn'. This is thereby an intervention into one of the 'epic intellectual struggles' of the day – between subjugated knowledge, epistemologies, stories, praxis, and that which is dominant. With this in mind, we suggest that a decolonizing perspective on community development engages with *at least* the following.

Firstly, a decolonizing perspective accepts and endeavours to understand how colonial histories trace into the present, shaping people's lived experience. While we do not conduct substantive analysis on this, we do draw on the likes of Frantz Fanon's work, seminal in post-colonial thinking, and also more recent attempts to link community development with ongoing woundedness, as per van der Watt's work in the Richtersveld among the Nama people (a clan of the San) (2016; 2018). Issues of intergenerational, along with social and political trauma become pertinent as communities seek to both heal individual and social bodies, along with transforming their material and political realities. We add, drawing on the disrupting thought of Tuck and Yang (2012), that a decolonizing perspective also offers 'a different perspective to human and civil rights based approaches to justice, an unsettling one, rather than complimentary one. Decolonization is not an "and". It is an elsewhere' (2012: 36). Such an 'elsewhere' will be disruptive, not necessarily enabling easy coalitions between those struggling for different kinds of social justice.

Secondly, we consider how the actual project of community development, holding those contradictory traces of both emancipatory hopes alongside colonial concepts – such as 'development' – can be decolonized to be a practice of solidarity and collective social change. Recognition of the colonial traces then invites practitioners to be aware of the 'ideas' (or myths) often hidden unconsciously in their practice (often linked to colonial, racist, sexist, or classist assumptions). In turn, this recognition insists on pertinent questions such as: how will stolen lands be returned to original owners?

Thirdly, a reflexivity on the project of community development subsequently engages with the vexed question of 'the professional', professionalization, and positionality. Who are 'we' doing this work, and what do 'we' bring? In turn, what does a decolonial perspective offer to questions on the professionalization of community development, and also what it might mean to be a professional reflexively engaged with positionality, as well as being accountable to Indigenous peoples.

Fourthly, while exploring the 'project of community development', we also consider the actual community development practices that support a decolonizing approach. It is not enough to 'talk' about the decolonial turn – the issue is *what is done differently* as a result of this turn. We want to ensure decolonization is not an empty signifier, but is a disruptive set of practices unsettling everyone (the politics of land being taken from settlers and/or returned to original owners would be an example of unsettling practice – and land reform politics in South Africa certainly evidence this unsettling space).

Finally, below, we present a criteria framework that enabled us to decide what stories and practices we would examine within our inquiry. After all, we opted not to seek out many stories of colonial practice, which would require systematic critique, but instead opted to 'sing-up' decolonizing stories and possibilities.

Analytical framework (3) Does community development work?

Understanding how community development works is both a complex philosophical and social science question. Adding a post-structural and decolonizing perspective makes it even more complex. To engage with this key question, we have therefore developed another analytical framework, briefly identified here and discussed further in Chapter 4.

Firstly, we approach the question of 'how does community development work?' through the lens of effectiveness. Within this lens, we are concerned with the 'effect' that is both intended and unintended, by both people in a community and also practitioners and organizations drawing on community development approaches. A beautiful piece of artwork is effective if the effect on anyone gazing upon it is 'oh, what beauty'. We probe the equivalent for community development.

Secondly, while foregrounding effectiveness in a particular way, we also engage with the question of evidence, and particularly consider what is understood as the 'politics of evidence' (for example, the politics of quality versus quantity; the politics of what is observed when thinking about evidence).

Thirdly, and linked to the above, questions of evidence and effectiveness are intimately linked to the challenge of measuring. What is measured is what is seen, which is then what is valued. This becomes a vexed question when we consider the often invisible processes of real social change. How do we measure what is not easily seen? And, making this even more complex, what happens to the invisible when made visible through measuring? (Because we all also know that to observe something is to change it.)

Finally, our framework of 'what works' – linked to previous discussions – aims for a contextual and responsive 'good practice', eschewing the contemporary preoccupation with the falsities of so-called decontextualized 'best practice' (which we suggest is probably just the 'next practice', borrowing a phrase from the hermeneutic philosopher John Caputo). Contextual and responsive good practice is good enough.

Perhaps too ambitious. As we get older, we desire to be ambitious.

Our methodology

In the same way that community development practice is sometimes reduced to a set of frameworks, methods or tools, so too is research. Sometimes researchers, and particularly new researchers who 'want to do it right', mistake well-designed methods with good-quality research. And while acknowledging such research methods is important, we suggest that what is crucial is the work of honing the qualities of the researcher and the intention/s of the inquiry. As co-authors, this has been part of our journey together, and in the relational and dialogical encounters along the way, we have endeavoured to bring a quality of curiosity, rigour, astuteness, nuance, accuracy, and boldness to our work.

In doing this, initially, we reflected on our immersion in the field over many years. Then we did desktop work, reading the literature on community development in South Africa, collecting and analysing the policy documents of the government and so forth. And then, we went looking for community development stories that demonstrated change over a period of time, that is, effect – which suggests community development effectiveness. We hung out with people, practitioners, and policy-makers, interviewed, wrote about, and checked back with them about our interpretations. We looked for work with or among those who have been marginalized in South African society – those on the edges. And we looked for work that had sustained itself, evidenced by people's growth, through working with others. Importantly, the stories demonstrated the possibilities of community as both the site of change (in local places) and as the vehicle of change (people cooperating together). In light of this, we present a more precise set of criteria guiding the stories and possibilities we engaged with. The practices and stories:

- were committed to undoing at least one element of domination culture (class, race, gender, and so forth);
- were engaged with a tough substantive issue facing South Africa and linked to community development and decolonial aspirations, for example, education, land, housing;
- demonstrated the use of engaged and critical thinking and reflection in the praxis;
- fitted community development orthodoxies as per relational practices and collective change;
- demonstrated worker/practitioner reflexivity in terms of their own positionality (who they are; how their histories shaped practice), accountabilities (to those on the margins), and their everyday practices (they were able to do double-loop reflection, questioning assumptions); and
- recognized that people, groups, and communities had a right to their own story and their own definition of what was going on (not what a community worker or other decided was going on).

That is, the story was indicative of working with people from the 'inside-out', based on the particularity of a place and context. We spent time understanding these stories and then importantly distilled the practice and practices that enabled the work to unfold. As relatively experienced community development workers, sometimes our pre-existing knowledge and understanding – occasionally explicit, other times tacit – were confirmed. Other times, we learned new things, or our pre-existing interpretations were disrupted. It has been quite a journey. Ironically, during and after the social distancing of the global COVID-19 lockdowns, we will have to rediscover the essence of being interconnected in building more robust and resilient communities to deal with a precarious and unknown future.

Chapters of book

We now briefly outline what each chapter contributes.

Part I of the book consists of Chapters 2 to 4 and inducts or orients the reader into our approach to community development and questions of effectiveness. Chapter 2 shares our reading of the South African context, and also gives an update on where community development is within the Republic of South Africa.

Chapter 3 gives a brief glimpse into our autobiographies as authors, because engaging in a decolonizing perspective requires being transparent about backgrounds and assumptions.

Chapter 4 articulates how we approach the question of 'does community development work?' Concepts such as effectiveness and effect, evaluation, and measurement, and, finally, making the case for 'developmental evaluation' are addressed.

Part II of the book approaches the question of effectiveness through the lens of 'intentions and ideas'; that is, recognizing that questions of effectiveness have to be linked to what is intended, or the idea behind the practice. Intentions and ideas are grounded in two chapters exploring 'diverse traditions' and 'multiple frameworks' as a way of examining the diverse kinds of community development being drawn upon within South Africa.

Chapter 5 reaches towards a social reconstruction tradition of community development underpinned by a decolonizing perspective. This builds on an argument 'for traditions', using Campfen's (1997) conceptual lens of intellectual traditions. This chapter both carefully introduces the reader to those key concepts and discusses the findings of the historical and contemporary analysis of community development. Traditions such as social guidance, social mobilizing, and social learning are considered as well as linkages with the specific work of people such as Steve Biko.

Chapter 6 then pushes for a 'reconstruction of frameworks', recognizing that it is too easy for practitioners to simply draw on predetermined frameworks rather than reflectively developing their own. Along with several existing frameworks drawn upon within the South African context, Fanon's 'decolonizing framework' is foregrounded.

Part III is an assemblage of stories and possibilities for community development. This part of the book has been structured into seven chapters (Chapters 7–13), each discussing a key story from our dialogical and relational encounters with practice. Each chapter also articulates findings in relation to decolonizing yet effective community development practices.

Chapter 7 considers the linkages between community development and political practices, focusing on the case study of the Southern Cape Land Committee, based within the Western and Eastern Cape. The story is located within the ongoing challenges of farm workers and land reform in South Africa.

Chapter 8 considers the significance of action learning within community development in South Africa. The chapter particularly focuses on the case study of the Abalimi Home and Community Garden Initiative, an exemplary story located in the Cape Flats area of the Western Cape. The Abalimi Initiative works with over 3,000 women creating economic and livelihood initiatives. The chapter locates their story within the context of the unemployment crisis of South Africa, and also the literature that links community development and local economic development.

Chapter 9 considers the significance of community development and place-based practice within South Africa. The chapter particularly focuses on the case study of the Hantam Community Education Trust, an exemplary piece of emergent place-based community practice located in the rural Karoo area of the Eastern and Northern Cape. The chapter locates its story within the context of the educational crisis of South Africa.

Chapter 10 tells the story of how discontent and anger have erupted in the post-apartheid nation and have resulted in ongoing community protests currently endemic in South Africa. The chapter not only elaborates on the reasons for these community and service delivery protests, but also explores and explains how community voice, anger, violence, and protest are and should be an integral part of making sense of community development approaches.

Chapter 11 takes a different turn in illustrating why and how a historical approach, in this case the low-cost housing landscape of South Africa, is a *sine qua non* for community development work practice. This then sets the scene for arguing for the importance of working within a social justice and rights-based approach in dealing with low-cost housing issues in community development.

Chapter 12 considers our investigation into the interaction between supply-oriented, state-led community development and cooperative formation. Cooperative formation is a crucial element of the South African national development plan and has been well integrated into the national community development programmes. The chapter considers the challenges of state-led strategies such as cooperative formation, particularly when linked to a supply-oriented chain, and foregrounds the problematics of neo-colonial approaches to community development.

Chapter 13 (the Interlude), 'In dialogue with Es'kia', focuses on the community development process *from a decolonizing perspective*. The chapter departs from the dialogical encounter with people in the field, and instead reflects on an encounter and analysis of a piece of text about community development from the writings of South African exile and activist Es'kia (Mphahlele, 2002).

Chapter 14 (the Conclusion), brings all the practices together from the stories and interprets their meaning, more or less foregrounding our key framework for what makes community development work within post-structural, deconstructive, and decolonizing perspectives. It is what we would now say to the MIT professor.

Note

1. We acknowledge the work of Patrick Chabal and Jean-Pascal Daloz in *Africa Works* (1999) as triggering our thoughts about the analytical framing of this research.

References

Alexander N. 2013. *Thoughts on the New South Africa*. Auckland Park, South Africa: Jacana Press.

Campfens H. 1997. *Community Development around the World: Practice, Theory, Research, Training*. Toronto, London: University of Toronto.

Chabal P. and Daloz J. 1999. *Africa Works*. Oxford & Indiana: The International African Institute in association with James Curry.

Freire P. 1997. *Pedagogy of the Heart*. New York and London: Continuum.
hooks b. 2010. *Teaching Critical Thinking: Practical Wisdom*. London, New York: Routledge.
Human Rights Commission. 2016. *Report of the South African Human Rights Commission: National Hearing Relating to the Human Rights Situation of the Khoi-San in South Africa*. Johannesburg: Human Rights Commission.
Kelly A. and Westoby P. 2018. *Participatory Development Practice: Using Traditional and Contemporary Frameworks*. Rugby, UK: Practical Action Publishing.
Max-Neef M. 1991. *Human Scale Development: Conceptions, Application and Further Reflections*. London and New York: The Apex Press.
Mphahlele E. 2002. *Es'kia*. South Africa: Kwela Books in association with Stainbank and Associates.
Sandoval C. 2000. *Methodology of the Oppressed*. Minneapolis and London: University of Minnesota Press.
Tuck E. and Yang K.W. 2012. Decolonization is not a metaphor. *Decolonization: Indigeneity, Education & Society* 1(1):1–40.
Van der Watt P. 2016. Engaging the soil and soul of a community: Rethinking, development, healing and transformation in South Africa. Unpublished PhD thesis, Bloemfontein: University of the Free State.
Van der Watt P. 2018. Community development in wounded communities: Seductive schemes or un-veiling and healing. *Community Development Journal* 53(4):714–731.
Wright E.O. 2010. *Envisioning Real Utopias*. London and New York: Verso Press.

PART I
Context and perspectives

Part I, consisting of three chapters, inducts and orients the reader to where we are coming from, naming our perspectives so to speak. Chapter 2 speaks to the South African context; Chapter 3 identifies 'where we come from', including our positionality; and Chapter 4 inducts the reader into the issues of 'how do we know what we know?'

CHAPTER 2
The South African context: The double story

Abstract

Chapter 2 shares our analysis of the South African context through a double-story framework (what's going well and what's not going so well), and also gives an update on where community development is within the Republic of South Africa, including community development policy, programmes, and education/training.

Keywords: double story, community development policy, programmes, education and training.

In discussing the broader South African context, we have used a 'double story' approach. Double story refers to the fact that when we observe and listen to the South African context, we can focus on at least two stories. The first story is the complex tapestry of ongoing suffering, poverty, and distress; and the second story is of people's resilience, agency, and action. Such a double story could also be framed as understanding both needs *and* assets or poverties *and* capabilities. In this way, we focus on *both* 1) the enduring poverty and inequality, the legacy of apartheid's separations, the current struggles of the African National Congress (ANC) government, and so forth, and 2) the resilience of people, the successful changes since apartheid, the possibilities of individual and collective agency, and the experiences of community life and community 'experiments' that have transcended apartheid's objectives and continue to forge a transformative space.

With this double story in mind, firstly, we overview what is considered by many to be going well within South Africa. At the outset, it should be noted that many more people have access to clean water, sanitation, and housing than they did prior to 1994. Despite what some analysts call 'native nostalgia' (Dlamini, 2009), the ANC has 'delivered' many social and economic goods (Marais, 2011: 1; Statistics South Africa, 2015; 2017) albeit within a cultural context of rising expectations. It has reformed much of the public service, reallocating resources away from previous places of privilege and instead towards the underprivileged. The ANC has also succeeded by many international standards. South Africa has proven to be adept and successful at managing an economy along the lines of the so-called Washington Consensus, combining that economic success with the design and development of an effective and adaptive social protection framework and system that are the envy of Africa, known as *viva zola skweiyiya*.

As a result of this success, there has been an ongoing flow of foreign investment, international tourism growth, and financial markets into the nation. Credit must be given, from within a particular paradigm. However, the South African economy is in distress, with very high debt ratios and a weak macro economy. All the state-owned enterprises (for example, South African Airways, Eskom, and the South Africa Broadcasting Corporation) are bankrupt with the international credit rating agency Standard & Poor's, with Fitch downgrading South Africa to 'junk' investor status (see Cohen, 2019).

Secondly, in relation to the normal concerns of 'development practice', within South Africa poverty is enduring, development is uneven, and structural inequality is endemic. Unemployment grows and inequality stretches, and as acclaimed Kenyan author Ngugi wa Thiong'O (2007: 760) aptly puts it: 'potholes multiply and garbage mounts up'. Even more concerning is that South Africa's Human Development Index (HDI) rating had been heading steadily downwards (Buhlungu et al., 2007: 2), though there has been a recent increase. According to the United Nations (2018), South Africa is now ranked 113, up from 116 in 2015 and up from 123 in 2010 and 121 in 2006, with a current HDI score of 0.699.

In terms of inequality, Anna Orthofer's research (Orthofer, 2016) suggests that the South African Gini coefficient is around 0.7, which is higher than any other major economy that collects such data. Furthermore, data from the National Income Dynamics Study indicates that 10 per cent of the population owns approximately 90–95 per cent of all wealth. Clearly, such statistics are indicative of significant strains.

Summing things up, recent reports, such as the Nelson Mandela Foundation's 'Grappling with Poverty and Inequality' (Nelson Mandela Foundation, 2018), the Motlanthe Report 2017, all tell the story of enduring poverty and structural inequality. The analyses of these significant reports signal some key fault lines that cause enduring poverty and structural inequality, including:

- Structural economic decline, with South Africa's economic growth lagging well behind global trends, and unemployment on the rise.
- Rural economy and land reform failure, in which few livelihoods have been enhanced through successful agrarian reform, and apartheid patterns of land ownership remain.
- Early childhood development, particularly the first 1,000 days, with many children not adequately fed – a key form of deprivation determining intergenerational poverty.
- Education, with the public schooling system remaining what is referred to as 'bimodal', whereby research illuminates the way in which there is a huge disparity in learning between those in poor urban and rural areas and those in what were known as Model-C schools.

- Youth, with many young people dropping out of school prematurely, hindering entry to the labour market.
- Labour market, with at least 27 per cent of people still excluded from employment, and also significant pay differentials for those within employment.
- Urbanization, informality, and spatial inequality, in which – despite successful housing projects – many people cannot access places of work, which, of course, leads to rural–urban migration with the accompanying challenge of informal settlements and informal work, sometimes known as informalization.
- Transport, with a lack of investment in public transport, the lack of road space allocated to service public transport initiatives, and the failure of many state-owned enterprises. In turn, there is an overspend on road infrastructure.
- Health, with disparities in health funding across public and private health sectors and challenges of access for many, and significantly, a lack of accountability towards patients in terms of quality of care.
- Food security and food poverty, including nutritional needs, are critical issues for many, with one quarter of the population living below the food poverty line in 2015.
- Sustainable development, with the need for a particular emphasis on renewable energy to become a priority.
- Social cohesion (being the ability of people to cooperate, within and across group boundaries without coercion and/or pure self-interest) is a significant challenge, particularly in light of the structural inequalities mentioned earlier (Nelson Mandela Foundation, 2018: 18–41).

In summary, the key aspect that needs to be emphasized is that the great majority of South Africans continue to experience profound levels of social distress and social suffering (Bourdieu, 1999). Such concepts highlight the structural disjuncture that sits between people's aspirations and the barriers that exist for people to realize their 'life-projects' (Blaser et al., 2004) and the felt pain resulting from that disjuncture. People's aspirations, amplified since 1994, are being thwarted by this enduring trajectory of poverty and inequality. There is an increasing sense of social injury (Brown, 1995) and community woundedness (Van der Watt, 2018) that leads to frustration, humiliation, and growing rage. In some places, the rage is evidenced through phenomena such as increased violent crime, land invasion, worker strikes, consumer boycotts, and so-called service-delivery protests.

In this regard, Peter Alexander et al. (2013) refer to the rebellion of the poor in terms of rolling community protests. Lately, the term 'community protests' has become well entrenched in South Africa, referring to civil strife at community level expressing dissatisfaction with government's lack and/or pace of service delivery and inability to account for public service provision (Botes,

2016; Matebesi, 2017; Matebesi and Botes, 2017; Mkhize, 2015; Wasserman et al., 2018).

Community development as one approach to social change

It is in such a context that community development practice is one contributor, among many, of social change work approaches. Community development practitioners sit alongside lawyers, educators, unionists, activists, and others in utilizing different traditions, approaches, and methods of social change. Importantly for this book, the Nelson Mandela Foundation report suggests that:

> The Action Dialogues [that developed an analysis of enduring poverty and structural inequality] ... encouraged critical discussion about the need to replace failed top-down technical models of policy implementation to an 'inert', 'grateful citizenry' with no agency of its own with practices that engaged the citizenry from the outset and which recognized and gave respect to people's own efforts to change the quality of their lives (2018: 10).

Furthermore, we suggest that 'people's own efforts' are the key to community development as small, humble contributors to social change. From the perspective of a more macro or national level, particularly drawing on more state- and economic-centric orthodox views of development, community development would appear to be marginal. It would be easy to argue that the core 'developmental process' of South Africa is being worked out within the class-based struggles represented by mining and agricultural-related worker struggles, and also student revolts against rising higher education fees in struggles such as #FeesMustFall (2015 and 2016) (see Booysen, 2016) and those working against state capture. Here, endogenous development is at its crux, as South African workers and citizens struggle for their fair share of the surplus generated by the capitalist development trajectory of one of the BRICS (Brazil, Russia, India, China and South Africa) nations (Forslund, 2013). The 2012 Marikana mine workers' strike – where the police killed 34 workers – and accompanying state-led violence were a crucial moment in highlighting such ongoing class-based struggles (Pillay, 2013; Salooje, 2016; Sinwell and Mbatha, 2016).

In contrast, most community development work occurs at the margins, among what has been previously described as surplus people (Bauman, 2004). We tend to agree and, from a justice perspective, are comfortable with that assessment. However, from less-orthodox development perspectives, those that are more oriented towards the post-structural (Esteva, 1987; McMichael, 2010), community development represents an important people-centred tradition of social solidarity (Sennett, 2012) among the marginal and precariat, one that experiments with social change initially on a small scale. However, as per our earlier mention of micro-macro articulations, this small-scale work can grow significantly with appropriate inputs and support, and also offer visions and actions of 'contested development' (McMichael, 2010). McMichael's vision coincides with Neville Alexander's (2013) vision for community development, discussed in the previous chapter.

From the perspective of our key question – does community development work? – this vision is important to keep in mind. Community development will not transform the nation or overcome poverty for all – it does not claim to do this – but it does contribute. Hard-nosed social analysts might say, so what? They might be tempted to agree with the MIT professor mentioned in our introduction. Our response is that for the surplus people and/or the marginal, the contribution is significant – and if micro-macro articulation is taken seriously, there can even be more impact.

The current state of play of community development in South Africa

Frik De Beer and Hennie Swanepoel (1998: 2) provide a very useful overview of the history of community development, tracing it back to the various claims made about community development within the USA and India. For some commentators, the origins of community development were in the early 1900s the USA. However, this has been contested and most commentators now agree that the 'term community development was invented by the British in the 1950s to connote small-scale rural development programs that combined local labour with government resources' (Midgley and Livermore, 2005: 158). Importantly, such work was then institutionalized within the British Colonial Office, both in India and then in Britain's African colonies in the 1950s (ibid.; Maistry, 2012: 30). Further, the French and other European powers also created community development programmes knowns as *animation rurale* (Midgley and Livermore, 2005: 158).

While acknowledging the official use of the term 'community development', as per P.W. Botha's 1961 appointment as a minister with the portfolio of Community Development and Coloured Affairs (during which time he was responsible for the destruction of District Six), according to De Beer and Swanepoel, community development was never really popular within South Africa. It was mistrusted by those in government due to its potential for political change (De Beer and Swanepoel, 1998; Maistry, 2012: 31). After the then-named apartheid era, the Department of Cooperation and Development was tasked with studying the international experience of community development; the apartheid regime initiated a series of efforts within the former homelands, embedded within the policy of 'separate development'.

However, while government mistrust and misuse of community development took place, other traditions of 'unofficial' or popular community development were seeding and flowering (Maistry, 2012: 32). There has been a long tradition of NGO, civic, church, and labour organizations for community development within South Africa. Organic forms of self-help and mutual aid work such as Stokvels (self-help savings and loans groups / burial saving societies) proliferated. From the 1920s, Gandhi deeply influenced forms of community organizing within South Africa (Goswami, 2009). During the 1970s, more experimental and radical forms of community development oriented towards adult education also emerged through the work of Steve Biko, drawing on Paulo Freire's philosophy and practice (Mangcu, 2012), and the churches also brought into this adult education tradition via the Christian Institute, World Vision, and the World Council of Churches.

Current policy context

2003 provided a watershed moment for official community development, with the then president, Thabo Mbeki, announcing the formation of a National Community Development Programme. This was officially launched in 2005 and since then there has been a proliferation within the discursive field of community development in South Africa. This has culminated with more recent pushes to develop a National Community Development Policy Framework. This latter task and process have been led, or facilitated, by the National Department of Social Development from 2008 through to 2013, and at the time of writing is still unfinished. Currently, the Department of Social Development is in a process of changing the Social Services Act to make provisions for community development workers on par with the recognition of social workers.

Sitting behind the development of such a policy have been significant efforts to understand international, national, and sectoral policies relevant to community development. For example, the Department of Social Development conducted an audit of policies relevant to community development in 2008 (Luka and Maistry, 2012). Such a national community development policy is also situated within a broader legal policy context. Although the chapters in this book lean more towards the social-development-related policies, other integrated participatory-development-related policies and strategies are also important to mention in strengthening our reflections on community development and participatory actions. Some key policies include: the South African Constitution and Bill of Rights; Reconstruction and Development Programme of 1994; the White Paper on Welfare Services of 1997 and the White Paper on Local Government 1998; Local Government Municipal Structures Act of 1998; Integrated Sustainable Rural Development Strategy of 2000; Local Government Municipal Systems Act of 2000; Traditional Leadership and Governance Act of 2003; the Development Facilitation Act of 2005; and the Comprehensive Rural Development Programme of 2009.

This policy context leads to what many community development workers call an 'enabling environment'. There is recognition that at a legislative and policy level, there are many reasons to celebrate – the state has been heading in the right direction creating a context for effective, integrated, and participatory community development work.

Current programme context

Firstly, there has been a proliferation of *sectoral* government-led community work and development initiatives, focusing on particular sectors or issues; for example, agricultural extension work, community health nurses, adult education work, and the very successful 'care groups' – an initiative of health officials. This has continued beyond the 1990s into the present.

Some other important community development programmes, albeit focused on service delivery, include the Integrated Sustainable Rural Development and Urban Renewal Programmes, both of which aim to promote coordinated service delivery across all spheres of government to improve the lives of very poor communities. There is also the Extended Public Works Programme, which aims to create job opportunities while the participants are gaining skills for further placement in various long-term jobs in the industry.

Furthermore, during the 2000s, another kind of community development has emerged from the state, one which could be understood as *place-based* or *generic* community development. The two main initiatives are the already mentioned National Community Development Worker Programme, managed by the Department of Cooperative Governance and Traditional Affairs, and the National Community Development Programme situated as a sub-directorate within the National Department of Social Development (NDSD). In the NDSD's Annual Performance Plan of 2018, community development is cited as a sub-programme under the overarching Programme on Social Policy and Integrated Service Delivery (Programme 5). Here, it is clearly stated that this sub-programme of community development, 'develops and facilitates the implemented policies, guidelines, norms and standards for ensuring the effective and efficient delivery of community development service and programmes' (Republic of South Africa, 2018: 80). Both of these can be characterized as *ideally* focused not so much on predetermined sectoral concerns or issues, but rather on concerns or issues emerging from the local place-oriented context. Ideally, the latter programme determines these concerns, actions, and potential initiatives using community-based planning processes (combined with the sustainable livelihoods approach), and the former through processes of household profiling, establishing local municipal participation structures, and building local capacity to engage with government stakeholders. Chapter 12 focuses on state-led community development and cooperative formation, and on research conducted within these two programmes.

Moving on from state-led processes, there continues to be a tradition of NGO-led community development focused on service delivery using participatory understandings of development. An example would be the Mvula Trust's work fast-tracking delivery of sustainable water and sanitation services to communities, drawing heavily on Robert Chambers' philosophy and techniques of participatory development. Others could be identified particularly within the housing field (Abahlali base Mjondolo – Shack Dwellers Movement), health (the Health System Trust), adult education (Adult Basic Education and Training), youth (Girls and Boys Town SA), and so forth. And of course, in more recent years, in parallel with the explosion in social enterprise work, there has been a proliferation of private-sector-led community development. Some of these are linked to corporate social responsibility requirements and others to more embedded practice, such as the community development work linked to the roll-out of the Renewable Energy Independent Power Producers Programme (Baker and Wlokas, 2014; Davies et al., 2017).

Training and professionalization context

Accompanying the current community development policy and programme, proliferation is an increasing focus in the training and professionalization of community development practitioners. A 2012 edition of *Africanus*, a journal of South African Development Studies, was dedicated to exploring the issues involved in such professionalization. In 2014, the National Department of Social Development facilitated the development of a Community Development Occupation category within the Department of Labour, and standards for community development practitioners within the Social Service Professions Policy have been articulated. The Department of Public Service Management was tasked to regulate the community development field. With leadership coming from the Social Development Department, in collaboration with key individuals, there is also a 'push' to formalize a Community Development Association and even potentially create a Community Development Council. During November 2018, there has been some work in developing a draft policy for social service practitioners and a Social Service Bill, which will incorporate the community development worker.

Linked to such professionalization agendas are the upgrading and standardization of community development training and education. Again, the Department of Social Development has taken the lead and, in 2012, working with the South African Qualification Authority and the Department of Higher Education and Training, has accredited both National Qualification Framework (NQF) level 4 certificates in community development and NQF level 8 bachelor's degrees in community development. At the time of writing, this department was working with numerous universities around the country to develop and implement both qualifications, such as the 2017 launching of the University of the Free State Bachelor of Community Development degree and the establishment of a community development worker Higher Education Training Forum.

Such an agenda is linked to a particular analysis of the status of community development within South Africa. In attending a June 2013 workshop, the Community Development Chief Director (within the National Department of Social Development) argued the following:

- Community development is only an emerging discipline that is not yet fully recognized or accredited as an occupation or profession.
- Community development practitioners are not yet adequately skilled.
- Due to the multi-sectoral nature of community development, facilitated by numerous government departments, there is a plethora of definitions, leading to confusion.

- There is an absence of standardization, which blocks the development of career pathways.
- Community development is currently dominated by a 'service-delivery' mentality or approach, with a limited focus on actual empowerment.
- The practice is inappropriately resourced and is therefore not making its potential contribution to development.
- There is, as yet, no association or professional body.

Whether or not we agree with this analysis, it did galvanize ongoing efforts to address each point with a growing network of people, endeavouring to build a recognized and formidable 'community of practice'.

References

Alexander N. 2013. *Thoughts on the New South Africa*. Auckland Park, South Africa: Jacana Press.

Alexander P., Ceruti C., Motseke K., Phadi M. and Wale K. 2013. *Class in Soweto*. Scottsville: University of KwaZulu-Natal Press.

Baker L. and Wlokas H. 2014. *South Africa's Renewable Energy Procurement: A New Frontier*. Tyndall Centre for Climate Change Research.

Booysen S. (ed.) 2016. *Fees Must Fall. Student Revolt, Decolonisation and Governance in South Africa*. Johannesburg: Wits University Press.

Botes L. 2016. Service delivery protests in South Africa: A case for community development? In Meade R.R., Shaw M. and Banks S. (eds). *Politics, Power and Community*. Bristol: Policy.

Davies M.L., Swilling M. and Wlokas H. 2017. Towards new configurations of urban energy governance in South Africa's renewable energy procurement programme. *Energy Research & Social Science*. https://doi.org/10.1016/j.erss.2017.11.010.

Bauman Z. 2004. *Wasted Lives: Modernity and its Outcasts*. Cambridge: Polity Press.

Blaser M., Feit H.A. and McRae G. 2004. *In the Way of Development: Indigenous Peoples, Life Projects and Globalization*. London: Zed Books.

Bourdieu P. 1999. *The Weight of the World: Social Suffering in Contemporary Society*, trans. Priscilla Parkhurst Ferguson, et al. Stanford University Press.

Brown W. 1995. *States of Injury: Power and Freedom in Late Modernity*. New Jersey: Princeton University Press.

Buhlungu S., Daniel J., Southall R. and Lutchman J. (eds). 2007. *State of the Nation: South Africa 2007*. Cape Town: Human Sciences Research Council.

Cohen T. 2019. A look at what might happen if South Africa is 'junked' in two weeks' time. *Daily Maverick*. www.dailymaverick.co.za/article/2019-03-14-a-look-at-what-might-happen-if-south-africa-is-junked-in-two-weeks-time/.

De Beer F. and Swanepoel H. 1998. *Community Development and Beyond: Issues, Structures and Procedures*. Pretoria: JL Van Schaik Publishers.

Dlamini J. 2009. *Native Nostalgia*. South Africa: Jacana Media.

Esteva G. 1987. Regenerating people's space. *Alternatives* 12(1):125–152.

Forslund D. 2013. Mass unemployment and the low-wage regime in South Africa. In Daniel J., Naidoo P., Pillay D. and Southall R. (eds). *New South Africa Review 3: The Second Phase—Tragedy or Farce?* Johannesburg: WITS University Press.

Goswami P. 2009. A re-reading of Gandhi's Satyagraha in South Africa for contemporary community organizing. *Community Development Journal* 44(3):393–402.

Luka S. and Maistry M. 2012. The institutionalization of community development in democratic South Africa. *Africanus* 42(2):14–21.

McMichael P. 2010. *Contested Development.* London and New York: Routledge.

Maistry M. 2012. Towards professionalization: Journey of community development in the African and South African context. *Africanus* 42(2):29–41.

Mangcu X. 2012. *Biko: A Biography.* Cape Town: Tafelberg.

Marais H. 2011. *South Africa Pushed to the Limit: The Political Economy of Change.* Claremont, South Africa: UCT Press.

Matebesi S. 2017. *Civil Strife against Local Governance: Dynamics of Community Protests in Contemporary South Africa.* Berlin: Barbara Budrich.

Matebesi S. and Botes L. 2017. Party identification and service delivery protests in the Eastern Cape and Northern Cape, South Africa. *African Sociological Review* 21(2): 81–99.

Mkhize M.C. 2015. Is SA's 20 years of democracy in crisis? Examining the impact of unrest indicators in local protests in the post-apartheid SA. *African Security Review* 24(2):190– 206.

Midgley J. and Livermore M. 2005. 'Development theory and community practice', In Weil, Marie (ed.). *The Handbook of Community Practice.* Thousand Oaks, London and New Delhi: Sage Publications.

Motlanthe Report, 2017. *Report of the high level panel on the assessment of key legislation and the acceleration of fundamental change.* Parliament of South Africa. https://www.parliament.gov.za/storage/app/media/Pages/2017/october/High_Level_Panel/HLP_Report/HLP_report.pdf report of the high level panel on the assessment of key legislation and – Parliament of South Africa Report of the high level panel on the assessment of key legislation and the acceleration of fundamental change Chart 2.5: Employment in non-agricultural activities, various countries (2015) 117 SLOW ECONOMIC GROWTH 117 www.parliament.gov.za

Nelson Mandela Foundation. 2018. Grappling with poverty and inequality: A report on the process and findings of the Mandela Initiative. South Africa: Nelson Mandela Foundation.

Orthofer A. 2016. *Wealth Inequality in South Africa: Evidence from Survey and Tax Data.* REDI3*3 working paper 15 Cape Town: University of Cape Town – The South African Labour and Development Research Unit.

Pillay D. 2013. The second phase tragedy or farce? In Daniel J., Naidoo P., Pillay D. and Southall R. (eds). *New South Africa Review 3: The Second Phase—Tragedy or Farce?* Johannesburg: WITS University Press.

Republic of South Africa. 2018. *Annual Performance Plan.* Pretoria: Department of Social Development.

Salooje A. 2016. Social protests and the exercise of citizenship in South Africa. In Kepe T., Levin M. and Von Lieres B. (eds). *Domains of Freedom: Justice, Citizenship and Social Change in South Africa.* Cape Town: UCT Press.

Sinwell L. and Mbatha S. 2016. *The Spirit of Marikana: The Rise of Insurgent Trade Unionism in South Africa*. Johannesburg: Wits University Press.

Statistics South Africa. 2015. *Millennium Development Goals, Country Report*. Pretoria: Statistics South Africa.

Statistics South Africa. 2017. *Sustainable Development Goals: Indicator Baseline Report*. Pretoria: Statistics South Africa..

Sennett R. 2012. *Together: The Rituals, Pleasures and Politics of Cooperation*. London and New York: Penguin Press Group.

Thiong'O, N. wa., 2007. *Wizard of the Crow*. London: Vintage Books.

United Nations. 2018. *Human Development Indices and Indicators: Statistical Update*. New York: United Nations.

Van der Watt P. 2018. 'Community development in wounded communities: seductive schemes or un-veiling and healing'. *Community Development Journal* 53(4):714–731.

Wasserman H., Chuma W. and Bosch T. 2018. Print media coverage of service delivery protests: A content analysis. *African Studies* 77(1):145–156.

CHAPTER 3
Where we are coming from

Abstract

Chapter 3 expands on the perspectives of the book, focusing on post-structural, deconstructive, and decolonizing approaches. The methodology of the book is briefly explained and glimpses into the autobiographies of authors are provided, recognizing that a decolonizing perspective requires transparency about backgrounds and assumptions.

Keywords: post-structural, deconstructive, decolonizing, positionality, methodology

If there is no such 'thing' as community development, and there is no 'right' and certain way of knowing what makes community development work, then it is important to be clear about where we are coming from. You, the reader, need to have a glimpse of our assumptions, perspectives, *and our stories*, which, of course, shape those assumptions and perspectives. This chapter is about 'coming clean', so to speak – making these things explicit. In doing this, first we expand on the brief introduction to the post-structural, deconstructive, and decolonizing perspectives. We then present our understanding of community development. Later, we each give a glimpse into our stories, revealing our positionality.

A post-structural perspective

Development is a troublesome notion with many definitions. Sometimes we would prefer to ditch the word altogether. Like sociologist Phil McMichael, we sense that 'development is not only in crisis but is at a significant turning point in its short history as a master concept of (Western-based) social science and cultural life' (2012: 2). Like Swiss scholar Gilbert Rist (2011), we are aware of the devastating histories and practices of development. Like Indian ecologist Debal Deb (2009), we are cognizant of the colonizing mindset of 'developmentality'. Like Colombian-American anthropologist Arturo Escobar (2010), we constantly grapple with the ongoing traction of assumptions and paradigms that underpin developmentalist practices. Like Caribbean and African philosopher Nelson Maldonado-Torres (2011), we suggest a renewed search for trans-disciplinary decolonial thought and a rediscovery of indigenous knowledge.

Yet, as we locate this book within the citizen and professional project of community *development* – that is, we are using the idea of development – there is no escape from it.

However, in that 'no escape', we come at development from particular perspectives, in which we reimagine it in two ways. Firstly, development can be understood as a metaphor signifying a qualitative change (Kaplan, 1996, 2002; Escobar, 2010), which can be contrasted with the quantitatively oriented metaphor of development as growth still underpinning most practices and mindsets. Development is therefore essentially about positive change or improvement – change for the better and an improvement in human wellbeing. From our perspective, development is primarily a qualitative change that focuses on people-centred processes rather than growth-centred outcomes. Qualitative questions also focus practitioners on some of the most pertinent 'development'-related questions of our times, including:

- How do we ensure all people on the planet have a decent quality of life, without being held hostage to the current model of economic growth that is so fossil-fuel reliant? Or, put another way, how do we create the conditions for *Just Transitions* (Swilling and Annecke, 2012; Escobar, 2015)?
- How do we direct resources to women's literacy, enabling individual women to make more decisions about their lives (Sen, 1999)?
- How do we create sustainable livelihoods for the almost inevitable exponential growth of numbers of young people living in urban slums (Pieterse, 2013)?
- How do we reduce consumerism within a global context among those of us who are wealthy, thereby reducing both the planetary footprint and social inequalities?
- How can land be returned to sovereign original owners, reversing colonization / settler stealing of land?

As will be discussed, these final two points beg the question of whether community development becomes a tool of modernity's impulse and trajectory, aligned to an industrial paradigm, or, alternatively, whether community development can be guided by a decolonizing paradigm. In this latter paradigm, it would potentially contribute to more radical and robust practices of resistance to (some) aspects of modernity, reconnection to nature / mother earth, the returning of stolen land, and revitalization of the commons.

Secondly, development is reimagined within the post-structural tradition (McMichael, 2012), namely, what Escobar identifies as the:

> possibility of visualizing an era where development ceased to be the central principle of social life. ... the post, succinctly, means a de-centring of capitalism as the definition of the economy, of liberalism in the definition of society and polity, and of state forms of power as the defining

matrix of social organization. This does not mean that capitalism, liberalism and state forms cease to exist; it means that their discursive and social centrality have been displaced somewhat (Escobar, 2010: 12).

To align ourselves with this post-structural tradition is to be consistent in our reflections on effective community development practice also as a post-structural project. In examining community development within South Africa, we see many *diverse practices* aligned with different visions of the good life, different 'competing political visions ... of the ideal society' (McMichael, 2012: 3) or different 'life projects' (Blaser et al., 2004). It is to argue for a utopian vision such as Escobar's 'pluriverse' (Escobar, 2018), by which he means multiple diverse futures that are sustainable – that is, different visions of 'development'.

Also, a deconstructive perspective

If a post-structural perspective signifies diversity and the de-centring of capitalist visions of development and community development, a deconstructive approach urges for renewal. Not for the hell of it. Not new because new is in and of itself good; but because it is so easy to become, as Wittgenstein said, ossified in our thinking.

We use the idea of deconstruction, drawing on Jacques Derrida's philosophy. The word deconstruction, as used by Derrida, is a play on Heidegger's *destruktion* – which, in German and French, is not so much about destroying, but about a critical reconstituting – and consequently the need to reconstruct community development (as per the sub-title of the book). For Derrida, the deconstructive task is not so much destroying, but about opening up text, programmes, and institutions – not with the purpose of anarchy, but with a view to *more just* programmes and institutions (Smith, 2005: 11). These acts of opening-up and unveiling, we argue, are the essence of a decolonial attempt at reconstructing community development. *Dis-envelop* (opening-up, unfurl, unfold) is after all what de-velop-ment is all about.

Derrida's deconstruction is also understood to be messianic in the sense that it is one of profound affirmation about a future yet-to-come. His thinking invites a community development praxis that is 'yet-to-come'. As he said in his final interview, 'deconstruction is always on the side of the yes, on the side of an affirmation of life' (Derrida, 2007: 51). As James Smith argues, quoting Derrida directly, 'I cannot conceive of a radical critique which would not be ultimately motivated by some sort of affirmation' (Smith, 2005: 2).

Why the need for a 'community development yet-to-come'? Community development has engaged with many key historical issues, from marginalization and poverty, feminism and patriarchy, colonization, and the concerns of First Nations peoples, to name just a few (see, for example, the 2017 *Routledge Handbook of Community Development* (Kenny et al., 2017). However, a community development 'to-come' is also needed to address many issues around the world. For example, how is community development responding to the globalization of right-wing populism, identity politics, and its accompanying patriarchal politics? What does community development have to offer in light of endemic wicked problems related to land, education, housing, and livelihoods in South Africa? Does community development provide any robust responses to human-induced climate change, species extinction, and the ongoing proliferation of extractive industries within South Africa? What does community development say to the concurrent neoliberal assault on the university and democracy? What does community development have to say to the inequality crises facing South Africa? Could community development cast any light on the improvement of post-liberation governance to avoid state capture, corruption, and mismanagement in the future? These questions are all pertinent, and we occasionally touch on a few of them. However, our main focus of renewal is the reconstruction of community development in light of the decolonial turn.

There is certainly, as is always the case for any fields of practice, an urgent need to renew community development. We suggest Derrida's philosophy could play a role, albeit recognizing that community development scholars and practitioners rarely engage directly with philosophy, rightly because most practitioners are grappling with real everyday concerns (or the so-called *real politik* and pragmatism with issues to 'solve problems'), and also because scholars in the field are mostly influenced by the social and political sciences. Lately, management sciences and project management frameworks with log frames, goal setting, action plans, evaluation plans, impact measurement, and so forth also leave little space for philosophical reflections during the hurried lifecycles of many community development projects.

This is not to say that deconstruction has not been utilized by community development scholars. For example, Akwugo Emejulu's *Community Development as Micropolitics* (2016) deploys deconstruction to analyse the micropolitics of community development in the USA and Britain in the period between 1968 and 1997. Significantly, earlier editors of the *Community Development Journal*, Carpenter and Miller, suggest that deconstruction is relevant in the process of 'revitalizing community development in theory and practice' (Carpenter and Miller, 2011), the title to a special collection of selected papers presented at an international symposium in 2009.

Cutting to the chase, the take-home message of Derrida's episteme of deconstruction is that there are *at least* two readings of any text, programme, or institution. The first reading is reading for the truth, which reaches for the author's intent, or the originary concepts of a programme or institution. In contrast, the second reading is a reading for the contradictions, fissures, and tensions within any text or institution – for Derrida, they are always there, undermining, or bringing more complexity to the so-called truth of the first reading. This second reading is also an affirmation of something new, something that can arrive from a fresh living encounter with the text or institution, for example the 'community development yet-to-come'. Importantly, this new reading, as are any ongoing readings as per Derrida's *hauntology*, is also one that is haunted by the summons of justice.

In this deconstructive approach, Derrida *would* be – for he never talked of community development – wanting community development to be subject to the minimal 'two readings'. The first is a reading that reaches for the imagined truth of community development (its 'originary concepts' and traditions), delving into the traces of life deep within it. Of course, the originary concepts for community development are both liberatory and also tainted with the colonial ideals of progress and the Enlightenment (of 'development') (Carpenter, 2013), or even worse, in South Africa, with links to 'separate development'. Remember that at least within the UK, the first courses designated as community development, led by Margaret Read and T.R. (Reg) Batten, started as a result of the 1948 Cambridge conference of colonial administrators (Eversley, 2019).

Then, the second reading is *both* critical – seeing the multiplicities, tensions, and fissures within community development, acknowledging there is no truth – *and* affirmative, reaching for a community development-of-tomorrow. In terms of the critical – the multiplicities, tensions, and fissures – there are many within community development. For example, Gilchrist (2004) talks of conservative, reformist, and radical models of community development. Likewise, Campfens (1997) refers to the social guidance, mobilizing, and learning traditions of community development, which we draw upon in Chapter 5. Some community development praxis is animated by a post-development imaginary (Esteva, 2014), or post-capitalist aspiration (Gibson-Graham, 2006); others by cooperative aspirations (Restakis, 2010), or others towards local economic development imperatives (Shuman, 2007). The point is that there are many debates, discussions, and disagreements occurring.

In terms of the affirmative, Derrida would also insist that our love of community development praxis ensures we keep reconstructing it, reaching for a community development praxis that is haunted by the call for justice. Clearly, this de- and reconstruction has been going on for the last 50 or so years – the ongoing reforms are evidenced in debates within the 'architectures' of community development archived in the *Community Development Journal* (Oxford University Press), *Community Development* (journal of the USA Society), many easily accessible books, and many conferences.

For Derrida, within this constantly reforming process, to not be haunted by the summons of justice would be to slip into a deadened position and perspective – which echoes the thinking of Wittgenstein, who argued that universities are full of people whose thinking is ossified. It would be, using the idea of philosopher Francois Jullien, to 'become settled', which is to enter a state of decay (Jullien, 2016).

Derrida's contrast to death, decay, or a deadened settling, is to always affirm the 'yes', in fact making the case for what he referred to as a 'second yes' and even a 'third yes'. This affirmation, sitting at the centre of his final interview, recorded in the gem of a book *Learning to Live Finally* (Derrida, 2007), is an affirmation of the constant inauguration of a commitment. To affirm that a community development-of-tomorrow is haunted by the call to justice is a 'yes.' However – and here is Derrida's key point – tomorrow we must wake up and affirm it again – a 'second yes', and then again we must awake with a 'third yes'. And onwards, always with the inauguration of reform – the messianic-like *telos* that drives Derrida, which haunts him, and should each of us.

If we are not haunted by the spectre of justice, then it would be best to walk away from community development, to leave it alone, to do no more damage.

Note that this 'yet-to-come' is *not* a vision of a community development that is constructed by neoliberal logics (because that is 'likely to come' if powerful interests are not thwarted). Quite the contrary, Derrida's thought is radical in the sense of reaching for the liberatory roots of community development – the traces of those originary concepts that are not neoliberal, while also deconstructing the contradictions within them.

In turn, this deconstructive approach insists that practitioners should become skilled and knowledgeable about contemporary traditions, frameworks, and practices of community development. A deconstructive approach demands participation in the 'community of practice', which makes community development a field that is evolving. A deconstructive approach invites fidelity to the practice of social solidarity, decolonization, and collective work. However, beyond this insistence, demand, and invitation, a deconstructive approach calls for renewal, moving the old into the new, ensuring the work and the practices are re-contextualised into new spaces and historical challenges. It means those of us working in this field need to keep moving from the 'centre' (reading the journals, attending conferences, checking out the new books), but also engage from the 'margins' or edges, listening to what is going on in the world and the work, such that the centre is renewed.

And also, a decolonizing, or colonizing paradigm of community development

Right now, the margins, the edges, are calling for a decolonizing approach or perspective. This is our focus. Possibly, the margins always have been – but they have not been heard or have not had a voice. However, the call is now stronger than ever. We are in what some refer to as a 'decolonial turn' (Mamdani, 2016; Zondi, 2016), which does seem odd seeing as the decolonizing of Africa probably started before Ghana gained independence in 1957. Nevertheless, there is a renewed energy in South Africa for decolonizing, one that recognizes not only decolonization as a post-apartheid necessity but also grapples with colonization of Indigenous peoples such as the Khoi-San (Human Rights Commission, 2016).

However, we are also arguing for a decolonizing of community development itself.

This decolonizing needs a number of processes. Firstly, as already proposed, it needs a decolonizing of *how we think* about community development. In some ways there is no need to repeat ourselves, as we have said it above. We must no longer think of community development as a *thing, with an essence*.

Instead, it is a diverse array of theories and practices producing different types of praxis. As such, a post-structural perspective and deconstructive approach are our cornerstones of decolonizing. The perspective and approach open the 'project' of community development up to rethinking, for renewal, for disruption – and particularly from the margins.

Secondly, the *actual practices* of community development need to be rethought in light of this decolonial turn. For authors such as Guardiola-Rivera, South Africa, like many places in the world, is in the midst of a 'war' of paradigms, namely between an industrial and Indigenous or decolonizing paradigm (Guardiola-Rivera, 2010). The industrial paradigm represents unfettered expansion of modernity (Bauman, 2011), 'globalization from above', developmentality (Deb, 2009), capitalist surplus accumulation (Harvey, 2012), control over natural resources, and so forth. Even the mantra of the so-called Fourth Industrial Revolution is playing out according to the rules of global market capitalism. Community development, when aligned with such a paradigm, simply becomes a tool of modernity's impulse and trajectory: primarily a concern of economic growth and modernization, albeit at a more local level. Community development, then, focuses on what can be described as first-order social change: enabling people to 'survive' the current capitalist economic system through practices such as microfinance, attracting tourists into their community, and the development of small and medium-sized business.

Alternatively, community development, when 'guided' by an Indigenous or decolonization paradigm, is enacted by radical and robust practices such as resistance to (some) aspects of modernity, reconnection to nature / mother earth, revitalization of the commons, humanization, and disrupting settler perspectives. The focus would be more on what can be understood as second-order social change attempting to challenge the fundamental ordering of racist, capitalist, sexist, political economy. Understanding community development within South Africa requires discernment around which paradigms are framing practice, either consciously or unconsciously. The question arises: has community development become a part of modernity, or is it still a practice that incorporates at least some element of resistance?

Thirdly, there are implications for mentoring, reflection, and education of community development practitioners. In many ways, thinking about that is a whole other book, but for now we mention that implications would flow into what is understood as the 'hidden curricula' within tertiary education, but also within the non-formal education that often sits at the heart of community development praxis. Here, we are deeply wedded to Paulo Freire's approach of critical questioning, or importantly, for decolonizing the mind, learning to question. Yet, we add Tuck and Yang's insight (somewhat critical of Freire) that also requires disrupting settler perspectives, particularly 'settler moves to innocence' (Tuck and Yang, 2012: 35). Crucially, community development practitioners themselves must do the edgy and often painful work of *decolonizing their own mind and praxis*, questioning assumptions, bias, racism, sexism, classism, and so forth. For those from more privileged backgrounds, we suggest as per bell hooks' work, 'apprenticing to the margins' (hooks, 1992); that is, learning from the margins, listening deeply; and also making themselves 'accountable to Indigenous sovereignty and futurity' (Tuck and Yang, 2012: 35).

Importantly, such implications ensure a rethinking of the project of professionalization and 'the profession' within community development. Summing up the implications of a decolonizing perspective, consider these words from Loretta Pyles (2019: 183):

> The famous quotation from Lilla Watson, (an Indigenous Australian artist, activist and academic), 'If you have come here to help me, you are wasting your time. But if you have come because your liberation is bound up with mine, then let us work together', points not only to all of our shared fates but to a disruption of the often-rigid line between helper and helped.

Lilla Watson is insisting to anyone who comes to this work 'to help', which is often the stance of professionals, that 'you are wasting your time'. We agree and have, through many decades of experience, confirmed this wisdom. People smell and sense the gesture of helping and it is often not wanted. Instead, our approach is built on ideas of solidarity, friendship, co-motion (rather than 'intervention'), and animation (discerning how to support people, and ourselves, to get unstuck). It is not to be against professionalization as such, but to locate any such project within the broader call to solidarity, a recognition of 'development as freedom' (originary concepts for community development), and in keeping with Derrida's hauntology of justice.

Re-orienting community development

Aligned with the thoughts above, and as already said, community development is not a thing. From a post-structural perspective, it has many possibilities. Furthermore, mainly, it is not what we say it is, but what we do – and from this 'doing' perspective, community development is informed by various theories and practices. In its simplest form, we could think about the variations as conservative, reformist, or radical (see Gilchrist, 2004). From a more sophisticated perspective, which is what we offer in Chapters 5 and 6, it is possible to think about variations of traditions and frameworks. Each tradition – with particular inspirational and intellectual roots of practice – is varied: Freire, Gandhi, Biko, Alinsky, and many others. However, aware of this post-structural diversity, we do want to again lay out our assumptions and perspectives. We have made ours. Here they are.

Our first thought: community development is oriented by consideration of a number of axes, each of which names a tension within the process of theorizing and practice. Some of the many tensions are:

- Growth-centred versus people-centred development;
- Endogenous versus exogenous development;

- Top-down versus bottom-up practice;
- Service-oriented versus developmental practice;
- Product-driven versus process-oriented; and
- State-led versus community-driven.

Conceptualizing these tensions as axes provides the space to think in terms of primary and secondary rather than either/or. For example, we see community development as *primarily* drawing on endogenous resources (that is, resources internal to a community), and as *secondarily* drawing on exogenous resources (that is, resources supplemented from outside); and again as *primarily* bottom-up, even if the animating resources (for example, a community worker) are provided within a top-down initiative. In relation to the first axis, we are resolved that community development sits at the people-centred end of the spectrum, but we are also conscious that without a growth-oriented model of development, there could well not be enough taxation to provide the resources to support people-centred development; albeit there is a substantial body of scholarly work challenging the inevitability of growth-oriented development models.

Referring to the fourth axis listed above, a useful framework that can help re-orient community development practice is discussed by Burkett and Bedi (2007) from the International Association of Community Development. The framework clarifies one key paradigmatic struggle within community development, understood through the lens of a developmental approach versus a service-delivery approach.

The contrasting of developmental versus service-delivery approaches enables clarification of some key issues. Firstly, much of the language of community development is used by 'development practitioners' when they are in fact engaged in social development or service-delivery work. Such social development practitioners are working with predetermined models, ideas, and 'packages' of development goods. They are often similar to William Easterly's (2006) description of planners as opposed to searchers. And, do not get us wrong, some of these are very good (depending on where the plan/model/idea emerged from). However, such work is not grounded in the relationally oriented work of a developmental approach. The social developers/planners tend towards a colonial praxis, inevitably tainted by 'we know best' mentalities.

In contrast, a developmental approach starts with people, *engaging in relationships first and foremost,* reaching to be conscious of achieving some kind of understanding of the people's situation *as they see it* (Kaplan, 1996; Kelly and Westoby, 2018). The 'as they see it' is crucial because at the heart of a decolonizing practice is the ability to 'see what the people see'. Development *work* is therefore about relationships, and the struggle for equitable and just interaction between interest groups is at the heart of the struggle for development.

We often say to students something like: 'If you go into a community with a good idea of what to do, or a good model of what will work, then you have moved into social development/planner or service-delivery mode with development processes emerging from *your own social analysis* of the issues a hand'. Clearly, a well-trained professional will have such a social analysis. However, within the decolonizing and developmental tradition we align ourselves to, it is crucial for practitioners to put any such ideas or models 'on hold', 'carrying their analysis lightly' so to speak, enabling them to first and foremost enter into relationships with people to 'see what the people see' (see Lathouras, 2010). It is now a well-known maxim that only people can achieve true development and that development cannot be done to people. Representation, involvement, and having a voice are essential in community development work. It is the relational work between the practitioner and people, and the relational work between people themselves, that creates a community of people enabled to conduct collective conversations and work – which sits at the very heart of such community development work.

Creative ideas and great models might then come into play, but ideally, they are *the people's ideas*, or *a model the people have developed*, based on their ability to question, analyse, and strategize. It is not to say people are on their own. Practitioners can ask good questions and be asked questions. Practitioners have networks and can support communities to learn from others. Communities can be supported in searching for stories from other contexts – usually nurtured through a process of horizontal learning. This relational learning is perhaps the essential building block of growing networks of trust and cooperation that some refer to as social capital.

It is within the context of such practice that we understand the work of community development practitioners as primarily relational, communicative, emotional, educational, and political work, and secondly as technical work. To engage with people relationally requires strong communicative and emotional capacities, and to enable groups to 'move' through supporting a learning and organizing process (inevitably political in some way).

Any community development practice reduced primarily to the technical has been captured by an instrumentalist or reductionist approach to community development, whereby community development is understood through the lens of 'input' and 'output'; in other words, the logic that says that an investment, or transfer of money, skills, and projects into a community setting leads to good results. In contrast, the primary investment is relationship.

Alternatively, it is in a non-instrumental sense that community development sits within the people-centred tradition of post-development theory and practice. With people as the primary resource, relationships are centred on the practice alongside a responsiveness to the inevitable shifting relationships (Westoby and Kaplan, 2013). The practice becomes one of creating spaces and platforms for co-motion, rather than intervention (Esteva, 1987). It is about socially initiated work and not master plans that are socially engineered. If people cannot cooperate, or people engage in destructive kinds of conflict, then community development processes will fall apart, and from there will also fall the work, which is very fragile in nature. Technically oriented community development work usually puts financial resources at the centre of practice, with programmes or projects determining the development trajectory. People themselves remain at the periphery, subjected to being objects, as 'participants' or 'beneficiaries'.

Furthermore, it is worth noting that our perspective is also underpinned by a bias towards understanding the role of a community development worker as being *of, with*, or *among* the people – a stance that is troubled by the idea of working *for* communities, or *on their behalf*. The kind of work within which practitioners inhabit a stance of 'for' or 'on-behalf of' is usually community-service oriented.

Poverties, not poverty

Another thought about where we are coming from: development cannot be reduced to either economic, social, environmental, political, cultural, or spiritual/moral factors. Clearly, the enduring state of what Chilean economist Manfred Max-Neef (1991) calls *poverties* requires an equally sophisticated understanding of the holistic and systemic nature of the challenge. For example, South Africa's development challenge has not emerged just from apartheid's racial policies, but also from the ongoing exploitative class formations of a particular kind of capitalist development (Alexander, 2013; Andreasson, 2010; Marais, 2011; Mbeki, 2009).

People interviewed within the research work for this book argued for many kinds of analyses. For example, one senior practitioner argued that the main challenges facing South Africa are threefold, dealing with: 1) the failure to transform the education system; 2) the failure of land reform; and, 3) the failure to transform patterns of corporate ownership and power. Another argued that South Africa lies at a key juncture at this historical moment, focusing on an analysis of the state – with one direction being where the state would fragment and slumber into failure and the other where the state would rise with the best and brightest of human resources. Some commentators have talked about the problem of a 'shadow state' or 'state capture' (Pauw, 2017). In 2018, the incoming South African President, Cyril Ramaphosa, appointed the Zondo Commission to investigate and host hearings on state capture. As one witness after the other took to the bench, it became clear how state funds and state contracts were abused to benefit a few powerful elite. Some commentators have remarked that this may have resulted in billions of rands being lost from the nation's budget (see Ballim, 2018), even perhaps up to a third of the nation's gross domestic product. South Africa, clearly, could have been much further on the way to creating a better development path in terms of economic indicators.

A conflict transformation framework

The perspective of this book also takes into account that post-apartheid South Africa represents a post-conflict context. South Africa experienced many years of what can be considered as low-intensity warfare in which ongoing lines of separation were reinforced through state and non-state violent actions. Fear was a constant companion among many constituencies (fear of the state–military nexus, fear of the unknown 'others', fear about the future).

Such conditions also make contextual and particular demands of South African community development practice and theory. These demands sit within the realms of community healing or 'memory-work' (Harris, 2011), undoing the poverty of separation and fear, building *bridging* social capital across racialized boundaries, and communalizing the trauma of violence (Jansen, 2009), and healing memories (Lapsley, 2012; van der Watt, 2016; 2018). Understanding community development within South Africa therefore needs to incorporate an understanding that is inclusive of such analyses and perspectives. Good examples of work taking these issues into account would be the Community Peace Programme established in Cape Town (Froestad and Shearing, 2007), Michael Lapsley's Institute of Healing Memories work (2012), and, drawing on a broader frame of integrating socio-economic and psycho-cultural elements, the story of Bokfontein and the Community Works Programme (Langa and von Holt, 2011).

In light of this, our horizon is also informed by a commitment to *community healing*. Community development is therefore also concerned with collective healing as well as reparation. The conditions of colonization and the apartheid era remain spectral within the South African present, haunting individual and collective processes at all levels. Reparative requirements of justice, for example, returning stolen land, provide one narrative that could inform a decolonial tradition of community development within South Africa.

Attuned to this perspective, community development would need to also sit within a conflict transformation framework. Taking into account literature on conflict management, resolution, and transformation, this book frames social change through a conflict prism. Such an analysis leads to the proposition that the apartheid state was focused on *managing* escalating conflict and violence through a myriad of mechanisms. The late 1980s and early 1990s saw a process of conflict *resolution* leading to a 'negotiated' transition, with the new 1996 constitution providing the platform for genuine transformation.

Since this period, South Africa has been immersed in a process of conflict *transformation* whereby attitudes, practices, and structures related to the legacy of apartheid are shifting. Here, issues of reparation, reconciliation, and reconstruction take place within a context of individual, social, and structural change processes, or instead fail to do so, with accompanying social and political vulnerabilities arising. Some stakeholders resort back to a conflict management framework, utilizing the discourse of transformation, while in fact drawing on an approach that puts displacement at its centre (for example, transformation equals displacing 'whites') or continuing to propagate forms of white innocence such that nothing actually changes. Resorting to such a conflict management frame – that is, managing change processes, rather than engaging in deeper attitudinal, behavioural, and structural change processes – is one easy way out, albeit potentially a route to more conflict. Other stakeholders of course resort to reactionary ways of undermining transformational change, focused on entrenching 'white' power, primarily in the economic sphere, but also within the attitudinal-cultural sphere.

Bringing it together: criteria for our dialogical and relational inquiries

In light of these perspectives, we developed the following criteria to signpost the stories and possibilities we engaged with:

- Commitment to undoing at least one element of domination culture (class, race, gender, and so forth).
- Engagement with a tough substantive issue facing South Africa and linked to community development and decolonial aspirations, for example, education, land, housing, while recognizing the centrality of land.
- Demonstration of use of engaged and critical thinking and reflection in the praxis.
- Fitting community development orthodoxies in terms of relational practices and collective change.
- Demonstration of worker/practitioner reflexivity in terms of their own positionality (who they are, how their histories shaped practice), and their everyday practices (ability to do double-loop reflection, questioning assumptions).
- Recognition that people, groups, and communities have a right to their own story, and their own definition of what is going on (not what a community worker or other decided is going on).

That is, the story was indicative of working with people from the 'inside-out' based on the particularity of a place and context.

Positionality

While the above section informs the reader of where 'we' come from, now each of us briefly reveals our positionality. It is our sense that, in engaging in this research and writing project, it is important to provide a glimpse of our stories and perspectives, making explicit our bias when researching community development theory and practice within South Africa.

Peter

Peter is a 53-year-old white male. 'White' masks a lineage that includes Viking blood and English and Irish ancestry, and then a family move to Australia in 1980. His mum's side of the family grew up in the slums of Greenwich, England, and life was basically that of the underclass. On his dad's side, there are histories that include a great-grandmother who was an early suffragette, a woman who started the Meals-on-Wheels organization, and a Labour mayor.

Moving to Australia in 1980, Peter grew up in a lower-middle-class family on the outskirts of Brisbane (Yugara and Turrbal First Nation countries). He has made that his home, even while working in many parts of the world. It should also be said that, as a Queenslander (living in Brisbane, Queensland), Peter carries a deep sense of sorrow that Queensland and South Africa's apartheid regime have been so deeply bound together in colonial policy-making. The apartheid of Queensland linked to the apartheid of South Africa. This sorrow is shared in simple mutual recognition. In addition, in an ongoing parallel with South Africa, in Queensland there is a dual process of ongoing colonization (as Indigenous people still have their land stolen) and decolonization.

Importantly for this book, Peter first arrived in South Africa in 1994 and stayed for four years, working around Durban, the peri-urban townships of Umlazi and KwaMakutha, and the southern coast region of Umbumbulu. He spent 1998 working nationally, involved with many non-governmental organizations across the nation. He left for Australia in 1999, but has been back in the country every single year since, living there full-time again in 2011 and 2013. Basically, Peter is in love with South Africa, and as one friend says, 'it's your soul country'.

With that in mind, Peter's journey in decolonizing his mind and practice has been ongoing. Early encounters in his 20s with Gandhi's and Freire's work have continued to animate his thinking and reflexivity. bell hooks' engagement with Freire, and her own *opus* is an almost daily challenge to move beyond domination thinking and practice, towards a pedagogy of liberation and healing. Following the move to Africa in the early 1990s, initial readings of Biko's *I Write What I Like*, along with literary work such as *Things Fall Apart* (Achebe, 1958), gnawed at any self-confidence residing in a person from a white settler/colonial lineage. Yet these works, and so much more in Africa, inspire responsible engagement despite the regular loss of balance.

However, it has been encounters with, and apprenticeships to, many people from the margins that have been most transformative: learning from refugees Peter has journeyed with, or from people from favelas who have challenged his practice and positions; from a boss in Durban, and colleagues who have pulled him up for 'little things' that were not so little to some people in the room. Peter is still on the journey, ever aware of shadows of racism, sexism, classism, ableism, and so many more, that sit just beneath the surface. Freire's adage 'learn to question' involves creating community spaces where he too is accountable and can be questioned at any time.

Ultimately, Peter is still grappling with the heart of decolonizing work – how to relinquish stolen land?

Lucius

Lucius is a 57-year-old white African male and a pathological optimist who was born and raised in Namibia. His mother hailed from a family of white farmers in the semi-arid areas of rural South Africa (parts of the Kgalagadi and the Northern Cape in today's South Africa – bordering Namibia). His great-grandfather (on his mum's side) was a digger during the diamond rush in Kimberley, South Africa, with the turn of the 19th century. Lucius father grew up very poor with a stepmother and her two blind children in the small Karoo town of Phillipstown. Here, his stepmother, Luceia (whom Lucius is named after), spent time as a volunteer to help those living on the commons to survive. She did so while struggling to put bread on the table as a single mother of three children, surviving on doing washing and cleaning work for the more affluent white people who lived in the upper-town, the other side of the Hondeblaf (dog bark) River.

Lucius' father had the opportunity, as the first from his family to enrol for tertiary education, to become a teacher, later principal of a school, and mayor of the northern Namibian town of Tsumeb (the third largest town of Namibia at that time). He later became the human resource manager of Namibia's largest copper mine group and the first appointed post-independence Namibian CEO of the Namibia Development Corporation.

Lucius spent most of his adult years in Bloemfontein in the central rural Free State Province of South Africa. As a theologian and sociologist he drifted towards development studies. In his early career years (1990–1998) he did a great deal of community building and research work in the informal settlements of Central South Africa, in townships such as Freedom Square, Nonzwakazi, Huhudi, and Galeshewe. This was followed by extensive research work with multi-disciplinary teams in the areas of poverty alleviation, local economic development, and service delivery. Recently, he was involved in studying the first wave of community protests since 2004 and attempted to understand civil strife against a non-responsive and non-delivering government, despite an array of policies, programmes, plans, and projects.

What can I do?

In providing a brief sketch of these biographies, we also consider Biko's famous question, 'What can I do?' (Biko, 1978: 37), particularly referring to those with privilege, which we both clearly are. The answer is *a lot*. There is a huge responsibility, for all – including those who come from the settler/colonizer lineage and those fighting colonialism – to unravel what has taken place both within (our psychologies, our ways of being and thinking, decolonizing the mind and body) and without (in the material world of praxis). A friend of Peter's suggests that the responsibility of the privileged in South Africa is to, 'shut the fuck up, stay in our lane, and share the wealth'. While mostly agreeing with this suggestion, clearly the writing of this book implies a desire to say something despite the shaky ground we stand on.

Our final thought, riffing off the bell hooks wisdom that, 'I came to theory because I was hurting' (hooks, 1994), is that we acknowledge coming to the post-structural, deconstructive, and decolonizing because of our pain – our loss of a compass point in these turbulent times. Recognizing the borderlands that we are crossing, always with trepidation – because Biko might say to Peter something like, 'What are you doing here in South Africa? Go home and work in Australia', or some equivalent to Lucius – we step into uncertainty yet yearning for that justice that Derrida says must haunt us.

Conclusion

This chapter provides the reader with a sense of where the authors are coming from in terms of story, perspective, and therefore bias. It is hoped that our perspectives and subjectivities have been made more transparent, which, in turn, enables the reader to interpret the findings, analyses, and conclusions embedded within the whole book through an understanding of the lenses applied. It is posited that such an approach constructs the possibility of a more honest dialogue between author and reader. This is the cornerstone of post-structural, deconstructive, and decolonizing perspectives.

References

Achebe, C. 1958. Things Fall Apart. London: William Heinemann Ltd.
Alexander N. 2013. *Thoughts on the New South Africa.* Auckland Park, South Africa: Jacana Press.
Andreasson S. 2010. *Africa's Development Impasse: Rethinking the Political Economy of Transformation.* Zed Books: London.
Ballim G. 2018. Political uncertainty and the impact on business and the regional economy, Standard Bank. *Insights.* Johannesburg: Standard Bank.
Bauman Z. 2011. *Collateral Damage: Social Inequalities in a Global Age.* Cambridge: Polity Press.
Biko S. (ed.). 1978/88. *Steve Biko: I Write What I Like: A Selection of his Writings.* Johannesburg: Penguin Books.
Blaser M., Feit H.A and McRae G. 2004. *In the Way of Development: Indigenous Peoples, Life Projects and Globalization.* London: Zed Books.
Burkett I and Bedi. 2007. *What in the world...? Global Lessons, Inspirations and Experiences in Community Development.* Scotland: International Association for Community Development.
Campfens H. (ed.). 1997. *Community Development around the World: Practice, Theory, Research and Training.* London and Toronto: University of Toronto Press.
Carpenter M. and Miller C. 2011. Editorial: Revitalizing community development in theory and practice? *Community Development Journal* 46(1):i1–i6.
Carpenter M. 2013. Editorial: Community development in a postcolonial age. *Community Development Journal* 48(2):175–178.
Deb D. 2009. *Beyond Developmentality: Constructing Inclusive Freedom and Sustainability.* London: Earthscan.
Derrida J. 2007. *Learning to Live Finally: The Last Interview.* New Jersey: Melville House Publishing.
Easterly W. 2006. *The White Man's Burden: Why the West's Efforts to Aid the Rest Have Done so Much Ill and so Little Good.* New York: Penguin Books.

Emejulu A. 2016. *Community Development as Micropolitics: Comparing Theories, Policies and Politics in America and Britain*. Bristol, UK: Policy Press.
Escobar A. 2010. Latin America at a crossroads. *Cultural Studies* 24(1):1–65.
Escobar A. 2015. Degrowth, postdevelopment, and transitions: A preliminary conversation, *Sustainable Science* 10:451–462.
Escobar A. 2018. *Designs for the Pluriverse: Radical Interdependence, Autonomy, and the Making of Worlds*. USA: Duke University Press.
Esteva G. 1987. Regenerating people's space. *Alternatives* 12(1):125–152.
Esteva G. 2014. Commoning in the new society. *Community Development Journal* 49(1):i144–i159.
Eversley J. 2019. *Social and Community Development*, USA & UK: Red Globe Press.
Froestad J. and Shearing C. 2007. Effecting security and deepening democracy through 'peacemaking' and 'peacebuilding' forums. In Southall R. (ed.). *Conflict and Governance in South Africa: Moving Towards a More Just and Peaceful Society*. Lyttelton: Conflict and Governance Facility.
Gibson-Graham J.K. 2006. *A Post-Capitalist Politics*. Minneapolis: University of Minnesota Press.
Gilchrist A. 2004. *The Well-Connected Community: A Networking Approach to Community Development*. Bristol: Policy Press.
Guardiola-Rivera O. 2010. *What if Latin America Ruled the World? How the South Will Take the North Through the 21st Century*. London, Berlin, New York: Bloomsbury.
Harris V. 2011. *Madiba, Memory and the Work of Justice*. Alan Paton Lecture 2011, Nelson Mandela Foundation.
Harvey D. 2012. *Rebel Cities: From the Right to the City to the Urban Revolution*, London and New York: Verso.
hooks b. 1992. *Black Looks: Race and Representation*. Boston: South End Press.
hooks b. 1994. *Teaching to Transgress: Education as the Practice of Freedom*. New York and London: Routledge.
Human Rights Commission. 2016. *Report of the South African Human Rights Commission: National Hearing Relating to the Human Rights Situation of the Khoi-San in South Africa*. Johannesburg: Human Rights Commission.
Jansen J. 2009. *Confronting Race and the Apartheid Past: Knowledge in the Blood*. Stanford: Stanford University Press.
Jullien F. 2016. *The Philosophy of Living*. London: Seagull Books.
Kaplan A. 1996. *The Development Practitioner's Handbook*. Chicago and London: Pluto Press.
Kaplan A. 2002. *Development Practitioners and Social Process: Artists of the Invisible*. Chicago and London: Pluto Press.
Kelly A. and Westoby P. 2018. *Participatory Development Practice: Using Traditional and Contemporary Frameworks*. Rugby: Practical Action Publishing.
Kenny S., McGrath B. and Phillips R. 2017. *The Routledge Handbook of Community Development: Perspectives from around the Globe*, London & New York: Routledge.
Langa M. and von Holt K. 2011. Bokfontein amazes the nations: Community Work Programme (CWP) heals a traumatised community. In Daniel J., Naidoo P., Pillay D. and Southall R. (eds). *New South Africa Review 2: New Paths, Old Compromises?* Johannesburg: WITS University Press.
Lapsley M. 2012. *Redeeming the Past, my Journey from Freedom Fighter to Healer*. Mary Knoll, NY: Orbis Books.

Lathouras A. 2010. Developmental community work—a method. In Ingamells A., Caniglia F., Lathouras A., Wiseman R. and Westoby P. (eds). *Community Development Stories, Method and Meaning*. Illinois: Common Ground Publishers.

McMichael P. 2012. *Development and Social Change: A Global Perspective*. LA, London, New Delhi, Singapore, Washington DC: Sage.

Maldonado-Torres N. 2011. Thinking through the decolonial turn: Post-continental interventions in theory, philosophy, and critique. *Transmodernity: Journal of Peripheral Cultural Production of the Luso-Hispanic World* 1(2):1–15.

Mamdani M. 2016. Between the public intellectual and the scholar: Decolonization and some post-independence initiatives in African higher education. *Inter-Asia Cultural Studies* 17(1):68–83.

Marais H. 2011. *South Africa Pushed to the Limit: The Political Economy of Change*. Claremont, South Africa: UCT Press.

Max-Neef, M. 1991. *Human Scale Development: Conception, Application and Further Reflections*. New York & London: The Apex Press.

Mbeki M. 2009. *Architects of Poverty: Why African Capitalism Needs Changing*. Johannesburg: Picador Africa.

Pauw J. 2017. *The President's Keepers: Those Keeping Zuma in Power and out of Prison*. Cape Town: NB Publishers.

Pieterse P. 2013. *Rogue Urbanism: Emergent African Cities*. Cape Town: UCT Press.

Pyles L. 2019. Ethics and transformative community organising in the neoliberal U.S. context. In Banks S. and Westoby P. (eds). *Ethics, Equity and Community Development*. Bristol, UK: Policy Press.

Restakis J. 2010. *Humanizing the Economy: Co-operatives in the Age of Capital*, Gabriola Island, BC: New Society Publishers.

Rist G. 2011. *The History of Development: From Western Origins to Global Faith*. London and New York: Zed Books.

Sen A. 1999. *Development as Freedom*. New York: Knopf.

Shuman M. 2007. *The Small-Mart Revolution: How Local Businesses are Beating the Global Competition*, San Francisco: BK Publishers.

Smith J. 2005. *Jacques Derrida: Live Theory*, New York, London: Continuum.

Swilling M. and Annecke E. 2012. *Just Transitions: Explorations of sustainability in an Unfair World*. Cape Town, South Africa: UCT Press.

Tuck, E. and Yang, K.W. 2012. Decolonization is not a metaphor. *Decolonization: Indigeneity, Education & Society* 1(1):1–40.

Van der Watt P. 2016. Engaging the soil and soul of a community: Rethinking, development, healing and transformation in South Africa. Unpublished PhD thesis, Bloemfontein: University of the Free State.

Van der Watt P. 2018. Community development in wounded communities: seductive schemes or un-veiling and healing. *Community Development Journal* 53(4):714–731.

Westoby P. and Kaplan A. 2013. Foregrounding practice – reaching for a responsive and ecological approach to community development – a conversational inquiry into the dialogical and developmental frameworks of community development. *Community Development Journal* 49(2):214–227.

Zondi S. 2016. A decolonial turn in diplomatic theory: Unmasking epistemic justice. *Journal of Contemporary History*, 41(1):18–35.

CHAPTER 4
Community development effectiveness – how do we know what we know?

Abstract

Chapter 4 articulates how we approach the question of 'does community development work?' Concepts such as effectiveness and effect, evaluation and measurement, and, finally, making the case for 'developmental evaluation' are addressed.

Keywords: effectiveness, effect, evaluation, measurement

Let us return to some of our opening statements in the previous chapters. Firstly, we stated that there is an *unambiguous* history of people working together in their communities to make a better life. From this perspective, community development – as a citizen-led way of people learning, cooperating, and organizing together – works. History provides the evidence in the many stories of people coming together, organizing, and forming organizations. Such stories are key indicators of effectiveness, made substantive in the many organizations that are now taken for granted, often started from these grassroots initiatives.

This is not to say that many experiments have not also failed. Any process that puts people and relationships at the centre is frail. Relationships can be fragile. Groups can struggle to hold together in light of pressures, sickness, weariness, or conflict. People's organizations can flounder or fragment as energies are dissipated or pioneers leave. Therefore, along with evidence that citizen-led community development works, there is also evidence of plenty of failings. This is the ever-present gift and reality of social process. Failure is the shadow-side present of so-called success, of non-manipulated processes in which people are fully free to continue or walk away at any time.

We also suggested that two particular things cannot be conflated. Rather than the citizen-led community efforts, we asked about the 'practice' of community development, deployed by practitioners, workers, civic organizations, NGOs, states, and, increasingly, private-sector commercial enterprises. By 'practice' we mean community development practice that is recognized as a professional project, supported by an architecture of the profession – that is, journals, conferences, training, tools, and so forth. In applying the question,

'Does community development work?', we are really asking about the effectiveness of community development as a *professional project*, although we have previously problematized the 'professional' project from the decolonizing perspective.

The answer to this question is more complex than when considering citizen-led work, particularly when coming from post-structural, deconstructive, and decolonizing perspectives, recognizing that there are many kinds of community development praxis.

With that complexity in mind, our introductory answer to the question was that from our combined experience, community development is certainly not perfect, not revolutionary, not solving the endemic structural problems of power, powerlessness, and poverty; perhaps, community development is even marginal to the big picture of society – yet, it is making *some people's lives a little better* and it is *creating alternative futures*, experimental though they might be. In this *humble* sense, community development works. This is our claim.

However, this chapter goes deeper into the question and possible ways forward in shaping a more reflexive answer that also takes the post-structural, deconstructive, and decolonization perspectives seriously. To do this, we consider 'how do we know what we know?' by discussing topics such as effectiveness, evaluation, and evidence. We particularly make a case for 'developmental evaluation' as an iterative and adaptive, yet rigorous, approach to ensuring community development is effective – but understood 'from the inside-out' and from a complexity-systems approach (acknowledging the desire for micro-macro articulation and systemic change). We also make a case that this developmental evaluation approach aligns with a decolonizing approach to community development. Although we do not directly refer to issues of sustainability in the framework, the stories presented in Chapters 7 to 12 were all selected from contexts and sectors where the development interventions (projects and programmes) were or will be running for 10-plus years. In this sense, effectiveness can be thought of as 'sustainable' because they generate long-term results benefiting communities after extended support has ended. Many of these interventions also occur without significant, if any, ongoing external support. Hence, sustainability can be a key indicator of effectiveness, but is not primary within our framework, for reasons discussed in this chapter.

Revisiting the analytical framework

As we stated in Chapter 1, understanding how community development works is both a complex philosophical and a social science question. We therefore draw on philosophy, particularly in relation to discussing 'effectiveness' or 'effect', before turning to more orthodox development and social science traditions to examine the politics of evidence and evaluation.

Effectiveness

The challenge of development effectiveness and evidence is a real one. Today, many government international development departments have established 'development effectiveness' offices. Peter directed a Master's of Development Practice for many years, and a review committee looking at the programme insisted on including a new 'development effectiveness' course. Peter is also, at the time of writing, a member of the governance committee of a Research Development Impact network, ensuring that the evidence base of research is translated into effective policy and practice. 'Clients' seeking tenders for development initiatives and interventions insist on certainty about effectiveness and want assurance that the presenting 'problem' can be 'fixed'. So, this question of effectiveness, and how to measure it, is a significant one. We need to talk about effectiveness as it is clearly popular.

Those of us in positions of policy and practice also wonder about effectiveness as we want to feel somewhat assured that we are not wasting our time or scarce resources. Where there is also an ever-present emissary of a crisis, there can be an overwhelming sense that ecological, social, and economic decay is at pandemic levels. With a pulsating heart, we genuinely fear for future generations. To give ourselves then to trying to bring change in the world, is to invite this question of effectiveness.

From a critical perspective, it is also tempting to take a defensive, or perhaps even 'radical', position on the question of evidence, effectiveness, and 'what works'. From this position, the argument would be that questions of effectiveness are themselves symptoms of dominant and somewhat hegemonic paradigms with accompanying discourses linked to 'what you can't measure you can't see'. Evidence then gets tied up with issues of measuring and becomes a colonized space of what is easy to measure: the 'bums on seats', 'how many people attended the workshops or participated in the activities', or 'how many jobs were delivered', or 'homes for the homeless' kind of measuring, which is easy for the bean-counters. Within this defensive stance, the whole question of effectiveness is then interpreted as a dominating system's desire to control things, to make everything fit into its own predetermined, abstract ideas of what makes a better life or society.

Such a defensive or perhaps radical position can also be predicated on the idea that community development practice must be kept alive and protected from the bean-counters' colonization. Our job, particularly from a radical perspective, would be to then keep our work away from regimes of audit, evidence, and evaluation.

However, in this book, we will avoid this dismissive approach, recognizing as per the introduction to this chapter that it is important to have some assurance that the work is effective. No-one wants to be wasting their time and scarce resources.

Yet we do suggest that this kind of radical perspective poses poignant questions around the unexamined use of certain words that have the potential to diminish the efficacy of community development practice. A more radical perspective on effectiveness necessitates seeing the often hidden stories of people, or the quality of a process – what we think of as 'the invisible' (as per Kaplan, 2002). For example, consider the following excerpt from van der Watt's article on community development and healing in South Africa (2018: 17):

> A granny in the programme explained what happened to her: I have talked and now I feel better, even though nothing had changed. I don't even know why I feel better.

Linked to this participant quote, van der Watt cites Kaplan:

> Through the art of conscious seeing we change nothing of what is seen, but everything changes, because we see that which was invisible to us before (Kaplan, 2002: 26).

So, how do we talk about understanding effectiveness if the effect of the work can be, and often is, invisible? Often, the mere exposure to a process could have a significant development impact for people. It is very hard to know the answer, because it depends on where the invisible process of growth and the impetus for the change have come from. It is impossible to make assessments without knowing context, history, and energies at play. It would be akin to asking if a person who loved once and long had a more effective love life than someone who loved five times but over shorter periods. In this sense, thinking about the effectiveness of community development alludes to the now famous words of Socrates, spoken in his trial: 'The only thing I know is that I do not know'.

In a sense, language is always discursive. Words attached to meanings – and part of a capillary-like web of powerful instruments and institutions – are not neutral. They carry power and meaning. The use of the word 'effectiveness', much like evidence, implies an agenda: the idea of 'in order to'. Instrumentality is then part and parcel of the constellation of discursive power linked to effectiveness. How would such instrumentality measure the 'in order to' captured in the granny's reflection above? However, as per our musings on 'development effectiveness' offices, it is an emissary that is really hard to avoid. We have to talk about it.

A phenomenological understanding of effectiveness

We have found a useful and intriguing philosophical angle into the conversation, relevant to deconstructive and decolonizing perspectives, through drawing on Francois Jullien's poignant book, *A Treatise on Efficacy* (2004). At the heart of Jullien's book is effectiveness as understood through the classical Chinese philosophy of war, or Jullien's interpretation of it. In many ways, it offers a phenomenological perspective on the question of effectiveness. For Jullien, effectiveness comes from being able to observe carefully to see the 'fissure' that will become a crack, a crevice, a chasm. To 'see' the potential fissure and then 'intervene' into that space, expanding it, is to ensure the goal is reached. From this perspective, the efficacy of community development is linked to seeing, discerning, and sensing our way into *what energy is already at play* within people, a group, or a community, or supporting a process of people discerning their energy and accompanying pathway for change. It is not so much to intervene in an instrumental way. It is to see the invisible process of change already at work within a place, region, community, or group and then, in turn, support or nurture that.

From this tradition of practice, practitioners and organizations need to move from active-passive, to receptivity, responsivity, and enabling resourcefulness. In some ways, the question of effectiveness is thrown back onto questions to do with the quality of the practitioner. Is the community development practitioner responsive? Are they capable of being receptive to what is unfolding in a person, group, community, or locality, as opposed to imposing a 'development agenda'?

When we think of effectiveness in the community development field, we tend to think of what we (as experts, professionals, outsiders) *will do;* the goal we set out to achieve, the ideal we wish to reach (sometimes determined by the donor or the organizations worked for), but a phenomenological approach invites a slightly different way of thinking.

Jullien asks, as per this tradition, what is possibly the most crucial question: how – and under what conditions – is an effect possible? (Jullien, 2004: 104). For example, when is an art piece producing a particular effect, such as beauty? Would that not imply that the art piece has been effective? Or that there is effectiveness within that piece of art?

What does this question mean in the social field, and what might it mean for community development effectiveness? Surely it is as we have already been saying – in the same way that an art piece can be measured as effective by the effect of beauty, a person, group, community, or locality (that is, a social phenomenon) can be measured by the effect of *it being itself*. It is not about a community development process leading to an outcome predetermined by a practitioner, policy-maker, or funder. It is about community development being a process of people or groups in communities, discovering their pathway to change, gaining more options in their life, which is ultimately 'development as freedom' (Sen, 1999). It is therefore about a practitioner accompanying such a community in that process – an act of solidarity in opening up life choices and life chances for people to foster optimal living. In this wisdom lies some key criteria for thinking about effectiveness, to do with the quality of the practitioner and the capacity to accompany and respond to what is unfolding.

Community development pays attention to effect, but ...

The big caveat, which will run like a line of gold through this piece of writing, is that 'we can never be sure' of effectiveness, or that what we will do will work. Even if the practitioner has a profound quality of presence and responsivity, uncertainty, humility, and 'letting go of control' sit at the heart and soul of effective community development practice.

However, it is not only about the practitioner, as research knowledge can also produce a sense of the conditions and practices as well as routines and rituals that lead to the most fertile ground for flourishing community development work. This book does also offer some of that knowledge.

In some ways, we are searching for a new 'myth', as Denzin (2009: 139) quoting Hammersley suggests:

> To serve evidence-based policymaking we probably need to invent a ... myth for qualitative work, that is we too have clear-cut guidelines and criteria, maybe not randomised control trials, but we have our criteria (Hammersley, 2005: 4).

At the same time, effectiveness through this kind of lens invites practitioners to constantly 'look for effect', recognizing that effect is not always so obvious, much like the 'granny' quote earlier. And it is this constant looking that we now think about, often considered within the frame of 'evaluation and evidence'.

The problem of more conventional evaluation and evidence approaches

Acknowledging the relevance of questions around effectiveness we do also bring the critical analysis mentioned above. Many decades of 'development practice' have now been shaped by the ideology of *impact* effectiveness. One way of approaching the question of impact has been framed as quantitative versus qualitative (Denzin, 2009). Other critiques recognize that whether the impact is evidenced quantitatively or qualitatively misses the key point of where the indicators come from – inside or outside. Generally, 'impact' becomes the siren call of an ideology usually steeped in colonial traces of externally oriented indicators.

Impact can mean what we, the professional, or the policy and programme context, want to see happen. The literature will therefore often refer to ideas such as 'strengthening management for impact'. This kind of ideology has penetrated more or less all development organizations and one of the outcomes is the accompanying growth of organizations filled with functionary positions or personnel – for example, data capturers, monitoring and evaluation (M&E) officers, proposal and report writers, and communications officers. Problematically, the organization responsible for 'carrying' a participatory community development programme then becomes middle-heavy and evidence seems to suggest that in the 'snake pit' of such professionals, the king becomes communications imperatives – the need for the annual report. M&E becomes driven by the communication imperative rather than real M&E concerns. In turn, the accountability mechanism of the work turns upwards. Accountants and auditors want the project to do exactly what they had in the proposal three years ago, and the communications expert wants their equivalent of the one-pager. The question of real effect tends to become somewhat marginal. Instead, while using the language of effectiveness, the real gaze is on efficiency. Therefore, while effectiveness in development evaluation implies some kind of success and impact, efficiency implies success and impact but always within financial boundaries (the budgetary constraint).

You could say that the great sociologist Jürgen Habermas (1972) anticipated this nearly 40 years ago, suggesting that:

> the link between empiricism, positivism and the global audit culture is not accidental and it is more than just technical. Such technical approaches deflect attention away from the deeper issues of value and purpose. They make radical critiques much more difficult to mount ... and they render largely invisible partisan approaches to [evaluation] ... under the politically useful pretense that judgments are about objective quality only. In the process human needs and human rights are trampled upon and democracy as we need it is destroyed (Habermas, 1972: 122).

What also flows from this is that development successes are quantified, documented, and communicated to a greater extent than failures – ethics and discussions around purpose, democracy, and human rights are marginalized. Reflective practice, essential for decolonizing work where people share their lessons learned, is not encouraged. Ironically, in theoretical discussion, development experts will readily agree that failures are an important part of the learning process. However, when considering their own projects, development experts at all levels in the process have an interest in presenting a picture of success. Success is rewarded, while failure, however potentially informative, is not. The result of this is that the knowledge of the failure, the very information that could allow a specific community development programme or intervention policy to improve, is lost (Botes and Van Rensburg, 2000).

The politics of evidence

Because of this, there has also been pushback among development practitioners committed to fidelity in the work. One manifestation of this has been 'The Big Push', whereby practitioners are consciously engaged in a process of deliberation and debate called the 'politics of evidence'. Returning to Denzin (2009: 142), the key idea embedded within the 'politics of evidence' is that:

> evidence is never morally or ethically neutral ... the politics and political economy of evidence is not a question of evidence or no evidence. It is rather a question of who has the power to control the definition of evidence, who defines the kinds of materials that count as evidence, who determines what methods best produce the best forms of evidence, whose criteria and standards are used to evaluate quality evidence?

Consequently, the politics for evidence is evidence. And of course, this takes us right to the heart of reconstructing community development in light of the decolonial turn, because such questions are focused on issues of power: who gets to set the agenda, and, importantly, 'whose and what knowledge counts?'

At the same time, there has been pushback from those at the forefront of rethinking, or reclaiming, questions of evidence and the practice of evaluation. This includes cutting-edge thinking connecting the field of complexity studies and developmental/evaluation methods, evolving whole new approaches such as outcome harvesting, most-significant change, and valuing voices. Susan Kenny summarizes that, generally, evaluation might involve a 'final overview and judgment of a program *or* it might be an ongoing process involving monitoring' (Kenny, 2011: 386). This latter ongoing work is really about 'keeping an eye on things', which is aligned to a developmental evaluation approach, although rigour is also crucial – which we discuss later. Other earlier ways of framing this 'ongoing approach' include 'participatory action and learning' (see Pretty et al., 1995), or the likes of what Yoland Wadsworth called a culture of evaluation 'on the run' (2008). Such learning, in turn, ensures that activities and action are adjusted to meet the goals of those participating.

Denzin (2009: 140) usefully suggests that the way forward is to align our assumptions:

> with the call by First and Fourth World scholars for an indigenous research ethic. This call opens the space for a discussion of ethics, science, causality, trust, and a reiteration of moral and ethical criteria for judging qualitative research.

In this sense, Denzin has named some of the key partners to thinking about effectiveness who take decolonization seriously.

Ann Ingamells and Peter Johnson frame this politic of evidence and the search for new evaluation innovations as a struggle between the 'conventional policy approach' with its predilection for 'command and control' versus 'experimentalism' (Ingamells and Johnson, 2018: 162). In relation to command and control, they suggest that even when governments recognize the need for locally developed and adaptive work and accompanying evaluations processes – and even use the nomenclature of community development – they still *do not usually really mean* locally developed or adaptive (ibid.). While couched in developmental lingo, their emphasis is on summative kinds of evaluation that are concerned with making judgements.

The case for experimentalism and developmental evaluation

In contrast, Ingamells and Johnson suggest 'experimentalism' (ibid.). Within this framework, there is the acknowledgement of stakeholders agreeing to a direction with a timeframe for review – but there is an understanding that a locality or community needs to take up the authority to design and act – creating space for all those kinds of discussion that Denzin suggests are crucial. These include discussions about ethics of the work, the science being used to collect data, the challenges of understanding and causality, the deep layers of trust required in community development, and, finally, a reiteration of moral and ethical criteria for judging evaluative research. Such an approach is infused with a social learning ethos and reciprocal accountability. The shift from command-control to experimentalism requires new mindsets, sensibilities, new forms of relationships, and new skills at every level.

Ingamells and Johnson, building on this understanding of an experimentalism, within a contextual and adaptive approach to community development, recognize that evaluation has to also be emergent and adaptive. In line with our thinking, they also suggest that 'developmental evaluation' is most appropriate within contexts of uncertainty, which adaptive and experimental communities are (Ingamells and Johnson, 2018: 163).

Developmental evaluation

Most clearly articulated by Michael Patton (2015), developmental evaluation is summed up as 'using evaluation to inform innovation' through 'adapting evaluation to the particular needs and challenges of social innovation and systems change' (Patton, 2015: 1). Our suggestion that developmental evaluation is the most appropriate evaluative form – alongside other considerations about effectiveness – sits within some keywords in that statement. For a start, the 'particular needs and challenges' is crucial. This is not an approach that imposes outsider universal benchmarks or criteria. Therefore, it works from the 'inside-out', which we have named as crucial for reconstructed, decolonizing community development. It is to work with the singularity of each person, group, community, or locality, not imposing anything predetermined, pre-modelled or pre-designed.

Furthermore, 'social innovation' coincides with what professional community development is trying to do, accompanying groups or communities. Finally, 'systems change' can be aligned with a decolonizing goal of structural change. Patton also argues that the niche for developmental evaluation is the evaluation of 'innovations in complex dynamic environments' (ibid.). Much else does not need to be said for, of course, people, groups, or communities that are experiencing intergenerational forms of poverty are certainly entangled in complex dynamic environments.

From that premise of evaluation supporting innovation, developmental evaluation ultimately aims to help community development practitioners succeed. Effect then – to do with the quality of practitioner and practices, a cultivated ability to see the invisible, and the phenomenological (from the inside-out) – is also committed to success.

However, at risk of repetition, it is not then about judgement (from outside/summative work); it is about bringing together all the elements that can ensure practitioners know they are being successful in the work – seeing or sensing the invisible transformations, recognizing processes at play such as the decolonization of the mind, as well as material and structural changes. This approach also draws on data and is rigorous, so it avoids the fallacy trap of 'throwing the baby out with the bathwater', so to speak. To critique the misapplication of measuring, evaluation, and evidence-politics is not to dismiss the rigour and discipline of practice.

What appears to be crucial is the iterative dance between the constant reflective practice, deep listening about what is unfolding in a community development process, and feedback mechanisms from 'the people' who are setting their pathways of development (evaluative data and rigour). These, together, ensure constant adaptation from practitioners, and those supporting them as programme managers and/or policy-makers.

In summary, some of the key tenets of developmental evaluation, while not described here in detail (because readers can access material elsewhere), include:

- **Developmental purpose**: Knowing the purpose of the work but also recognizing the adaptive element, because often: 1) the context changes; 2) people participating shift; 3) people change through learning as they engage in the community development process; and 4) some new ideas have emerged so there is innovation by a community.
- **Evaluation rigour**: Ensuring the process is data driven, systematic, and not just reliant on hunches or perceptions. There is a commitment to challenging not only reflective questions about whether a community development practitioner is doing what they say they are doing but also whether their assumptions are accurate.
- **Use of complexity perspective and systems thinking:** Recognizing that we can only see complex realities *in part*, that it is more or less impossible to 'see the whole', but that we can still be 'methodical, informed, pragmatic and ethical about what we leave out' (Patton, 2015: 8). Specifically, systems thinking enables practitioners to understand the interrelationships between component parts of an initiative, along with recognizing perspectives and boundaries. Complexity theory, in turn, helps understand emergence, non-linearity, dynamic movement, and adaptation in the social phenomenon of change.
- **Co-creation is crucial:** The key adage, of 'not for us, but with us', sits within the developmental evaluation process itself.
- **Timely ongoing feedback mechanisms:** Aligned to the reality of community development processes on-the-ground, and everything else said above, timely feedback is crucial. Change sometimes occurs fast and, as Patton suggests, 'dynamic complexities don't slow down or wait' (2015: 12). It is because of this that a developmental evaluator should be embedded within a community development programme, constantly attentive, rigorously collecting data, and providing feedback to everyone within the system.

We would add to this that the process of co-designing and implementing developmental evaluation needs to also be informed specifically with the practice of decolonizing the mind and imagination. This requires the setting up of very specific places where the so-called margins of a process can speak to the mainstream, and those forms of domination – whiteness, patriarchal dynamics, and so forth – can be challenged.

Towards criteria for thinking about 'effect'

As we said we would, we have made a case for 'developmental evaluation' as an iterative and adaptive, yet rigorous approach to ensuring community development is effective – but understood 'from the inside-out'. We also made a case that this developmental evaluation approach aligns with our calls for a renewal or reconstructed community development that is responsive to the decolonial turn. As such, one of the tasks of our inquiry throughout writing this book has been to distil some key criteria for thinking about 'effect'. These are clearly articulated in Chapter 14 as we reflect on the stories and assemblages of Part III.

Conclusion

For those more oriented towards the positivistic, this chapter might well be frustrating. But we think such people would probably have not got to this chapter. For those more interested in the fine nuances and subtleties of thinking about effectiveness, we hope the chapter has offered some wisdom. We move mostly between the phenomenological, practical, and critical, suggesting some ways of reconstructing our thinking about effectiveness in light of the call to renewal and decolonization. Rigour and discipline are important, but underpinned by a people-centred, adaptive, culturally and linguistically sensitive, developmental, and experimental ethos.

References

Botes L. and Van Rensburg D. 2000. 'Community participation in development: Nine plagues and twelve commandments'. *Community Development Journal* 35(1):41–58.

Denzin N. 2009. The elephant in the living room: Or extending the conversation about the politics of evidence. *Qualitative Research* 9(2):139–160.

Habermas J. 1972. *Knowledge and Human Interests*, 2nd edn. London: Heinemann.

Hammersley M. 2005. 'Close encounters of a political kind: The threat from the evidence-based policy-making and practice movement'. *Qualitative Researcher* 1:2–4.

Ingamells A. and Johnson P. 2018. The Martu Leadership Program: Community-led development and experimentalism'. In Shevellar L. and Westoby P. (eds). *The Routledge Handbook of Community Development Research*. London, New York: Routledge.

Jullien F. 2004. *A Treatise on Efficacy.* Honolulu: University of Hawai'i Press.

Kaplan A. 2002. *Development Practitioners and Social Process: Artists of the Invisible.* Chicago and London: Pluto Press.

Kenny S. 2011. *Developing Communities for the Future,* 4th edn. Cengage Learning.

Patton M. 2015. *Qualitative Research and Evaluation Methods,* 4th edn. Thousand Oaks, CA: Sage.

Pretty J.N, Guijt I., Scoones I. and Thompson J. 1995. *A Trainer's Guide for Participatory Learning and Action.* London: International Institute for Environment and Development.

Sen A. 1999. *Development as Freedom.* New York: Knopf.

Van der Watt P. 2018. Community development in wounded communities: seductive schemes or un-veiling and healing. *Community Development Journal* 53(4):714–731.

Wadsworth Y. 2008. Is it safe to talk about systems again yet? Self organising processes for complex living systems and the dynamics of human inquiry. *System Practice Action Research* 21:153–170.

PART II
Intentions and ideas

Part II of the book approaches the question of effectiveness through the lens of 'intentions and ideas'; that is, recognizing that questions of effectiveness have to be linked to what is intended, or the idea behind the practice. Intentions and ideas are grounded in two chapters exploring 'diverse traditions' and 'multiple frameworks' as a way of examining the diverse kinds of community development being drawn upon in South Africa.

Part I of this book oriented readers to where we as authors come from, particularly making transparent our approach to community development along with our positionality, and also our understanding of how to consider the complex question of effectiveness. Part II now orients the reader on how we approach the complexity that comes from acknowledging the diversity of a post-structural perspective and even contradictory elements within community development. Firstly, in Chapter 5, diverse traditions are examined, underpinned by what we refer to as deep normativity. Importantly, different traditions are explored, acknowledging that each holds different intentions for the work. Ultimately, we reach for how a decolonizing perspective underpins a social reconstruction tradition, linked to Gandhi and Biko. Secondly, in Chapter 6, multiple frameworks are foregrounded, highlighting the different kinds of ideas that shape practitioners' practice. Fanon's decolonizing framework is offered as a particular guide.

CHAPTER 5

Reaching for a social reconstruction tradition

Abstract

Chapter 5 reaches towards a social reconstruction tradition of community development underpinned by a decolonizing perspective. This builds on an argument 'for traditions', using Campfen's (1997) conceptual lens of intellectual traditions. This chapter both carefully introduces the reader to those key concepts, and discusses the findings of the historical and contemporary analysis of community development. Traditions such as social guidance, social mobilizing, and social learning are considered as well as linkages with the specific work of people such as Steve Biko and Mahatma Gandhi.

Keywords: traditions, social guidance, social mobilizing, social learning

When attempting to make sense of community development in South Africa from post-structural and deconstructive perspectives – that is, acknowledging diversity and contradictions – one immediately runs into a problem. The diversity leads to a conceptual challenge about 'what community development is' before even working out how to understand effectiveness. For example, in acknowledging diversity and contradiction, does it mean that just because someone says, 'I'm doing community development', they are? How does one judge the effectiveness of *community development* practices, as opposed to some other practice that uses the language of community development? It begs the question, 'Does anything go?' Can any boundary be put around what is or is not community development?

We understand this conceptual problem in relation to the question of what some people call normativity, but which we extend to what we call 'shallow' versus 'deep' normativity. Shallow normativity is an ahistorical and decontextual way of thinking about community development in terms of ideas expressed as 'community development practice is *always* locally oriented' or 'community development is a participatory practice'. Within this approach, the norms and customs (that is, normativity) of community development thinking and practice are said to be shallow because there is no discussion of where these norms come from. They are discussed as being self-evident and are usually framed ahistorically. Community development becomes a set of abstract principles and aspirations.

Alternatively, *deep normativity* is a way of rethinking community development in terms of a diverse set of norms and customs that are situated within diverse historical traditions of community development. The norms and customs of practice, also potentially discussed in terms of principles and orthodoxies, do not determine what community development is, but rather what a *particular tradition* of community development is. There is depth to the norms, because they are grounded in the historical and other dimensions that are particular. Of note, we have opted to use the term 'tradition' simply to imply a historical element. We could easily replace 'tradition' with 'paradigm' or 'approach', or some other similar term. In turn, the effect of community development will be somewhat determined by the tradition or paradigm, because those evaluating effectiveness are 'looking' at different things (which will become clearer as we progress).

Another way of discussing the issue is to think in terms of *essentializing* versus the *traditions* of community development. To essentialize, like the shallow normativity mentioned above, is to revert to the essentializing or *defining solution*. It is to put a hard circle around what community development is. Within this approach, writers or practitioners of community development predetermine what is 'true' or 'authentic' community development, in line with a particular dogma or ideology. They then evaluate community development practice through this lens. Many different authors of community development theory and practice tend to drift in this direction by outlining key normative principles (Lombard, 1991; Ife, 2002; Kenny, 2011) or using the essentializing language of 'authentic' community development (de Beer and Swanepoel, 2012). This essentialist approach to community development would also easily jump to notions of so-called 'best practice' when searching for community development that is effective.

Some benefits can be seen within this approach. It gives scholars and practitioners alike some certainty about what community development is and is not, what is 'in or out of the community development family', so to speak. Community development academics such as Bhattacharyya (2004) argue that for community development to be universally relevant, the essence of the term 'community and development' has to be extracted. Alluding to Chapter 3 of this book, the reader could potentially discern our own drifting towards this approach. We have explicitly identified some key elements of community development, for example, contrasting development versus service delivery. We are even reaching for a decolonizing approach. However, a more accurate reading of that chapter reveals that our positions or understandings about community development do not arise from an essentialist or definitional stance of saying, 'this is community development' and 'that is not community development'. In turn, we do not suggest that a decolonizing approach is the only approach to community development. Instead, our perspective simply states where we are coming from based on the *clarity of the tradition* that we situate our practice within.

This brings us to the key point of this discussion. The second way of dealing with the question of diversity and proliferation is to carefully theorize the notion of 'traditions of community development'. Within this approach, theorists and practitioners do not so much worry about what is real or authentic community development but about what tradition of community development is being talked about, written about, deployed, or operationalized within a particular piece of work or writing. The task becomes deconstructive rather than definitional, opening up inquiry rather than being narrowly reductionist. This is not to remove the normative, because in many ways each tradition of community development, as has been said, has core orthodoxies or principles, within its own historical trajectory; but it is to resist a shallow ahistorical understanding of normativity and instead insist on a deep understanding of the norms and customs of a community development tradition.

Moreover, the benefits of this approach are that more spaces are provided to 'read' or make sense of what is actually going on within community development on the terms of the tradition – that is, to 'get inside' the ideas and intentions embedded within a tradition – rather than assessing what to look at from some outside, normative, so-called objective truth.

The gift of traditions

Anyone experienced in community development, with some sense of order in the work, knows that all positions are incomplete; each commitment to the work is somehow less than what is required. But community development workers who know the origin of the norms and ideas they use, and know the ups and downs of the story of their use, at least know an approximation of the tradition of their practice. In knowing the origins and the ideas, a practitioner can also discern what the effect is meant to be, and therefore be attuned to the question of effectiveness.

In acknowledging the importance of tradition, a community development practitioner has also experienced the richness of development work because of the presence of the many efforts of those who have done the work before.

One of the most formative influences in community development work is the pioneering work of Gandhi, because he was able to articulate an action methodology, a political and economic vision, and a personal and public value base. We link ourselves to this tradition as it also represents a crucial tradition in the decolonizing struggle (albeit, as readers will perceive, we link to others too, particularly from the African continent). Many people have taken his seminal ideas and shaped their own work practice directly from these. The great Jayaprakesh Narayan and Vinobe Bhave would be examples of this immediate and direct influence. Others have taken some of his ideas and married them with other sources of inspiration. For example, Fritz Schumacher, the author of *Small is Beautiful* (1973), was a key influence in the promotion of the community economy. Martin Luther King, that charismatic civil rights leader from the USA, is another who was influenced by this tradition.

It is openly acknowledged here that Gandhi (despite his faults) has very deeply influenced one of the writers of this book. Gandhi's influence has been so widespread that work borrowing from his ideas and example can be identified as part of a particular tradition of community development practice. Which, of course, is highly pertinent to South Africa, considering the 20-plus years he spent there. Later in this chapter, we will articulate this decolonizing perspective as a social reconstructive approach to community development, a lineage that became very much South African in the work of Es'kia and Biko.

What community development practitioners are able to offer, from moment to moment within development work, is greatly strengthened with the wisdom of a tradition. Yes, workers take risks – but with help. Although no one-liner lasts forever, there are 'rules' that encapsulate distilled points of wisdom that each can turn to. These points of wisdom are guidelines, not laws to be obeyed. *They are essentially tested good ideas* (and consequently historically formed norms), which are sometimes referred to as guidelines for a practitioner to register and take notice of. As points of advice about recurring difficulties, it is precisely this interface of difficulty and wisdom that makes them so useful. Part of learning a community development tradition is learning 'the guidelines' so that practitioners can have access to them when needed, associating them with problematic situations that are inevitably faced. Practitioners can trip-off these 'guidelines' in their mind through a learned response to these situations. At that stage, practitioners can then decide whether or not they wish to take the advice of the tradition or not. This approach also indicates that the reflective community development practitioner is alive to their tradition of practice and aware of questions of effect and effectiveness in an ongoing way. Rather than asking, 'Is community development effective?' they might instead ask, 'In what way have I been alive to this tradition of community development, and practised it with some integrity?'

When community development practitioners face recurring and seemingly insoluble dilemmas, the importance of wisdom elicited from tradition is incalculable. Take, for example, the issue of power and control. Community development work struggles to be a force of liberation. Power-based, controlling behaviour is so often at odds with that aspiration – and yet authority and control can be helpful when things are everywhere and all over the place, when order needs to be restored. But when is the right time to intervene and take control? When is it time to hand back control? Who controls the controller? These questions have a recurring and political quality, carrying all sorts of assumptions and potentially different answers.

It must be understood that the guidelines contained within community development traditions are neither absolutes nor commandments that demand conformity. The guidelines always need to be interpreted within the actual context and culture of a particular piece of work – there is no 'monolithic' interpretation. Individual differences of interpretation are important. Some practitioners, for example, are very collegial and peer-based, while others move forward by sharing more technical knowledge and information. Others still rely on charismatic qualities of sacrifice and bravery. People have different gifts they bring to bear to the community development task – calmness, a delicious sense of humour, a photographic memory – the list is as long and diverse as human nature. While knowing the guidelines of the tradition a practitioner is using may be one level of understanding, knowing what underpins the interpretation of those guidelines is another, and both are necessary.

Although all community development traditions have some common values, such as a commitment to justice and upliftment of the poorest, there are also fundamental differences between them. For example, in the participatory (see Kelly and Westoby, 2018) and dialogical traditions (see Westoby and Dowling, 2013), the community development process is based on relationship, not role and executive power. What practitioners bring to the work from these traditions is not the full story, nor the only path, but we know that without some minimum level of relational trust and cooperation, community is impossible – and it is this element that these traditions seek to protect and nourish. People hunger for that trust and cooperation, and those of us who belong to this particular tradition seek it out wherever it may be. Even with very dispersed, fragmented, and oppressed peoples, there are always small signs of hope – maverick, and sometimes the unexpected – and it is with these people and with this energy that community development workers from the participatory tradition stand to craft a path forward.

Thinking, for example, about these participatory and dialogical traditions, effectiveness becomes intrinsically connected to questions to do with the quality of relationship and community 'generated' or formed within the community development process. Other concerns become less important.

Now we consider a way of thinking about community development traditions through the lens of Campfens' work (1997), but we then stretch further, insisting that Derridean renewal, discussed in Chapter 2, is reaching for a reconstruction tradition underpinned by the 'decolonial turn'.

Intellectually rooted traditions of community development

Campfens (1997), in reviewing the many disparate intellectual traditions that underpin the field of community development, categorizes them into the broader traditions of societal guidance, social mobilization, or social learning thought, based upon what their key agenda is for society and social change. In many ways, this three-fold framework has proven to be useful, helping cluster thinking and practice into these traditions. However, our sense is that the three are inadequate, particularly when reaching for renewed possibilities in community development, underpinned by the realities of decolonizing imperatives.

Because of this, and through our research within South Africa, we also posit another intellectual tradition conceptualized as a social reconstruction tradition – mentioned earlier as linking Gandhi to Es'kia and Biko. It is this four-fold framework that we will draw on to 'read' what is taking place within South Africa.

This 'reading through traditions' approach groups various intellectual families into an overarching tradition based upon their core normative agendas, assumptions, and prescriptions about social change. In this sense, the broad traditions have clear ideas and intentions for change, which, in turn, profoundly shape how the question of effectiveness is approached. We will discuss this below when considering traditions within South Africa, but for now, key ideas of each tradition are briefly articulated.

For Campfens, the societal guidance agenda of community development is underpinned by the 'power of technical reason'. For example, Rostow (1960) sits within this tradition and, as such, practitioners or theorists tend not to question existing power relations. They are sometimes known as 'institutionalists', focusing on weaknesses of existing organizations and institutions to deliver a 'programme of development'. In many ways, some of the origins of community development are shaped by this tradition, reflecting the emergence from the British Colonial Office, and the desire for governments to shape what is good for communities. This tradition, now often supported by larger non-government organizations (NGOs) and even by corporations, continues to proliferate as organizations seek to implement 'community-level' initiatives based on government policy and priorities. Within this tradition of practice, the question of effectiveness is often linked to states' policy and programme goals. If the state wants more citizens to be participating in local government mechanisms for community decision-making, then effectiveness can be measured by the number of participants who 'come to the table', the impact of that 'coming to the table' in terms of people being heard, policy or programmes being reshaped accordingly, and so forth.

Secondly, within Campfens' framework, there is the social mobilization tradition of community development. For Campfens (1997), within this overarching family are a further three categories. The first is 'confrontational politics', as reflected, for example, in the work of Saul Alinsky (1964, 1971) and his classic books *Rules for Radicals* and *Reville for Radicals*. There has also been a global resurgence in this tradition, linked to the earlier industrial areas foundation work, and now diffused through writings such as that of Loretta Pyles (2019). Then, there is the 'politics of engagement' reflected in the utopian work of activists such as Robert Owen (Claeys, 1991). Again, this kind of approach is also alive and well, linked to the resurgence in cooperative community work (Restakis, 2010), commoning (Poteete et al., 2010), and community economies (Gibson-Graham, 2006). Finally, there is the anarchist category of the 'politics of free association and mutual aid' reflected in the work of social anarchists such as Proudhon (1979) and Kropotkin (1989). Overall, the question of effectiveness within these social mobilization agendas is linked to the impact of people's organizing and mutual aid efforts.

Thirdly, there is the social learning tradition of community development, which draws on a diversity of practices and ideas. These include American empiricism, particularly the pragmatism of John Dewey (1946, 1963), 'action learning', and organizational development. Then there are the ideas linked to Mao Zedong's seminal and influential essay *On Practice* (1968), which was viewed as a critical juncture representing a social learning tradition that integrated 'theory and practice' through class struggle. Importantly for community development theory and practice, there are the ideas of popular education, particularly theorized and practised by Paulo Freire (2006) as critical consciousness through dialogue. Freire's work has profoundly shaped contemporary community development, representative of key works such as Margaret Ledwith's *Community Development* (2005) or the long-term work of Myles Horton's Highlander Institute (Bell et al., 1990). This social learning tradition has also been grounded in a body of work that reconstructs the 'development expert' within social learning, disrupting 'expertise' within hierarchical practices. Somewhat differently to the previous two traditions, effectiveness of the social learning tradition is not so much measured in terms of instrumental impact, but instead is linked to questions about what people in communities learn – whether they are successful or not in what they set out to achieve.

Traditions and South African community development

A social guidance tradition of community development within South Africa

Applying the conceptual lens of social guidance to South African community development immediately illuminates many of the state-led community development programmes. They are drawing on a societal guidance tradition, whereby the state determines priorities and allocates resources accordingly. Within South Africa, the goals of such programmes are development, growth, and modernization – to lift people from economic and material poverty primarily although the unstated goal is often 'jobs, jobs, jobs'. For example, the particular role of community development workers is to draw communities into the terrain of the paternalistic or 'developmental state' activities, aligning people's goals with their own.

Clearly, as per our brief historical account in Chapter 1, there has been a history under apartheid of state-led community development situated in a particular social guidance framework. While drawing on 1960s United Nations definitions of community development, the guidance was predominantly influenced by the logics of apartheid thinking – that is, community development as 'separate development'. There have clearly been substantial changes since the end of apartheid – and our dialogical and relational encounters with many of the workers and practitioners employed within these programmes have been rich. However, it could be argued that the social guidance tradition is still somewhat tainted by colonial aspirations, mainly to do with economic development, rarely engaging with people's woundedness, the deeply torn social fabric of a society still entangled in post-colonial struggles. At the time of writing, there are numerous examples of programmes that embody this social guidance tradition. We mention just a few here.

The high-profile, and already referred to, National Community Development Programme is a substantive state investment. This programme was launched in 2005 under the presidency of Thabo Mbeki and continued during the Zuma era. It is coordinated by the National Department of Cooperative Government and Traditional Affairs. It employs upwards of 4,000 community development workers, with the goal being one community development worker per local municipality ward.

The Community Development Practitioner Programme is hosted by the Department of Social Development. Community workers in this programme focus on: household and community profiling; developing new and supporting existing non-profit organizations, (with some) focused particularly on early childcare development centres; and using community-based planning processes based on the sustainable livelihoods approach to develop initiatives such as community-based cooperatives and community gardens.

The Community Works Programme (and Expanded Public Works Programme) is also placed within the Department of Cooperative Government and Traditional Affairs. The focus of this programme is linking communities into the Local Economic Development Programme and particularly the development of cooperatives. However, it is primarily a social protection initiative supplementing people's grants with a small wage.

There is a large community health worker and community care initiative, focused on primary health practice and HIV-AIDS amelioration. Furthermore, there is a long-standing agricultural extension programme, using community-based trainers to support small-scale farmers – usually only in sporadic short-term ways, although critics argue the extension programme is still focused on supporting large-scale commercially oriented farms, rather than small-scale emerging farmers.

Of significance is the Rural Development Strategy with its five key directions, namely sustainable agrarian reform, home-garden and food security, improved service-delivery models, establishment of economic livelihoods, and creating enabling institutions.

Finally, there have been numerous adult education programmes over the years, with the most recent being the *Kha Ri Gude* campaign, focused on adult literacy.

While there is much literature available on the dominant state-led programmes in the country, relatively little is available on the thousands of NGOs and community-based organizations (CBOs). Many NGOs also initiate similar kinds of community development programmes and employ community workers, essentially working for the same state goals. Such NGOs essentially act as subcontractors of the state. Alternatively, some NGOs simply become subcontractors of international non-government organizations (INGOs), guiding communities into the kind of development envisaged from outside. The social guidance is not so much linked to state goals but to the stated goals of each INGO with their strategic hopes, often aligned to international donor hopes (a good example would be the Millennium Development Goals).

However, some NGOs draw on more reformist and radical traditions of community development, taking as their compass points Freire's and Alinsky's 'radical turn'. It is to these that we now turn.

The social mobilization tradition

Clearly, within South Africa, the social mobilization tradition has had a rich history. The anti-apartheid movement engine room consisted not only of politically oriented liberation movements such as the African National Congress (ANC), but the grassroots networks of civil society community-based organizations. Many such grassroots organizations were involved in either self-help or self-reliance-oriented work, but also supported people in struggle work.

However, the post-apartheid years have also seen a flowering of social mobilization, or social action. One obvious manifestation of this tradition is the so-called 'service-delivery protests' (Botes et al., 2008; Botes, 2018; Buhlungu et al., 2007: 13; Matebesi, 2017). These are often depicted by the South African state as illegitimate expressions of resistance against the liberation movement, but are interpreted by others as an expression of effective organizing and mobilizing, usually led by inspiring and committed young leaders. Such mobilization is indicative of people's growing impatience with their enduring experiences of social distress. People's life dreams are being thwarted by a lack of effective services, delayed infrastructure, corruption, and so forth. Some people's impatience is being directed into what Dlamini has named as 'native nostalgia', a somewhat destructive, backwards-looking gaze at so called 'better days of apartheid'. Other people's impatience is being directed more constructively into the service-delivery protests or lately coined community protests (Alexander and Pfaffe, 2014). Questions do arise over the use of violence, mainly towards property, but for many people their analysis is that, based on experience, violence alone triggers a responsive government. To avoid violence is to be ignored.

Other manifestations of the social mobilization tradition include social movements such as the Durban-based Abahlali movement (Gibson, 2011). The Abahlali movement is also associated with Shack Dwellers International (SDI), which, while being an international movement existing in over 30 countries, has offices within South Africa. For some commentators, the particular stand-out approach of SDI is to argue that 'self-responsibility, or self-help is a foundation for the mobilization needed to claim rights and draw the state into being a co-producer of services, rather than a deliverer of development' (The

Second Barefoot Collective, 2011: 9). Their practices include: moving from self-help to self-reliance; using community-to-community solidarity; self-research and self-knowledge; community visioning; and engaging the state in co-creation. This approach reminds us of the isiZulu expression of Zilweleni, which means 'fight for yourself'. The logic is that, once a community realizes the inherent potential within themselves, they can to a large extent improve their own living conditions.

A similar social movement, called the Federation of Urban Poor (FEDUP), also aligned to SDI, has been researched and documented by Swilling (2013). For Swilling, what is significant about FEDUP's approach is that it 'explicitly acknowledge[s] the complex and relational nature of the state and the need, therefore, to both engage it and contest the focus of its interventions, as well as the need to preserve and protect an autonomous base within the poorest homeless communities' (2013: 501). The mobilization, then, is not just towards the state, but also towards creating their own platform for dialogue within an autonomous space. Such an approach could be said to reflect an evolution of the mobilization tradition, reaching beyond Alinsky and other trade-union-oriented practices.

Another important expression of this tradition of social mobilization was the Coalition Against Water Privatisation and Johannesburg Water (Veriava and Naidoo, 2013). According to Dale McKinley, one of the founding directors, 'as a result of the privatization of water provision ... poor communities in and around Johannesburg found themselves unable to access and/or afford water and [have] responded with active resistance' (ibid.: 85). He argues that, 'one of the new social movements that arose to lead such resistance is the Anti-Privatisation Forum, an umbrella organization for grassroots community groups mostly located in Gauteng Province' (ibid.: 85). Here again is an example of local community groups, realizing they cannot act effectively on an issue that is 'beyond the local', and therefore coming together in a coalition.

There is also an emerging social movement particularly focused on the Karoo region, which is the anti-fracking coalition or movement (Fig, 2013). This movement is against underground gas exploration and extraction (led by Shell), and is organized both within the Karoo and at a national level. While the Abahlali and FEDUP movements, well documented and discussed internationally and locally (Swilling, 2013) are movements of the poor, focused on the obvious and immediate need of secure shelter and housing, the anti-fracking coalition is a 'middle class' movement that brings many different players together, crossing traditional class and race barriers.

The social learning tradition

In 1972, Steve Biko approached community animators/educators Anne Hope and Sally Timmel to help the Black Consciousness Movement. Their task was to train some adult educators in the Freirean literacy method. Biko had become aware of this method through his readings of Freire's then recently published *Pedagogy of the Oppressed* and was impressed with the potential relevance to South Africa. Timmel, with Biko, developed a one-week-per-month training programme implemented through most of 1972, equipping 15 adult educators, selected by Biko, with the literacy method. However, most of these people, along with Biko, were imprisoned by Christmas of that same year. The Freirean approach was part of Biko's hope for a holistic community development approach based on social learning.

Hope and Timmel went on to write the celebrated *Training for Transformation* (1984) educators' manuals, which represent the thinking of one manifestation of the social learning tradition applied to community development.

Other apartheid-era manifestations of such a tradition include NGOs such as Progressive Primary Health Care and Umtapo (Ngcoya, 2009). More recent examples of such practice include (the then) IDASA's grassroots popular education initiatives, Mvula Trust's citizen voice initiatives, and REFLECT groups run by the INGO ActionAid. This latter exemplary work is worth considering further. Sitting within the social learning tradition, it combines collective learning and social change. As stated within the Community Development Resource Association's Barefoot Guide (2011: 11), on using the REFLECT approach:

> people sit together in Circles (groups), analyse different problems and find solutions – Action Points. Techniques such as drawing, drama, songs, dance, writing, speaking, numbers, and visuals, for example calendars, maps and matrices, are used. These tools enable people's capacity to think about their lives more actively and to collectively organise to engage with the world.

In many ways, this statement about REFLECT groups represents the core processes of the social learning tradition for community development. The generalized lessons include what can be understood as: circle work (people sitting in ways that enable dialogue rather than monologue); discussion leading to analysis, where sometimes the discussion needs codes, or practical exercises to trigger new learning and new analysis (as it is particularly easy for people to get stuck in old analyses); and, finally, a choice, based on the analysis, to act in particular strategic ways.

Biko and Es'kia: A social reconstruction tradition

Mahatma Gandhi's work is well known globally. His work in South Africa – or at least the extent of it (over 20 years) – is less known. His approach can be understood as a 'reconstructive' tradition. This reconstructive tradition of community development (which aligns means and ends) focuses on nonviolent but purposeful relationships, includes both intentional community development (as per Gandhi's ashrams), and also practises self-reliance, stewardship, and trusteeship within village-level and national-level development. It is also an approach that recognizes the intersections between cultural liberation and economic/political liberation. Gandhi himself recognized that India's political liberation from British colonial rule would not necessarily lead to better lives for the poor unless it was linked to economic and cultural liberation.

Indeed, most analysts would argue that it is safe to say that Gandhi's *satyagraha* approach to social change was developed within the crucible of South Africa's early struggle years (Guha, 2013). His work also influenced many Africans' understanding of their struggle. For example, during Peter's three years living near Durban, he worked in the township area of Adam's Mission, a location famous for hosting Luthuli College, a training school for South Africa's black teachers. Luthuli College is named after Albert Luthuli – one of the founders and a key leader of the ANC – who was also a 'passionate disciple of Mahatma Gandhi' (Mandela, 2010: 52) and understood his non-violent approach to social change in terms of principle, not just pragmatics. That is, he saw nonviolence as a moral imperative, not just a strategic one.

However, as Luthuli and Mandela (the ANC) became more aligned to an activist approach to social change, rather than community development – Luthuli representing the elders' hope for nonviolent social activism, and Mandela representing the new guards' loss of hope about nonviolent efficacy and instead advocating for violence – Luthuli and Mandela become less relevant in tracing community development wisdom. After all, community development per se was not their focus. In contrast, the work of Steve Biko, and our subsequent discovery of the work of Es'kia Mphahlele, offers traces that form an intellectual tradition which we describe as a social reconstruction tradition.

Within our initial readings of both Biko and Mphahlele's approaches to community development, we were tempted to see a social learning approach, particularly when considering their emphases on both formal and non-formal education within community development practices. Certainly, the account of the social learning tradition above discusses Biko's desire to draw on the social learning trace of Freire, with his focus on adult education and literacy work. However, a closer reading of Biko's and Mphahlele's work has led us to conclude that while the form of the community development work might be understood within a social learning frame, the intellectual roots are different. For Mphahlele, the roots were what he called African humanism (Mphahlele, 2002: 185ff) and for Biko it was black consciousness, informed by the likes of Malcolm X, Frantz Fanon, and James Cone.

For example, for Biko, a key rationale in setting up health clinics was that they were health clinics run for blacks and by blacks, with both black medical staff and black management. The health clinic was important, per se, but for Biko, what was more important was 'reconstructing' a cultural consciousness that blacks can manage and run their own affairs. The key 'developmental' problems were *cultural* – if black people only see good things coming from white people then they will inevitably develop a sense of inferiority that saps the soul – and *structural* – recognizing the role of capitalist modes of production and accumulation within exploitation. Development activity then was focused on the practical, but also on the cultural-conscious. Biko, drawing on Fanon's insights, recognized that many 'black people were operating from a position of non-recognition' and that 'To be black was to be rendered invisible and illegitimate' (Mangcu, 2012: 200). In turn, this required engaging with a 'psycho-cultural challenge', with a transformation such 'that black people needed to believe that they were worthy of freedom and its responsibility' (Mangcu, 2012: 278). Biko himself states that:

> We try to get blacks in conscientisation to grapple realistically with their problems, to attempt to find solutions to their problems, to develop what one might call an awareness, a physical awareness of their situation, to be able to analyse it, and to provide answers for themselves. The purpose behind it really being to provide some kind of hope; I think the central theme about black society is that it has got elements of a defeated society; people look like they have given up the struggle ... now this sense of defeat is basically what we are fighting against; people must not give in to the hardship of life, people must develop a hope, people must develop some kind of security to be together to look at their problems, and people must in this way build up their humanity. This is the point about conscientisation and Black Consciousness (Stubbs, 1988: 85).

From this, it is clear that, like Gandhi, Biko understood cultural independence as being as important as political independence.

Conclusion

At the heart of the rationale for this chapter is the idea that the practice of community development requires practitioners to have an astute understanding of traditions. Several reasons can be articulated and argued for. Firstly, such an understanding ensures that a practitioner understands the possible traditions of community development that exist, enabling them to consciously work within one, or across several. Secondly, it ensures that they understand their own approach historically, being knowledgeable of the norms and customs associated with their tradition of practice. In a sense, then, they are released from trying to do any 'pure' or 'authentic' community development, but can instead reflect on the congruency of their stated norms and customs and actual practices. Thirdly, it enables a community development practitioner to deliberate with other practitioners more carefully, making their own tradition more transparent and eliciting an understanding of others' perspectives within the deliberative process. This disrupts the possibilities of talking at cross-purposes, ensuring that people elicit each other's associated meanings with concepts used. Finally, understanding community development in a way that is inclusive of tradition provides a rationale for creating 'communities of practice', whereby community practitioners can come together with others who share their tradition (and with those who do not) to enhance reflective and educational spaces.

As a final comment in this chapter, what has struck us as practitioners and engaged scholars within the South African context is the rich source of local material available to South African community development workers. Gandhi matured here within South Africa; Biko was a shining light – someone who drew on important ideas from people such as Paulo Freire, Malcolm X, and

Frantz Fanon – but who put them together in a concrete expression of the black community programmes; and then Es'kia articulates the practice beautifully, as will be explored more thoroughly in Chapter 13. These endogenously oriented traces, situated alongside the classic social guidance, social mobilization, and social learning traditions, provide a solid ground for reflection, learning, and action.

References

Alexander P. and Pfaffe P. 2014. Social relationships to the means and ends of protest in South Africa's ongoing rebellion of the poor: The Balfour insurrections. *Social Movements Studies* 13(2):204–221.

Alinsky S. 1964. *Reville for Radicals*. Chicago: University of Chicago Press.

Alinsky S. 1971. *Rules for Radicals: A Pragmatic Primer for Realistic Radicals*. New York: Random House.

Bell B., Gaventa J. and Peters J. (eds). 1990. *We Make the Road by Walking: Conversations on Education and Social Change: Myles Horton and Paulo Freire*. Philadelphia: Temple University Press.

Bhattacharyya J. 2004. Theorising community development. *Journal of the Community Development Society* 34(2):5–34.

Botes L. 2018. South Africa's landscape of social protests: A way forward for local government? *African Journal of Public Affairs* 10(4):241–256.

Botes L., Lenka M., Marais L., Matebesi Z. and Sigenu K. 2008. *The Cauldron of Local Protests: Reasons, Impacts and Lessons Learnt*. Centre for Development Support, University of Free State.

Buhlungu S., Daniel J., Southall R. and Lutchman J. (eds). 2007. *State of the Nation: South Africa 2007*. Cape Town: Human Sciences Research Council.

Campfens H. 1997. *Community Development around the World: Practice, Theory, Research, Training*. Toronto, London: University of Toronto.

Claeys G. (ed.) 1991. *Owen, Robert: A New View of Society and Other Writings*. UK: Penguin Classics.

Dewey J. 1927/1946. *The Public and its Problems: An Essay on Political Inquiry*. Chicago: Gateway Books.

Dewey J. 1938/1963. *Experience and Education*. London: Collier Books.

De Beer F. and Swanepoel H. 2012. A postscript as an introduction: Do we know where to go with the professionalization of community development in South Africa? *Africanus* 42(2):3–13.

Fig D. 2013. Hydraulic fracturing in South Africa: Correcting the democratic deficits. In Daniel J., Naidoo P., Pillay D. and Southall R. (eds). *New South Africa Review 3: The Second Phase—Tragedy or Farce?* Johannesburg: WITS University Press.

Freire P. 1970/2006. *Pedagogy of the Oppressed*. New York: Continuum.

Gibson N. 2011. *Fanonian Practices in South Africa: From Steve Biko to Abahlali base Mjondolo*. KwaZulu-Natal, South Africa: UKZN Press.

Gibson-Graham J.K. 2006. *A Post-Capitalist Politics*. USA: University of Minnesota Press.

Guha R. 2013. *Gandhi before India*. London: Allen Lane/Penguin Books.

Hope A. and Timmel S. 1984. *Training for Transformation: Handbook for Community Workers: Vol I-IV*. Zimbabwe: Mambo Press.

Ife J. 2002. *Community Development: Community Based Alternatives in an Age of Globalisation*, 2nd edn. Melbourne: Pearson Education.

Kelly A. and Westoby P. 2018. *Participatory Development Practice: Using Traditional and Contemporary Frameworks.* Rugby: Practical Action Publishing.

Kenny S. 2011. *Developing Communities for the Future,* 4th edn. Cengage Learning.

Kropotkin P. 1914/1989. *Mutual Aid: A Factor of Evolution.* Montreal: Black Rose Books.

Ledwith M. 2005. *Community Development: A Critical Approach.* Bristol: Policy Press.

Lombard A. 1991. *Community Work and Community Development: Perspectives on Social Development.* Pretoria: HAUM-Tertiary.

Mandela N. 2010. *Nelson Mandela: Conversations with Myself.* UK and Australia: MacMillan.

Mangcu X. 2012. *Biko: A Biography.* Cape Town: Tafelberg.

Mao Zedong. 1937/1968. On Practice. In *Four Essays on Philosophy.* Peking: Foreign Language Press.

Matebesi S. 2017. *Civil Strife against Local Governance: Dynamics of Community Protests in Contemporary South Africa.* Berlin: Barbara Budrich.

Mphahlele E. 2002. *Es'kia.* South Africa: Kwela Books in association with Stainbank and Associates.

Ngcoya M. 2009. Ubuntu: Globalisation, Accommodation, and Contestation in South Africa. Unpublished PhD thesis. American University.

Poteete A., Janssen M. and Ostrom E. 2010. *Working Together: Collective Action, the Commons, and Multiple Methods in Practice.* Princeton and Oxford: Princeton University Press.

Pyles L. 2019. Ethics and transformative community organising in the neoliberal U.S. context. In Banks S. and Westoby P. (eds). *Ethics, Equity and Community Development.* Bristol, UK: Policy Press.

Proudhon, P. 1863/1979. *The Principle of Federation.* Toronto: University of Toronto Press.

Restakis J. 2010. *Humanising the Economy: Co-operatives in the Age of Capital.* Canada: New Society Publishers.

Rostow W. 1960. *The Stages of Economic Growth.* Cambridge: Cambridge University Press.

Schumacher E.F. 1973. *Small is Beautiful: Economics as if People Mattered.* London: Abacus.

Stubbs A. (ed.) 1978/1988. *Steve Biko: I Write What I Like: A Selection of his Writings.* Penguin Books.

Swilling M. 2013. Beyond cooption and protest: Reflections on the FEDUP alternative. In van Blonk M., Swilling M., Pieterse E. and Parnell S. (eds). *Consolidating Developmental Local Government: Lessons from the South African Experience.* Cape Town: UCT Press.

The Second Barefoot Collective. 2011. Barefoot Guide Connection. Available at www.barefootguide.org. [Accessed 14 January 2019].

Veriava A and Naidoo P. 2013. Predicaments of post-apartheid social movement politics: The anti-privatisation forum in Johannesburg. In Daniel J., Naidoo P., Pillay D. and Southall R. (eds). *New South Africa Review 3: The Second Phase—Tragedy or Farce?* Johannesburg: WITS University Press.

Westoby P. and Dowling G. 2013. *Theory and Practice of Dialogical Community Development: International Perspectives.* London: Routledge.

CHAPTER 6
Reconstructing frameworks for practice

Abstract
Chapter 6 pushes for a 'reconstruction of frameworks', recognizing that it is too easy for practitioners to simply draw on predetermined frameworks rather than reflectively developing their own. Along with several existing frameworks drawn upon within South Africa, Fanon's 'decolonizing framework' is foregrounded.

Keywords: frameworks of practice, decolonizing, Fanon

Jim Ife's text on community development states that, 'every community worker will conceptualize practice in a different way and will build a different practice framework that will develop and change with experience' (Ife, 2002: 265). In this statement, Ife recognizes that community development cannot be objectivized, and that the practice is far more than applying a set of abstract propositions or a standardized toolkit. Coming to an understanding of community development requires practice, constant effort, and reflection based on a person's own experience and context. Ife further argues that:

> To seek to impose a single framework on all community workers is to fall into the positivist and modernist trap of assuming there is only one 'right' or 'best' way to do community work. This would be contrary to the principle of diversity and the need to establish 'bottom-up' constructions of wisdom. It is important to develop one's own framework (ibid.).

Ife's approach is aligned to our post-structural and deconstructive perspective, recognizing diversity as a core principle of community development.

Linking to the previous chapters on diverse traditions, this chapter considers the multiple frameworks that have shaped the work of South African community development. In doing this, a number of lenses are applied. Firstly, we recognize that many community practitioners have not developed their own personal practice framework, and instead draw on frameworks 'given to them'. This acknowledges that there are stages of professional development for a community development practitioner. The use and development of different frameworks and the evolving complexity of those frameworks are indicators of the various stages of the professional development of a practitioner. A more detailed depiction of these stages is outlined in Box 6.1.

The seven stages identified in Box 6.1 indicate a journey common to many in community development practice. Recognizing that many community

http://dx.doi.org/10.3362/9781788531320.006

> **Box 6.1 Stages of professional development**
>
> 1. The practitioner enacts aspects of a community development task but without a wider perspective about that task.
> 2. The practitioner enacts part of the task and, with the benefit of a situational framework, understands both the purpose and context of that task.
> 3. The practitioner is able to understand and enact a complete task and sees the whole through another person's practice framework.
> 4. The practitioner is able to understand and enact, both in part and in whole, another person's framework, and see this task in relationship to other tasks and other contexts (it is at this stage that practitioners are able to undertake professional supervision of another worker).
> 5. The practitioner is able to develop and enact, both in part and in whole, their own practice framework (at this stage they are often considered to be senior colleagues or, more frequently and less reverently, 'old hands' or the 'old brigade').
> 6. The practitioner is familiar with a number of practice frameworks and has the capacity to appreciate the strengths and limitations of each (at this stage a practitioner could make their way, confidently, with international work).
> 7. The practitioner is able to use and explain their own framework that has wide appeal to others (at this stage writing could become attractive).

development practitioners are not at a stage to develop their own personal practice frameworks, we offer some useful existing frameworks. A couple are organizational, as per the work of the Community Development Resource Association (CDRA) and Training for Transformation. Another is a version by Frantz Fanon, particularly helpful as we also reach for a decolonizing perspective.

Secondly, recognizing that many South African community development practitioners draw on organizationally diffused frameworks, we suggest that, like traditions, established community development frameworks are a great gift because they mean even the beginner worker need not begin at the beginning, reinventing the wheel. It is not mandatory that every practitioner must have a unique framework, but whatever the choice, the framework needs to fit the context. As a beginner practitioner, most are grateful for a relatively straightforward practice framework that they can try out for themselves, especially while they find their feet in the work. However, if there is only one framework on offer, it can become orthodoxy instead of an aid, and people can get stuck. The framework drives the practice rather than acting as a reflective compass point. On the other hand, if too many frameworks are on offer, it gets a bit like trying to choose a cleaning product from a thousand varieties available in the supermarket but not choosing any and, in turn, not doing the cleaning.

As trained practitioners, the first and minimum qualification for the job is becoming conscious of the practice framework being used and being able to articulate the framework to share with others. This is to become clear, transparent, and accountable in terms of the intentions and ideas behind practice.

Again, this is the only way to 'get inside' someone's practice, which is the way to inquire into the effectiveness of their work on their terms. To not have any framework is to not be clear about the ideas and intention behind the practice which, in turn, undermines any transparency and accountability regarding the question of effectiveness.

In our research journey, particularly our relational and dialogical encounters, we found ourselves regularly rubbing up against several frameworks. In reflecting on these experiences, we have opted to call them the 'big four'. We start with exploring these. Our inquiry also involved close relations with three particular organizations, and we give voice to them in an assemblage of possibilities. Finally, we have been intrigued by the resurgence or renewal of interest in Frantz Fanon's work within South Africa, indicative of the decolonial turn, and so we offer an interpretation of his framework to be used for practitioners searching to integrate a decolonizing perspective into their practice.

The 'big four' South African community development frameworks

What became abundantly clear when reading about, talking to, and visiting community development practitioners was that people were familiar with what we call the 'big four' frameworks that are being diffused throughout South Africa.

Community-led development

The first of these 'big four' is the framework known as community-driven or community-led development. This has historically been internationally championed, particularly by the World Bank (Everatt and Gwagwa, 2005), but has a global reach now within many organizations (see, for example, the website of The Movement for Community-Led Development, MCLD). Some of the key tenets of this approach include a phased engagement process as follows:

1. *Phase I: Transforming the mindset* of both citizens and government representatives from seeing people living in conditions of hunger and poverty as 'subjects/beneficiaries' to 'change agents' and rights-bearing, active citizens.
2. *Phase II: Supporting capacity.* As people begin to gain voice, agency, and confidence in their ability to take action to improve their lives, they need to begin building the 'social infrastructure' necessary for sustainable social and economic progress in all areas of life.
3. *Phase III: Impact.* Once communities are organized, they are equipped to achieve measurable progress in health, education, livelihoods, and all aspects of their vision.
4. *Phase IV: Sustainability.* The process is designed to restore citizens' control over their own lives and destinies. The process includes specific actions

to ensure that this outcome is sustainable, and resilient to political, economic, and other shocks (see MCLD, n.d.).

Within South Africa, this approach has been used by NGOs such as Khanya-aicdd. Other examples of this would be the People's Housing Process – ideally a self-help and community-driven approach to deliver housing to people. What appears to be appealing is the emphasis of 'community' being at the centre of decision-making and agency. While often designed by outsiders (such as the World Bank), authority is transferred to communities around decision-making, and resources are made available to communities to invest in their priorities.

Rights-based community development

Some practitioners drew on the second of the 'big four', which is rights-based community development. Rights-based approaches to community development focus on people's rights and the duty-bearers of those rights (which authority is responsible), for example people's rights to education and government as the key duty-bearer of that social right. This is a particularly tricky issue in South Africa, which has one of the most progressive constitutions in the world, implying not just 'traditional civil rights', such as free speech, assembly, property, and so forth, but also social rights such as housing, health, and education. This approach eschews self-help-oriented work, instead pointing to more structural approaches to change. Rights-based approaches are built on the assumptions that poverty, inequality, and marginalization are the products of embedded social structures and practices established during colonial and post-colonial times. This cannot be challenged and changed through programmes and projects, and deeper, more fundamental social structural change is necessary to make enduring human development possible. Rights-based approaches are diffused internationally by numerous INGOs (e.g. ActionAid) and some UN programmes.

Asset-based community development

Asset-based community development (ABCD) is the third of our 'big four' approaches, and is flourishing globally and within South Africa at the time of writing this book. Researched and internationalized by the Coady Institute, ABCD is experiencing a renaissance within South Africa (Schenck et al., 2010: 62; Wilkinson-Maposa 2008), evidenced by organizations such as Ikhala Trust in the Eastern Cape and the CDRA's engagement with it.

In this approach, the emphasis is on identifying, mapping, and using endogenous assets within a community, including physical, financial, and social assets. People come together and engage in their own participatory action research to assess these assets, and then design community-based initiatives that draw upon them. The intent is not to avoid any exogenous resources from the outside, but to emphasize the endogenous.

Sustainable livelihoods approach

Finally, the fourth of our 'big four' is the sustainable livelihoods approach (SLA). This approach has historically been diffused by the UK's Department for International Development and draws on the research and writing of Robert Chambers. In South Africa, the approach has been used extensively by the Department of Social Development, particularly within their Community Development Practitioner Programme. Furthermore, for some years, drawing on the training of Khanya-aicdd, the SLA framework was integrated as a tool of analysis within a community-based planning approach. Similar to the ABCD framework, the SLA seeks to assess the core assets within a community and mobilize them, while also assessing how communities can be vulnerable to external shocks (climate, economic downturns, and so forth). Distinctively, the SLA also tries to make more explicit micro-macro articulations, linking the grassroots issues to policy.

These four 'big' frameworks dominate the discursive and practice field South Africa, and most community practitioners are familiar with the language of one or several of these organizationally diffused frameworks. One of the challenges of this domination is that many practitioners often seem to think that the framework they understand (one of the above) equals 'real' community development. They are not necessarily aware that there are other frameworks available. Practice seems to be reduced to being able to utilize the steps, procedures, or methods of the framework understood (usually having been inducted into it 'on the job').

An assemblage of possibilities: Three organizations that welcomed us

However, there are a few frameworks being diffused not via large government or international organizations (as per the 'big four'), but through smaller South African organizations. Our research inquiry led to rich and rewarding relationships with three such organizations: Peter's engagement with the work of the CDRA and its 'developmental approach' or organic approach; the work of the Grail Centre and the 'Train-the-Trainer' (TtT) approach; and Lucius' long relationship with Khanya-aicdd, and their work in promoting an integration of the sustainable livelihoods approach within community-based planning methods (although it is acknowledged that they are working closely with the Department of Social Development).

CDRA and a developmental framework

Peter got to know the work of CDRA firstly at a distance when doing some work with an organizational development NGO (OLIVE) in Durban in the late 1990s, and then more closely in the past decade, often being invited to offer workshops from their most beautiful base in Woodstock/District Six, Cape Town. During the 1980s and 1990s, OLIVE and CDRA were two of the key organizations working to support the organizations that themselves were seeking to do effective community development. There was recognition that the organizations, along with their practice, needed support.

The developmental approach has best been articulated in CDRA's 1997/8 annual report (1998). This report, written in the form of an extended essay, considers some of the problematics of what is named as the conventional development paradigm, and then argues for an alternative developmental paradigm. For example, in discussing the conventional paradigm, the essay considers many of its assumptions and practices, such as (among others):

- Development can be created and engineered.
- Development is then something that is brought to, and is intended for, some, by others who are presumably more developed.
- Development can be done on behalf of third parties – that is, development practitioners bring interventions that are designed and financed by third parties, not by the communities who are the subjects of intervention.
- Ultimately, the paradigm is fundamentally about the 'delivery of resources' (see CDRA, 1998: 8–9).

The essay then goes on to outline an antithesis to this conventional development paradigm. At the core of this alternative paradigm is an understanding of 'development that is an innate and natural process found in all living things' (CDRA, 1998: 13). In this sense, development workers do not 'bring' development but intervene into development processes that already exist. The key practice for community development practitioners then is to be able to 'read' or discern where a group, community, or organization is on its own development pathway. The shift is from 'bringing resources' to 'facilitating resourcefulness' (CDRA, 1998: 17). Contrasting with some of the key tenets of the conventional paradigm identified above, this developmental paradigm argues that:

- Development cannot be engineered; it exists independently of the practitioner.
- In turn, a development practitioner can only facilitate processes that are already in motion.
- Development practitioners can only assist in the flow of a development process, nothing more.
- Interventions can only emerge from an accurate and sensitive reading of a situation.
- Because situations are constantly changing, a development practitioner must remain responsive and flexible, able to reflect, learn and manage such change (CDRA, 1998: 17–18).

The intellectual traces of this framework have then been gradually forged into a developmental framework through more than 25 years of work within the Cape Town-based CDRA (Fowler and Ubels, 2010), and, more recently, the work of 'the Proteus Initiative'. CDRA's work has been diffused during that time both within South Africa and internationally through consulting and facilitated learning programmes. Such an approach to social practice has been most clearly articulated by Allan Kaplan (1996, 2002) and Ubels et al. (2010).

As a whole, this framework provides guidance to a community practitioner in how to think about the social phenomenon of a community/organization, how to observe, how to make sense of the dynamics of community/organization and change, some of the possibilities of change processes, and, finally, the arts and design of actual practice.

Training for Transformation: Critical framework

Peter made numerous trips to the Grail Centre, Kleinmond, during the 2000s. He initially spent time getting to know Anne Hope and Sally Timmel, the original writers of the *Training for Transformation* series, and then checked out some of the post-Hope and Timmel work, carried by some dynamic women working with people from across Africa.

As already discussed, the social learning tradition of community development has a long history within South Africa, and one of the cornerstones of that tradition is Paolo Freire's intellectual work. In turn, one world-known interpretation of Freire's work is that of Hope and Timmel.

Hope and Timmel (1984) have taken the core of Freire's work on adult education, integrated it with other sources of practice (for example, organizational development, social analysis, human relations practice), and created an accessible, workable practice framework for community development workers within their resource *Training for Transformation: Books I–IV*.

When interviewed for this inquiry, Hope and Timmel explained that for them 'development is primarily a spiritual practice' and Freire's combination of spiritual awakening and social justice is what makes it Freirian. That word 'combination' was important to them, critiquing what they understood as people often wanting to take 'bits of Freire', either his spiritual practice or his justice work (literacy), but not all. They believe the real power in Freire is the combination – the 'whole package' so to speak.

They both met Freire when studying at Boston in the late 1960s as adult educators, and then again in Tanzania. These encounters consolidated their understanding and commitment to the approach. In 1973, Timmel was out of South Africa and found she could not return and so ended up in exile until 1990. During the exile years, she and Hope worked for many years in Kenya and other parts of East Africa. It was during these years that they developed many handouts (using old stencils), which became the first volume of *Training for Transformation* (TfT). It was then restructured when working in Zimbabwe and published by Mambo Press. They also argue that the success of their work in Kenya was partly achieved by working through the Catholic Church structures, giving them access down to village level, enabling a movement to grow.

84 DOES COMMUNITY DEVELOPMENT WORK?

Their analysis is that, currently in South Africa, the work is unfortunately fragmented, as there is no national structure to 'carry the work'.

Their long-term links have been not only with Freirian adult education, but also the international women's movement, particularly the Grail organization, with about 1,000 members around the world. In 1999, the South African Grail Centre was set up in Kleinmond, Western Cape, and in 2002 they started the TfT Diploma in partnership with the Centre for Development Studies at Kimmage College, Ireland. At the heart of their TfT framework are the following signposts for practice:

- Work with the poor and oppressed, not for them.
- Development is an awakening process.
- Let the people grow.
- Build up the people's solidarity.
- Build up the people's organization (Hope and Timmel, 1984: 27).

Within this framework, the community worker acts primarily as an *animator* – enabling critical consciousness, group learning, and organizational development – through a constant process of action–output–reflection.

Khanya: Integrating the sustainable livelihood approach with community-based planning

Lucius has been involved with Khanya for 10 years, both as board member and an evaluative researcher. Founded in Bloemfontein and then moving to Johannesburg, they worked across the nation, particularly training community development practitioners within the South African Department of Social Development and other NGOs. Their main contribution has been to integrate the SLA approach with community-based planning. They have developed numerous community-based planning toolkits (available online) and also have facilitated community-based economic development courses (over two- to three-week periods). Khanya-aicdd also has a footprint across Africa.

For Khanya, SLA theory is the conceptual framework for the practice of community-based planning and their main goal is to connect community to government using these tools, ensuring the micro-macro articulation takes place. While arguing that government really needs to adopt community-based planning (CBP) approaches, practitioners at Khanya are also critically reflective, arguing that:

> the missing bit in CBP is immediate local action based on what they have thought through themselves. The reason this is happening is that – the shortcoming is when the dialogue is a little limited (practitioner interview).

This comment recognizes that, often, despite the intention of enabling communities (or more accurately, groups-in-community) to do their own analyses and action planning, there is rarely time. The same practitioner acknowledged that, 'In hurrying it through it was really consultancy-driven, not community-driven'. Indicative of some tensions here undermining a decolonizing approach, the practitioner is suggesting the importance of time for communities to make sense of their reality, and therefore to do accurate analyses.

Crucial to Khanya's approach, as per the SLA framework, is the forging of connections between the community micro-level, the meso-level *local* government, and also the macro-level *national* government. Khanya works with each level of the system, articulating issues from below to above, and vice versa. In short, in community development, they are looking for maximum community participation and maximum government support. One practitioner we talked to argued that the key metaphor is 'walking together'. This same practitioner also explained the context for SLA and community-based planning, suggesting that:

> If you look at the history of [the Republic of South Africa] before 1994, there were communities engaged, but there was only disengaged government. Development was slow, community-driven, but without government support. Post 1994 through to 2005 we moved from this to a position of government-driven development and non-engaged communities. It could be described as the hand-out or entitlement era. In my organization we call this 'walking behind' government – a process of entitlement, with people saying, 'Government should do this. If the house breaks, government will come to fix it'. But we are now seeing situations in which shifts occur, in communities, where they see government is not working; and in this situation sometimes there is 'walk apart' – people want to go alone. We see there is no hope for walking alone, walking apart, or walking behind. The only sustainable community-driven development is 'walking together' where communities and government are engaged, from a different viewpoint, from a supportive role – really together, doing things together with them (ibid.).

This analysis provides a useful frame for understanding the dilemmas of community development work, particularly the community–government interface.

An interpretation of Frantz Fanon's decolonizing practice framework

Alluding to the previously mentioned revival in South Africa, and his significant contribution within the decolonial turn, we now turn to the wisdom of Frantz Fanon and what he can offer community development practitioners.

One of the most influential people in helping us understand community development practice and management of conflict within the colonial context was Fanon. Fanon developed his understanding in the latter stages of European colonial rule in Algeria in the 1950s. Both his personal and professional history gave him a profound insight into the turbulent events that surrounded him. He experienced the sweep of historical events that forged the colonial legacy, along with the struggle to rectify those events in the decolonization period.

One of Fanon's key insights that contributed significantly to community development practice, like many other profound insights, was essentially a simple one. He appreciated that traditional life did not finish with the invasion of the colonizers, that war did not end when the shooting stopped, nor poverty when welfare came. The events of history and public policy continue their impact long after they were officially over. Take, for example, the South African Land Act of 1913. Such a policy did not die when apartheid ended, but is still alive and well in the impact trail it created. Fanon understood that the events of history and the policies that shaped the times, whether they were helpful or harmful, attached themselves and added to the unfolding story. Even when the hard, upward decolonizing struggle began in earnest, all that history of hurt came into the birth of the new nations and new organizations, even though they were founded on the dreams of liberation.

What is so practical about this framework is that it helps community development practitioners understand the depth and grip of poverty among the people with whom they are working. Even though the oppressor might no longer be there, the level of anger expressed on a daily basis, even towards people they love, and to the very people who are most concerned and doing most to help, or the senseless in-fighting within, and between, colleagues, families, and communities, which is destructive and self-defeating, reveals the residual forces of the oppressor. These and other behaviours begin to make sense, and when the framework is shared and discussed, it enables a profound journey of self-awareness and personal growth (see also Gobodo-Madikizela, 2016). Fanon shows workers how to hear these phases of history and the different public policies in the day-to-day talk of the people. We could understand so much if we took notice of the buried meanings in the very words used to tell the story. This insight was to be developed much more fully by Paulo Freire in the following decade, to the point where this use of text has become a central principle of relational practice (see Kelly and Westoby, 2018). We have illustrated Fanon's framework and analysis in Figure 6.1.

Each of the ideas in the diagram is indicative of a historical phase and experience that, of course, would be contextualized to the particular histories of a given struggle. However, generally, starting with the right-hand side at the top, many communities that have experienced colonization (and continue to, even as they struggle for decolonization) had or still have a rich set of traditions, customs, or law. These traditions shaped relationships and responsibilities within family and community life, relations with nature, governance, conflict resolution, and so on. Invasion inevitably disrupted or destroyed many of those traditions, even as some continued either secretly or marginally. Warfare was an almost inevitable part of the conflict, not just between colonizer and colonized, but also between communities among the colonized – usually created through slavery, the selling of arms, co-option, and so on. Poverties became part of the story of the colonized – with households

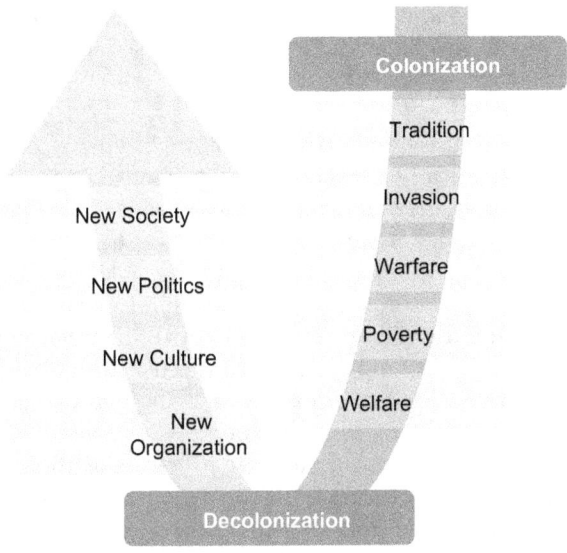

Figure 6.1 The colonizing-decolonizing cycle

and communities having lost resources such as land, culture, and social ties. Such communities became, and continue to be, ripe for welfare-oriented responses, experienced by some as 'sit-down money', further destroying the dignity and very fabric of communities.

Within Fanon's framework, the process of decolonization, signified in the left-hand part of the diagram starting at the bottom, reverses some of those experiences, with a combination of building new organizations, a new culture, new politics, and ultimately a new society. New organizations flourish as the colonized build community and social infrastructure – their networks, their *indabas*, and their federations. Within these dynamic spaces, there is usually a reaching for a new culture, some hybrid combination of the old and new, some kind of resurgence of Indigenous or endogenous knowledge and practices. In time, the resurgent culture and reorganization provide the cradle of a new politic in which the decolonizing process fosters a new voice, new social power, a movement from dialogue to demands, treaty, recognition, and so on; and finally, a new society can emerge, rocked and riddled with the new social forces from 'below'.

In line with Fanon, Van der Watt (2016) refers to former colonies as 'wounded societies in transition'. She echoed this in her thesis, 'Engaging with the soil and soul of community: Rethinking development, healing and transformation in South Africa', where she suggests that:

> [Community development] does not manage to ameliorate the psychological damage of centuries of discrimination and oppression – and some actions or inactions are actually aggravating the woundedness.

> The complexity and woundedness of the communities are not theorized or even mentioned. Practice for a healing approach is thus not touched upon (ibid.: 81).

The importance of this framework is that if we listen, we can hear all these phases of colonizing history as a daily, lived experience. People speak proudly of the glory of the past, inevitably mixed with violence then and now, all permeated with the humiliation and powerlessness of their current reality. This lived reality is what colonized people bring to the table, even as they work to build their new organizational and political futures. Fanon brought history into the moment and the voice of the people, enabling black and white, colonizer and colonized, to see that each was connected to and inevitably part of the other's story, and it was only in acknowledging that connection that the grip of colonial forces could be lessened and progress made.

This historical framework can then help both practitioner and people appreciate, understand, and work with this complex, deep-seated vortex of hope and despair. In the authors' experience, the use of this framework has provided transformative moments not only for the practitioner, but also for the people immersed in their decolonizing struggle, giving them a tool with which to understand and order their pride, their anger, and their hurt, as well as their hope for the future.

Conclusion: Towards personal practice frameworks

In offering these multiple community development frameworks, it is apt to return to the opening quote by Ife, that 'every community worker will conceptualize practice in a different way and will build a different practice framework that will develop and change with experience' (Ife, 2002: 265). This quote alludes to the diverse kinds of practice frameworks that experienced community workers will develop.

In previous writings by Westoby and Ingamells (2011), these have been called 'personal practice frameworks' as a way of describing how practitioners eventually combine the wisdom of numerous frameworks, along with their personal experiences. Ideally, experienced practitioners then combine tacit knowledge, learned 'on the job' so to speak, with the knowledge learned from these frameworks. Such personal practice frameworks usually enable practitioners to combine elements of the 'self' with more abstract knowledge and skills and develop what is sometimes known in the social professions as 'practical wisdom' (Dunne, 2011). The framework then provides conceptual guidance to the worker, enabling them to be responsive to the situation at hand, drawing on the resources of self, alongside diverse frameworks.

Within this inquiry, what was clear to us was the lack of personal practice frameworks. People tended to adopt one of the 'big four' frameworks or to have no coherent framework at all.

This creates difficulties when thinking about effective community development work. Drawing on externally given frameworks, a practitioner soon can become lost in the complexity of everyday practice. The big frameworks rarely give conceptual guidance in practice issues that arise in the hustle and bustle of people-in-context. Some of the difficulties of evaluating effectiveness is that only external indicators can be drawn upon, such as how many new livelihoods were created, or what kinds of assets were mobilized for particular purposes. In contrast, as per our Chapter 4 framework, evaluating from the inside, based on a dynamic, ongoing, rigorous process of what is actually unfolding, becomes difficult. Practitioners steeped in externally oriented frameworks rarely have the flexibility or adaptable responsivity that is usually indicative of good practice.

From an effectiveness perspective, it is argued that what is needed for community workers is *both* a clear organizational community development practice framework (so that workers can locate themselves within their organizational context) and recognition that such an organizational framework will be interpreted and reinterpreted by practitioners *in situ*. The integration of a normative organizational practice framework with such factors as context, personality, and experience, leads to a personal practice framework that, over time, should be easily articulated publicly by practitioners, and which then enables them to hold rigorously, transparently, and accountably the 'ideas and intentions' behind their work.

This is the core material for communities of practice to then create opportunities for mentoring, reflection, and supervision – oriented towards reflective practice, constructing a personal practice framework that mixes community workers' personal experience with the organizational framework (see Ife, 2002; Westoby and Ingamels, 2011).

At present, there appears to be little space provided within workplaces for community workers to reflect on how those frameworks could be integrated into the personal (their own histories and so forth). The consequences are such that, when practitioners were accompanied into the field and social situations occurred that were beyond the bounds of the framework – such as the procedures of community-based planning – the community worker was found wanting. The craft of community work, the capacity to dance 'a responsive dance' (Westoby and Kaplan, 2013), was lacking.

References

Community Development Resource Association (CDRA). 1998. *Annual Report: Crossroads: A Development Reading*. Cape Town: CDRA.

Dunne J. 2011. Professional wisdom in practice. In Bondi L., Carr D., Clark C. and Clegg C. (eds). *Towards Professional Wisdom: Practical Deliberation in the People Professions*. Surrey, UK: Ashgate.

Everatt D. and Gwagwa L. 2005. *Community Driven Development in South Africa, 1990–2004*. World Bank, Africa Region, Working Paper Series No. 92. Washington DC: The World Bank. Available at <http://documents.worldbank.org/curated/en/612931468302490147/Community-driven-development-in-South-Africa-1990-2004> [Accessed 11 May 2020].

Fowler A. and Ubels J. 2010. Multiple dimensions: The multi-faceted nature of capacity: Two leading models. In Ubels J., Acquaye-Baddoo N. and Fowler A. (eds). *Capacity Development in Practice*. London: Earthscan.

Gobodo-Madikizela P. (ed.). 2016. *Breaking Intergenerational Cycles of Repetition: A Global Dialogue on Historical Trauma and Memory*. Toronto: Barbara Budrich Publishers.

Hope A. and Timmel S. 1984. *Training for Transformation: Handbook for Community Workers: Vol I–IV*. Zimbabwe: Mambo Press.

Ife J. 2002. *Community Development: Community Based Alternatives in an Age of Globalisation*, 2nd edn. Melbourne: Pearson Education.

Kaplan A. 1996. *The Development Practitioner's Handbook*. Chicago and London: Pluto Press.

Kaplan A. 2002. *Development Practitioners and Social Process: Artists of the Invisible*. Chicago and London: Pluto Press.

Kelly A. and Westoby P. 2018. *Participatory Development Practice: Using Traditional and Contemporary Frameworks*. Rugby: Practical Action Publishing.

Movement for Community-Led Development (MCLD) (no date) Analytic framework. <https://mcld.org/analytic-framework/> [Accessed 4 March 2019].

Schenck R., Nel H. and Louw H. 2010. *Introduction to Participatory Practice*. South Africa: UNISA Press.

Ubels J., van Klinken R. and Visser H. 2010. Bridging the micro-macro gap: Gaining capacity by connecting levels of development action. In Ubels J., Acquaye-Baddoo N. and Fowler A. (eds). *Capacity Development in Practice*. London: Earthscan.

Van der Watt P. 2016. Engaging with the soil and soul of a community: Rethinking development, healing and transformation in South Africa. Unpublished PhD thesis, Bloemfontein: University of the Free State.

Westoby P. and Ingamells A. 2011. Teaching community development personal practice frameworks. *Social Work Education* 31(3):383–396.

Westoby P. and Kaplan A. 2013. Foregrounding practice: Reaching for a responsive and ecological approach to community development – A conversational inquiry into the dialogical and developmental frameworks of community development. *Community Development Journal* 49(2):214–227.

Wilkinson-Maposa S. 2008. Jansenville Development Forum: Linking community and government in the rural landscape of the Eastern Cape Province. In Mathie A. and Cunningham G. (eds). *From Clients to Citizens: Communities Changing the Course of their Own Development*. Rugby, UK: Practical Action Publishing.

PART III
An assemblage of stories and possibilities

Part III is an assemblage of stories and possibilities for community development. This part of the book has been structured into seven chapters (Chapters 7–13), each discussing a key story from our dialogical and relational encounters with practice. Each chapter also articulates the findings in relation to decolonizing yet effective community development practices.

Part III tells the stories we have assembled, each representing possibilities for a decolonizing approach to community development. Some readers might ask why stories open up possibilities for reconstructing community development. Our reply is that stories are crucial for the process of reconstructing community development. They are the light switches of imagination and a great deal of imagination is needed in community development practice and development evaluation.

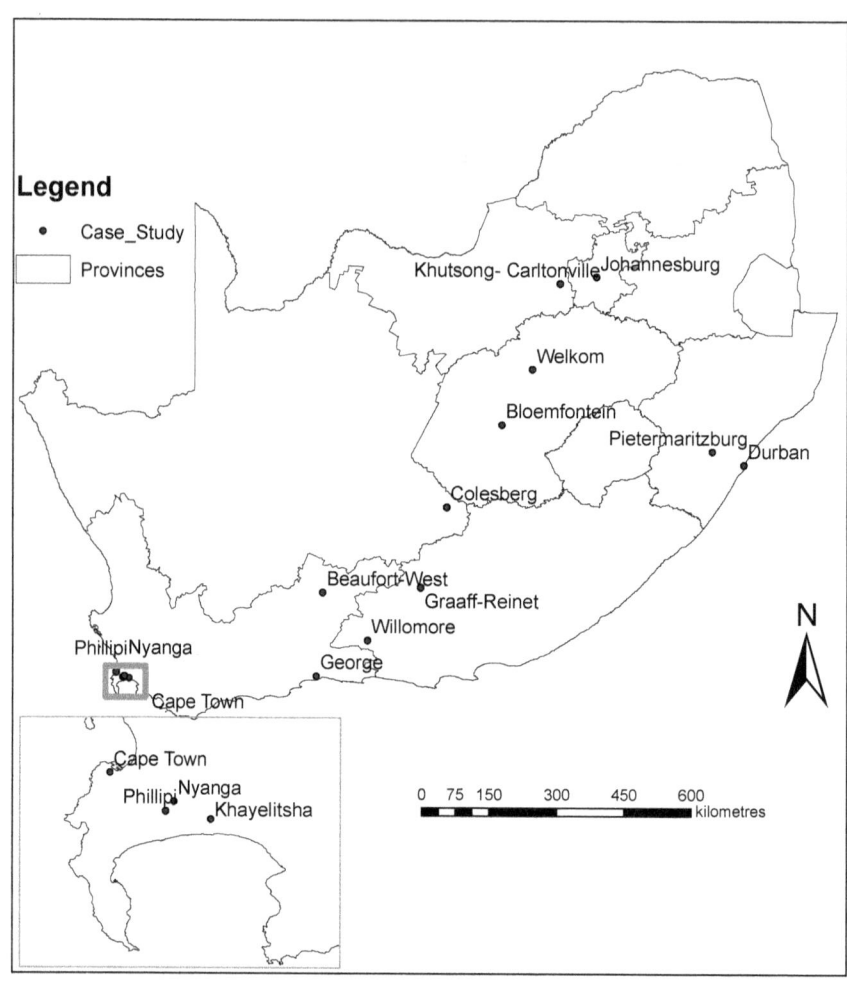

Map 7.1 Locational map of the Republic of South Africa with markers for the stories and case studies

CHAPTER 7
Accompanying, horizontal learning, and structuring: Political practice and the Southern Cape Land Committee

Abstract

Chapter 7 considers the linkages between community development and political practices, focusing on the case study of the Southern Cape Land Committee, based in the Western and Eastern Cape. The story is located within the ongoing challenges of farmworkers and land reform in South Africa.

Keywords: land reform, politics, democratizing, accompanying, structuring, co-creating

Introduction

Peter has driven some 450 km from Bloemfontein to the Karoo town of Graaff-Reinet to visit one of the site offices of the Southern Cape Land Committee (SCLC). It is a stunning drive – the scenery striking in both its serenity and also its vastness. The stark mountains rise up from the rolling plains, and the vistas regularly take the breath away. At the site office, there is a meeting with several community development practitioners who have a three-day programme of field visits ready. We travel out to a number of farmworkers, some of whom are still working on large, white-owned commercial farms, and several others facing eviction from these farms. We then drive another 170 km to the town of Willowmore and are introduced to several members of the Baviaans Land and Agrarian Reform Forum (BLARF) who are organizing 17 cooperatives of emerging black farmers within the municipality boundary.

It is into this context that we locate the exploration of community development that has a 'political edge', and, within this story, a political edge focused on the issue of land reform. Clearly land sits at the centre of any decolonizing perspective for it is land that has been stolen within South Africa's history.

The story is of the work of the SCLC, one representative of a community that is grappling with the decolonial turn, for land sits at the heart of the issue. However, that decolonial turn helps us foreground not only the land issue, but also a few of the practices that are used by the committee, articulated as 'accompanying' in contrast to 'helping'; 'horizontal learning' rather

http://dx.doi.org/10.3362/9781788531320.007

94 DOES COMMUNITY DEVELOPMENT WORK?

than experts 'educating the people'; and 'structuring' in the sense of 'community organizing'.

Within the chapter, we also foreground the importance of community development's engagement with local government, the level of government closest to 'the people'.

A caveat: one of our observations is that, within South Africa, people think about or talk about community development primarily in terms of infrastructure development or economic development – with either a focus on roads, footpaths, streetlights, or on livelihoods, small business, enterprises, cooperatives, and so forth. In contrast, when people think of the story discussed in this chapter, they tend to think about activism, not community development. However, as per our examination of traditions in Chapter 5, this dismisses not only a whole tradition of community development, built around political activism, community organizing, and social mobilization, but it also fails to take seriously one of the crucial demands of community development within democratic settings – that is, politics. Again, part of the challenge is removing the technical or 'project bias' from community practice. At times, community development does have a strong political edge, which becomes obvious when observing community development practice 'on the ground' in South Africa.

The context

Within South Africa, the issue of land is central to transformational hopes, and the Nelson Mandela Foundation's analysis locates the lack of land ownership transformation as one of the key causes of ongoing structural inequality.

Since early settlement, there has been an ongoing process of colonization that has seen land ownership predominantly in the hands of white commercial farmers. Different crucial moments, such as the Land Act of 1913, which both extended processes of forced removal and essentially codified existing patterns of land loss to black communities, simply represented part of an ongoing process of colonization. With apartheid ending in 1994, the previously dispossessed became hopeful – there was a perception that change was coming. However, since 1994, despite a post-colonial epoch, decolonization of land has failed miserably. The same pre-apartheid patterns of ownership, labour, and agrarian exploitation continue. While numerous laws claim to have made a positive difference (related to issues such as minimal wage increases, eviction, and tenure), enduring structures and relations continue.

Resistant regimes are also easily identified and analysed. People working within what can be described as organized agriculture are very fearful and resistant to change, often tending towards a defensive posture of 'this is mine', and 'without us food won't be grown'. Government has itself entrenched pre-apartheid patterns through, for example, how it structures departments. For example, the Department of Agriculture has a substantial budget and works with organized commercial (mainly white) farmers. Extension officers are well resourced and support such work. In contrast, the Department of Rural Development and Land Reform works with black farmers, mainly using commonage land (owned by cash- and capacity-strapped municipalities) for small-scale agro-ecological work. This department has few resources to support these initiatives. Any attempts for such farmers to access the extension workers of the Department of Agriculture comes to little, with their response being, 'we only support large-scale export-oriented commercial farming'. This reinforces and is itself reinforced by the assumptions around the world, whereby 'the simplistic formulation of "subsistence" farmers versus "commercial farmers" ... continues to hold currency among ministries of agriculture, national governments, donors, and others' (Peters, 2013: 551).

Market-led strategies of land reform have failed miserably in South Africa. As Pauline Peters again argues:

> the outcomes of the 'market-led', 'willing buyer-willing seller' model in programmes of land distribution have been poor and its premises and assumptions are flawed, especially by ignoring the political context where highly unequal social relations, such as those between rural poor and landowners, structure the supposedly neutral 'market' relations of prospective 'buyers and sellers' (2013: 543).

There is a huge body of literature on this, and readers could do well to refer to the repository of the Institute for Poverty, Land and Agrarian Studies (PLAAS) at the University of the Western Cape. Peters (2013: 552) summarizes the political issues arising from 'the inevitability of an agribusiness future centred on large farms, albeit with outgrower schemes absorbing (some of) the current rural populations'. Furthermore, Peters argues that:

> Over the past few years ... the posited disappearance of the smallholder population in Africa has come under reassessment, due to several factors. One is the new literature on the environmental and ecological costs of agro-industrial agriculture which provides a new type of critique of the posited inevitability of such a future. A second is the formidable rise of agrarian social movements, particularly in Latin America and Asia, which, along with the surprising links between these and similar movements in Europe, have helped fuel a challenge to seeing 'peasantries' as necessarily doomed, and provide a positive assessment of the economic, ecological and social benefits of rural-based livelihoods. A third is the fast-growing documentation of intensifying land appropriation ('grabs') by both foreign and domestic agents from peasant and smallholder populations ... a trend that has occasioned not only deep concern but a re-evaluation of conventional trajectories of 'development' (Peters, 2013: 552).

This commentary is summative of both the global and South African restructuring of the agricultural sector, away from smallholder farmers and towards large, commercially oriented farming; but also the second movement responses, as social movements organize resistance and reclaim spaces for revitalization of smallholder farming and other forms of agro-ecological practice.

It is into such a context that the SCLC, originally known as the Southern Cape Against Removals (SCAR), works across communities of the Western and Eastern Cape. They have offices in Graaff-Reinet, George, and Beaufort West. Their work is focused on farmworkers, emerging farmers, agro-ecological practices, political schools, and networking with government departments. They have a dual strategy. One is first-order social change work – enabling farmworkers and potential emerging black farmers to 'survive the existing system' through paralegal work, seeding, and supporting new agro-ecological initiatives. The other is second-order social change work, aiming 'to change the system' through community organizing, campaigning, and advocating for new models of land reform. There are both aspirational and pragmatic elements to their strategy, which are discussed in more depth below.

The project of democratizing

In thinking about community development and political practice, it is prudent to step back and consider the idea of democracy. However, rather than use the noun 'democracy', thought of as a 'thing', we prefer to imagine possibilities through the verb *democratizing*. This approach opens up thinking about how community development work can support active citizenship and governance around the democratizing project, something that must be made and kept alive by people's agency.

Thinking in terms of verbs enables people and practitioners to rethink democracy as a 'project of democratizing' requiring *constant renewal* with various potential trajectories. If people are lacking the freedoms to engage around their concerns or are not active as citizens in the governance of their own lives, many commentators would argue there is a problem for democrats. If some people are protecting entrenched powerful interests or some key people are purposefully blocking citizen engagement, then there is a risk that the project of democratization has reached a state in which it has stalled. On the other hand, if people are actively engaging around their concerns or are challenging elites, then the project of democratizing is a process that has some life in it, and diverse agents are determining its future. In this sense, a living democracy is always haunted by Derrida's hauntology of justice, and requires constant renewal. Our argument is that this renewal requires a response to decolonization, which locates land and politics front and centre to the work.

One of the key tasks as community development practitioners is to care for politics and politically oriented practice, because one of the key imperatives is the project of democratizing all our social, cultural, economic, and political contexts. Democratization is central to making the political sphere of participation and citizenship meaningful. Democratization is one of the cornerstones of an approach to community development in which people have a right to voice, can act publicly, and are able to influence decision-making processes (see Good Governance Learning Network, 2011). Many significant development outcomes – those that genuinely reflect the way people want to live – are dependent on people's democratic ability to participate in the process of deciding how they should live, not only in terms of civil and political rights, but also in relation to socio-economic rights (Jones and Stokke, 2005). While arguing for a 'universal project of democratization', we recognize that the *forms* of democracy emerging from that project will be shaped differently within different social, cultural, historical, and economic geographies. What *democracy* looks like within South Africa will be different to that emerging elsewhere.

So what does it mean to make the project of democratization central to community development? One of the classic essays on democracy was written by Alexis de Tocqueville, in which he used the key concept of the *agora*. Originally the marketplace and meeting place of the city states of classical Greece, the agora is used by de Tocqueville as 'the assembly', where people's concerns are discussed collectively and publicly. Bauman (1998: 86–87) likens the contemporary idea of civil society to the concept of agora, seeing it as an interface between the public and private spheres of social life. Historically, there has been an evolutionary process whereby the agora has, officially at least, been opened up to everyone. Originally, in ancient Greece, it was for 'citizens', defined as a particular group of men. In modern parliamentary democracy, it has opened up to include almost everyone through universal suffrage.

One challenge of democratization for community practitioners is to support people on the margins to learn about the political system and how they can use it to take what they have perceived as their private concerns into these public assemblies for discussion and deliberation. After all, feminist movements and others have taught us all that 'the personal is political; the private is often public'. In many ways, the process of present-day community development 'may be conceptualized as the late modern *agora* – as the site of political, or at least politicized, assembly of citizens' (Geoghegan and Powell, 2009).

In South Africa, there are many examples of organizations attempting to democratize through forceful participation in government deliberation and decision-making. As already mentioned in Chapter 5 of this book, when referring to the social mobilization tradition of community development, the Durban-based Abahlali movement (Gibson, 2011) is an excellent story. Of significance to their work is a combination of democratization through rights-based practice with a co-creative ethos, arguing for a different kind of relationship between state and civil society, not one founded only on a social contract for service delivery, but a different kind of politics. Their story represents a manifestation of political action, particularly in the form of social movements that are not just acting *towards* the state, but are also creating their own platform for dialogue within an autonomous space. Such an approach could be said to reflect an evolution of the politics, reaching beyond Alinsky and other traditional trade-union-oriented political practices.

There are also many other examples of community development processes that are politically oriented. Contemporary examples include what is being called 'social accounting', or 'social auditing', whereby local communities are organized in ways that hold governments to account in terms of their stated objectives.

Democratizing local government within South Africa

While the project of democratizing as a general rule is crucial, a focus on democratizing local government is particularly apt for community development practitioners. Both community development theory and practice, while being primarily focused on the collective action of people in communities, are also particularly concerned with the sphere of local government. After all, it is the level of government closest to the people. Such a concern ensures community development is not reduced to local self-help efforts or mutual aid alone, but also with citizen engagement and rights.

Within South African policy, there is also a commitment to participatory governance – which can be thought about as a 'set of structural and procedural requirements to realize public participation in the operation of [provincial] and local government' (Matebesi and Botes, 2011: 6). Citing Lovan, Murray, and Schaffer (2004), Matebesi and Botes (2011: 6–7) also argue that such participatory governance 'goes beyond public management to a more fundamental question of how the process of democracy can be adapted to help countries resolve the complex public issues with which they are challenged'.

Such an approach transforms the way government has been operationalized within South Africa. During the apartheid era, most South Africans were passive actors as recipients of government, rather than being active citizens. According to Matebesi and Botes (2011: 10), such a history ensured that 'formal participatory governance structures became an important feature of post-apartheid governance at all levels'. Some key contextual policies for such participatory governance in South Africa include the White Paper on Local Government, which highlights the role of municipal councillors as that of promoting involvement of community groups in the design and delivery of municipal programmes. Through such mechanisms, municipal councils are ideally accountable to their local communities. Furthermore, ward committees are mechanisms created to assess and approve budgets and participate in the planning and development of integrated development plans. More recently, multi-stakeholder forums have also been experimented with as a way of enabling more participatory forms of local government. Effective public participation also requires including as many structures and organizations that represent the community as possible, and from there the importance of stakeholder forums for participatory governance cannot be understated.

However, research seems to indicate that despite all the hopes of participatory local governance, the reality 'on the ground' is highly problematic. For example, Matebesi and Botes' (2011) research within the municipality of

Khutsong indicates that, despite all efforts for the community to participate within democratic structures, its voice was neglected or, more accurately, marginalized (other voices were considered more important). Eventually, after many efforts of dialogue and discussion, the community turned to the 'last resort' of initially peaceful protest and civil disobedience, and eventually violent protest. In this case, the disjuncture between local needs/voices and national priorities disrupted any effective efforts for local democratizing.

The conclusions of Matebesi and Botes (2011: 17) are that 'what was regarded as a participatory process was in fact tantamount to ... manipulation', and, furthermore, in this case, went on to 'reinforce the personal interests of strong leaders' (ibid.). Their conclusions remind us of an old saying learned as young community workers – 'for a local person a local tyrant is just as bad as a national tyrant'. It was a way of reminding us that while community development practice often focuses on local-level action and concerns, often idealizing the local as where decision-making should be focused (as per decentralization discourses), sometimes the result could be just as harmful. The local sphere of politics, along with the national, can be only as good as the mechanisms of checks and balances that exist to ensure that power is democratized. In reality, 'the struggle is not for democracy per se, but for processes of democratizing', putting the focus on democratizing as an ongoing endeavour. Many community protests and service-delivery protests are a healthy sign of the impulse among the marginalized for democratization. Protests are often the consequence of communities who have experienced not being heard and feeling that their voices have been silenced. South African citizens are turning more and more to creating these alternative spaces to express dissatisfaction and dissent (Good Governance Learning Network, 2011). To have reached the post-apartheid era of democracy is not enough. Democratization – whereby decision-making processes are truly transparent and decision-makers and agenda setters are held accountable – is an ongoing process and goal.

With such an understanding of the project of democratization, particularly within the complexities of local government, we now return to the story at hand.

The story: Southern Cape Land Committee

The SCLC was established in 1987 and was initially focused on fighting against forced removals in the George area of the Western Cape. However, from the 1990s, the work focused more on land reform issues, attempting to create spaces for people to participate in policy issues. In the 2000s, a process of reflection led to the conclusion that land reform was 'going nowhere' within South Africa and so the organization shifted its work towards community organizing. This refocus has led to several initiatives.

Firstly, their work aims to support *emerging farmers* to 'act as one voice'. The community development workers of the land committee support emerging black farmers through capacitation of leadership so that they can act with one voice within local-level multi-stakeholder forums. The focus, as per the literature on local government, is on engaging local municipalities with one voice. The analysis is that governments find it easier to relate to each individual group separately – it then becomes easier to utilize patronage forms of politics with some groups, or simply to ignore others. Some would refer to this as a divide-and-rule strategy by those in power. In contrast, when groups organize horizontally, and form a cooperative, network, forum, or coalition in the way that has been fostered by the SCLC, then it is difficult for local municipalities to discard the arising issues. Such networks of groups have a stronger force, which is harder to be ignored or manipulated by the powerful.

Secondly, they use a 'rights-based' practice to educate *farmworkers* about their (limited) rights. Their practices involve the formation of farm committees at very local levels, ensuring that farmworkers can work together. Again, such farmworker committees are then linked together, giving them a stronger voice.

Thirdly, the committee works among emerging black farmers to promote agro-ecology, as per the work demonstrated by the Latin American social movement *Via Campesina*. This work supports emerging farmers in producing their own food with the aim of food sovereignty. This requires engagement with local government, particularly to lever access to commonage land and also particular services, such as water.

Finally, their work focuses on people mobilization, raising awareness of poverty-producing processes and supporting initiatives and movements for change. Here, they work in close partnership with other civil society organizations such as Khanya College, an organization that is experienced in running 'critical schools', attempting to catalyse social movements.

From a broader perspective, the SCLC attempts to integrate these initiatives into the overall goal of building local leadership that can catalyse a rural social movement that demands change in the various spheres of influence. They attempt to integrate practical and strategic work – the former being work such as agro-ecology, supporting people to grow their own food, and the latter being more explicitly political whereby the organization accompanies people in learning about, and exercising, their rights along with campaigning work.

In talking to the workers of the organization, and meeting several constituencies they work with, we were also able to hear about and see some of their actual practices. For example, within the initiatives above, they often use participatory rural appraisal practices to support farmers in conducting their own analysis about the issues at hand and to also consider how to move forward. From workers' participation in this analytical process, leadership groups are then formed, which can participate in municipal forums. These practices embody a grassroots critical process that enables the marginalized to engage with formal structures of local government.

Another practice of the organization is to be closely embedded in the geographies they work within. This ensures that the community development fieldworkers are quick to hear about emerging 'hotspots', usually because farmworkers or emerging farmers call the worker. The organization can then quickly respond, organizing mass meetings within the hotspot, following these up with horizontal learning processes between different farmer groups, building cross-locality networks enabling local people to learn about their rights, and then farmers are supported to organize local structures that enable them to sustain their work of advocacy.

At a higher level, the SCLC is also committed to working closely in partnership with other NGOs, ensuring that they themselves do not have to do all the work, and also avoiding duplication of expertise. For example, SCLC is part of a national platform of nine civil society organizations working in the agrarian transformation sector, *Tshintsha Amakhaya*. National collaborations strengthen advocacy, support national campaigns, and enable sharing and learning.

Discussion of practices

Having considered elements of the story, and a few of the practices of the SCLC, we now turn to a discussion of four practices that are particularly relevant to the broader work of community development and political efforts. These have been distilled to: the delicate relationship of accompanying; the practices of horizontal learning; the practices of structuring the work; and co-creative approaches to state–community relations.

Towards accompanying

There is a delicate relationship between what we think of the community ecology of 'the people, the leaders, and the experts' and 'the practitioner' embodied in all community work. However, when community development is engaged with political efforts, this delicate relationship becomes even more complex. Questions arise, such as how a community practitioner engages or supports poor marginalized workers (in this story, farmworkers and emergent leaders) in a way that does not abuse the authority of being a professional, being deployed by a reasonably well-resourced organization, and of bringing a particular political commitment themselves. In a nutshell, how does the community worker *accompany* the community they want to mobilize without manipulating them? Paulo Freire has talked about 'delicate relationship' (Bell et al., 1990) embodied within the complex relations between an educator and a student. A similar relationship is embodied within the relations between a community organizer and those being worked with.

One way of resolving these complex issues is to, as already discussed, imagine the practice as one of accompanying people (Watkins, 2019) or, to put it another way, engage in a process described by Gustavo Esteva as 'co-motion' (1987). For the SCLC, accompanying means starting where people are, engaging with their own realities and stories, then exploring together the root causes of skewed power relations and opportunities to challenge these. It requires careful listening, empathy, and an understanding of the context.

This idea of accompanying alongside Esteva's co-motion helps imagine the movement for both parties (community worker and farmworkers/dwellers), ensuring that while there is an agenda to bring change, that agenda is subject to a mutual process of co-learning, co-reflection, and co-strategizing. The worker has some ideas of what to do – they have at least collected or lived within the stories of other communities organizing themselves – but they also recognize the integrity of each story and do not impose another.

The possibilities of horizontal learning: Communities accompanying one another

While the practices embedded within the story above draw on numerous forms of community-based education efforts, such as participatory rural appraisal, critical schools, and information sessions on people's rights, a crucial component of their work involves what is known as horizontal learning.

Horizontal learning is a way of ensuring people both *learn* – whereby they learn from others who are experiencing or at least have experienced a similar set of issues (the real experts, so to speak) – and also *build* a network of support and solidarity at the same time. In this sense of building a network, it is also a way of enabling communities to *accompany one another.*

Embodied within the idea of delicate relationship discussed above is the idea that a community development practitioner's primary resources are: 1) their process expertise – accompanying people in a step-by-step process of coming together, building analyses together, and structuring together; and 2) the practitioner's access to stories and networks of other communities who have had similar experiences. It is not to say that a community itself will not have access to stories (and particularly so as social media and internet access accelerates). However, a community development practitioner has collected stories as a discipline. Therefore, rather than being able to provide solutions to community questions, the practitioner can link people to others (or to stories of others) who have worked on similar issues. The people are then left to find their own solution, but with access to the stories and networks of others. This is really the process of empowerment within community development work – for people to feel they have access to knowledge, confidence, networks, and resources themselves.

Structuring the work

The building of a network of support and solidarity, referred to above, can be understood as 'structuring the work'. It is a community development term for moving informal groups towards a stage of formalization, which enables the people to sustain the work over a longer period of time. We will discuss this more in the story of the Hantam Education Trust but, for now, structuring refers to the particular task of creating community-based structures – sometimes legally recognized, other times not – which are able to 'hold' an identity, name, funds, and clear decision-making processes. An example within the story of this chapter is the formation of BLARF, which is organizing 17 cooperatives of emerging black farmers within the municipality boundary. Such formation implies numerous levels of structuring.

Firstly, the initial structuring of local famers into place-based cooperatives. Such cooperatives formalize the non-formal pre-existing relations and enable the local farmers to work as one, to make decisions together, to access resources, and so forth. Secondly, there has been a process of structuring 'beyond the local' into a municipal forum of 17 cooperatives. This level of structuring gives the farmers leverage at a municipality level and enables them to consolidate leadership and other resources into a focused process of lobbying and campaigning. Local forums provide the basis for provincial and even national campaigns and solidarity actions. This structuring beyond the local ensures community development work does not remain overly focalized on only local issues but tackles the broader totality of concerns (Freire, 1970: 111).

A co-creative approach of community–state relations

One of the challenges of participatory governance processes within South Africa is that many people still locate governance within a service-delivery framework, whereby the participatory structures become another mechanism for government officials *to consult* with community stakeholders. This is often stuck within a somewhat paternalistic social guidance tradition of practice. However, one of the negative impacts of this consultation model is that usually the consultation leads to more demands for services, based on evident needs and people's sense of their rights and entitlements. Some people engaged within this inquiry argued that this fundamental paradigm has not changed despite the new structures. For example, one senior practitioner interviewed in our research discussed how:

> The state can't just deliver services into community as if it is a mechanistic, open hole into which you can pour water. In order for those services to be received they have to be adapted, they have to be re-created and taken into the fabric of community in a way that the community knows and understands it. And, most importantly, link it to the community's own resourcefulness so that they're not just these sort of cunning creations of government bureaucrats and policy-makers from, dare I say it, universities. So the challenge has to be co-creative and if you look at where things have worked (for example, shackdwellers) people can build their own houses with state support. And real community development takes place, not just building houses.

Within this story, community development practitioners of the SCLC have been pushing in the more 'co-creative' direction articulated by this practitioner, away from the often failed participatory and consultative mechanisms embedded within what is known as integrated development plans. Instead, the experimentation has been on multi-stakeholder forums whereby the community–state relations are reconfigured in a co-creative relationship that can even be imagined as an accompanying relationship. Such forums attempt to ensure that resources flow into the municipality in ways that link resources and needs more appropriately and effectively. Ideally, there is recognition from state actors that they cannot service the people based on their expertise alone. The forums harness the expertise of many actors into focused action. Here, there is the real possibility of genuine partnership, transformed by an accompanying mindset informed by a decolonizing perspective.

Conclusion

Edgy, politically oriented community work is necessary to keep democracy alive (Kenny, 2011). Community development with this orientation, sometimes understood as activism or community mobilization, is thriving in South Africa. As people and communities feel more alienated from the benefits of a growing economy and voiceless within the polity, some turn to community action. Such action can be explosive and violent, other action more incremental and strategic. The work of the SCLC sits within the latter category, with its community development workers accompanying people into the *agora* – the assemblies where decisions are made. Their work particularly supports farm-workers and dwellers to survive – through agro-ecological practices – but also to fight strategically for their land rights. It involves campaigning, conscientization through critical schools, horizontal learning processes, structuring local farmer groups, and structuring forums 'beyond the local'. It is edgy because sometimes the work is fraught – challenging vested interests (commercial farmers, wage levels, labour practices), which inevitably relate to issues of power. And power is never just given away, it needs to be taken! However, from a decolonizing perspective of community development, it is the key idea of accompanying that we wish to foreground. Eschewing or disrupting any colonial traces of helping or guiding, accompanying is a way of negotiating the delicate relationship among 'the people', 'leaders', 'experts', and the community development practitioner who holds to the integrity of working from the 'inside-out' of a community process.

References

Bauman Z. 1998. *Globalisation: The Human Consequences*. Cambridge: Polity Press.
Bell, B., Gaventa, J. and Peters, J. (eds). 1990. *We Make the Road by Walking: Conversations on Education and Social Change: Myles Horton and Paulo Freire*. Philadelphia: Temple University Press.
Esteva G. 1987. Regenerating people's space. *Alternatives* 12(1):125–152.
Freire P. 1970/2006. *Pedagogy of the Oppressed*. New York: Continuum.

Geoghegan M. and Powell F. 2009. Community development and the contested politics of the late modern agora: Of, alongside or against neoliberalism. *Community Development Journal* 44(4):430–447.

Gibson N. 2011. *Fanonian Practices in South Africa: From Steve Biko to Abahlali base, Mjondolo*. KwaZulu-Natal, South Africa: UKZN Press.

Good Governance Learning Network (GGLN). 2011. *Recognising Community Voices and Dissatisfaction: a Civil Society Perspective on Local Governance in South Africa*. Cape Town: GGLN.

Jones P. and Stokke K. (eds). 2005. *Democratising Development: The Politics of Socio-Economic Rights in South Africa*. Boston: Martinus Nijhoff Publishers.

Kenny S. 2011. Towards unsettling community development. *Community Development Journal* 46 (suppl 1):i7–i19.

Lovan W.R., Murray M. and Shaffer R. 2004. *Participatory Governance: Planning, Conflict Mediation and Public Decision-Making in Civil Society*. Aldershot: Ashgate Publishing.

Matebesi S. and Botes L. 2011. Khutsong cross-boundary protests: The triumph and failure of participatory governance? *Politeia* 30(1):4-21.

Peters P. 2013. Land appropriation, surplus people and a battle over visions of agrarian futures in Africa. *The Journal of Peasant Studies* 40(3):537–562.

Watkins M. 2019. *Accompaniment and the Creation of the Commons*. Cambridge, MA: Harvard University Press.

CHAPTER 8

Action learning and research, food security, and Abalimi Bezekhaya

Abstract

Chapter 8 considers the significance of action learning within community development in South Africa. The chapter particularly focuses on the case study of the Abalimi Home and Community Garden Initiative, an exemplary story located in the Cape Flats area of the Western Cape. The Abalimi Initiative works with 3,000-plus women creating economic and livelihood initiatives. The chapter locates their story within the context of the unemployment crisis of South Africa, and also the literature that links community development and local economic development.

Keywords: food security, social-solidarity economy, action learning-research, observation, community gardens, urban agriculture

Introduction

An early observation in this inquiry was that community development in South Africa is in danger of being captured or colonized by an 'economic' vision of community development. In a sense, poverty is unreflexively defined as an economic condition or state, and, in turn, 'development' is understood as economic transformation or, even less reflexively, as economic growth or participation. Consequently, when talking of community development within South Africa, most people very quickly start talking about social enterprises or livelihood-oriented development. However, at the same time, we want to avoid the mistake of underestimating the centrality of some form of economic development to most poor South Africans. Therefore, the story of this chapter considers the issues of economic development, connecting the dots between food, jobs, work, and land.

While the context is a story around these issues, the thread highlighted from a decolonial perspective of community development is action learning and action research. Particularly, from an effectiveness perspective, this foregrounds the importance of ongoing iterative and adaptive learning and evaluation as per our conclusions to Chapter 4. Decolonizing practices ensure working with what is unfolding from the inside of a place or process, and constantly adapting to the movement at hand. It is posited that a key way of doing this is through action learning and research.

Context

In 2011, Peter first visited the Abalimi Bezekhaya (from now on referred to as Abalimi), a voluntary association supporting and catalysing an urban home and community garden movement, consisting of mainly female urban agriculturalists from the surrounding townships.

In 2018, as he again drove into Cape Town, he was struck by the accurate analyses of both Mike Davies' *Planet of Slums* (2006) and Edgar Pieterse and AbdouMaliq Simone's *Rogue Urbanism: Emergent African Cities* (2013) of the unfolding failure of capitalist systems of economics to transform the lives of millions of marginalized. The N1 highway cutting through Cape Town provides a poignant overview of the ongoing consequences of capitalist logics – some win, many lose – and the failure of African urban policy-makers to engage with the urban reality. In 2015, the township area being visited with a small group of other interested observers was also burning with community anger, another manifestation of so-called 'service-delivery protest'. In fact, tensions were so high that our host, the director of Abalimi, informed us that 'the locals insist we have a police escort'.

It is in this context that we chose to visit Abalimi, a hopeful story of community development work. Our impressions were that here was a story of innovative work, focused on women, on the building of solidarity, and of food security. Abalimi is focused pragmatically on poverty alleviation, but philosophically is also constructing a 'relational economy' that connects the urban poor, mainly women, with those who have cash incomes – the middle class – using a short food chain community-supported agriculture (CSA) mechanism.

Abalimi is located within some communities of the Cape Flats area, a huge region populated largely by economic refugees from the previous apartheid homelands of the Ciskei and Transkei in the Eastern Cape. New arrivals into Cape Town are officially estimated to be about 12,000 people per month and unemployment figures continue to be in the region of 30–40 per cent.

The Abalimi Bezekhaya, translated as 'the Farmers of Home', was founded in 1982/83, as a voluntary association, although discussions illustrated that the term 'non-profit' is contested and might in the future be changed to 'social profit' – a perspective that again triggers new ideas emerging within what is known as fourth-sector organizations. The organization attempts to alleviate poverty and create self-employment through micro-farming initiatives combined with other practices. For Abalimi, micro-farming means that people are growing vegetables and other food items in home gardens and community gardens, but there are many other benefits, such as the old and young being revived with energy from eating healthy food, as well as the therapeutic effects of working with the earth. Micro-farms can be anything from one square metre at home up to one hectare in size.

Recent research by Wynand Grobler and Steve Dunga (2019) revealed that food security among the elderly of South Africa is influenced by age, gender, source of income, and marital status. Older women who are receiving social grants (state old-age pension) and living alone are the most likely to be food insecure. This makes the case of Abalimi even more relevant if one wants to understand a community response to food insecurity and poverty in South Africa.

Abalimi runs an administrative office in the township area of Phillipi and works out of two people's garden centres (or demonstration gardens), nurseries, and training centres in the township areas of Khayelitsha and Nyanga. The majority of the core professional staff is female farmers who are recruited directly from among the beneficiaries. At the time of writing, they have a core full-time staff of (up to) 17, and part-time, contracted, or casual staff and volunteers of (up to) 14 persons at any one time.

The key beneficiaries are the marginalized, the poor, and the unemployed, particularly women – not because others are explicitly excluded, but because it is mainly women who come forward and actually do the work of micro-farming in the townships. Mothers and grandmothers, more often than not, represent whole families, and therefore the direct impact of the work goes well beyond individuals. While the organization would love to see more young people engaged in urban farming, they know it is a difficult task. As a result, in recent years, a young farmer training centre has been set up to support young people interested in urban farming as a career option.

Abalimi supports individual households and groups to implement home gardening, community gardening, and micro-farming projects. This includes a total of approximately 5,000 urban micro-farmers, or approximately 25,000 (with an average of five family members per farmer) direct beneficiaries per annum. It is an impressive piece of work, making a real impact to many lives.

Before telling the story in more depth, and also distilling crucial community development practices, we turn to the literature exploring community economic development.

Towards a social or solidarity economy

Having a job – a livelihood, employment – is crucial to people's futures. Like having a shelter over our head, many people want to have a meaningful job or, for that matter, any job at all. Engaging most people in conversation would soon see the topics of jobs, employment, livelihood, or incomes arise. Within the field of community development, such topics are usually encapsulated within the discourse of community economic development.

Clearly, community development has a long history of connection to community economic development practices, albeit there are very different traces of theory embedded within the practices depending on ideological leanings. Within the USA, 'community development' is almost synonymous within 'community economic development'. Within this book, community economic development is understood *as one possible pathway* of community development, one of profound importance within South Africa considering the endemic economic poverty.

In considering community economic development within the globalizing neoliberal project, people are often forced to rely more on their own individual or community agency to generate work or employment. In a sense, governments have given up on full employment as a goal and people are often left to themselves.

There are many community economic development practices that can be situated within this paradigm – with the role of community development being to harness people's abilities collectively to *survive or manage* within the frame of capitalist economics. Examples would be community development practice that is focused on levering tourism investment into a particular community, ensuring a geographical community attracts tourists, albeit at the expense of another geographical community.

However, there are significant other discourses of community economic development, and we particularly foreground the social or solidarity economy. These discourses and accompanying practices aim to fundamentally transform the logics of capitalist dominator culture. Recognizing the limited efficiency values of capitalism and the equalizing values of socialism, the discourse tries to steer a course that is more oriented towards cooperative, mutual, and reciprocal values. Proliferating around the world, and even penetrating mainstream institutions such as the International Labour Organization, the social and solidarity economy is creating and supporting whole new ways of cooperating, communing, and reviving the gift economy.

It should also be said that the economic sphere is increasingly understood to be intricately connected to the ecological – as two sides of the same coin – and in many ways community development, deeply influenced by the broader 'development literature', is being renewed and reconstructed by the ecological polycrises upon us (Swilling and Annecke, 2012). E.F. Schumacher's *Small is Beautiful* (1974) is the cornerstone of a flourishing lineage of work that has brought the economic and ecological together. This coincided with the analysis published within the Club of Rome's *Limits to Growth* (Meadows et al., 1972). Such publications have inspired generations of work and now there appears to be a gradual tipping point as people grapple with food sovereignty, soil health, de-growth possibilities for society, transitions, and broader sustainability. At a global level, the sustainable development goals also have a dedicated goal, Goal 2: Zero Hunger, to end hunger, achieve food security, improve nutrition, and promote sustainable agriculture. According to Statistics South Africa (2017), the proportion of people vulnerable to hunger decreased from 29.3 per cent (in 2002) to 12.1 per cent (in 2017). Despite this achievement, some three million South Africans are still reported to experience food insecurity from time to time. Targeting female-headed households with poverty intervention strategies is key in the South African government's attempts to achieve zero hunger for South Africa in 2030 (Statistics South Africa, 2015).

Making sense of the literature exploring this kind of work in recent years would be a huge task and is not necessary for this chapter. It is simply to make the point that the story of Abalimi brings these two historically disparate threads together beautifully – linking economic livelihoods and the ecological concerns of food security, healthy soils, and healthy bodies. As per Joanna Macy and Molly Young Brown's (1998) framework that suggests praxis be oriented to 1) analysing structural causes and creating alternative institutions, 2) focusing on changing hearts and minds through education, or 3) engaging in resistant practices or holding actions against those destroying the commons or the environment, the Abalimi story is one of new possibilities. It represents an alternative institution creating new economic-ecological futures for urban agriculture.

Learning from a case study: The story of the Abalimi Bezekhaya

We have chosen to structure the telling of this story through an account of learnings from three key site visits. In the discussion, we then explore the theory of development that has been distilled from Abalimi's long years of practice and reflection, foregrounding the significant role of action learning and action research.

During this inquiry, three important Abalimi sites were visited. The first site was one of the many community gardens run by groups of women. The garden is farmed using organic methods, natural wind barriers, and natural pest control (dual-cropping / companion planting). (It should be said that, while using organic methods, the work is not organically certified as it is using seeds from nurseries which cannot claim to have been organically produced. However, they are not genetically modified seeds.) Water, which is tested regularly, comes from underground, where there is an abundant supply.

What was immediately clear is that such a garden is like a small business and needs a great deal of work to make it productive. The women working on the garden have to choose whether they just want fresh food for their families, or to invest in labour and other costs to also make cash – that is, turn it into an enterprise that reaches beyond self-help. The particular group at the first site visit have a rule that in order to join their group an applicant must first work for a year for no cash income – they are only allowed to take home some fresh produce. It is a tough rule but the rationale is to stop new members benefiting too easily from the project after all the really hard work that has been done by elder women.

The women here, like most, have registered their collective as a non-profit organization (NPO), although all are being encouraged by the government to register as cooperative legal structures. As an NPO, they can access government financial support to buy water tanks, among other things. The advice Abalimi gives on these community structures is not to start an executive group, arguing that it is important to keep the groups small (six to 20 people) so all decisions can be made in plenary. They have learned 'the hard way', as someone put it, that 'executives' usually mean that either men or educated groups take control, marginalizing the less powerful or less educated workers/farmers. In fact, Abalimi has again learned that the real challenge of the work is not technical, but the social – such as how the groups are run and how people cooperate (or not) once money enters the picture.

In our inquiry, we also learned how important Abalimi's services are, and how people in the community get to know about such services via community networks, the radio, or community events. Abalimi essentially has two components, the first being the development service, which provides ongoing free technical support to the farmers. For Abalimi, while the women pay rent for the land and also costs of water and electricity, technical support is a free subsidy to the women. Their services are essentially those usually understood as 'extension services' – in this case provided by Abalimi because the state mainly focuses on providing such services to larger-scale commercially oriented farmers. The second service is the Abalimi business unit, understood as Harvest of Hope (HoH), discussed below.

The second site was one of the two People's Garden Centres with demonstration gardens, and in many ways these are understood as the real engine rooms of the work. Abalimi argues that if an urban farmer learns to cultivate 100 square metres of land, they can feed a family – provided good inputs are invested (such as labour and compost). The heart of where urban farmers learn how to make that 100 square metres of land fruitful are the two demonstration gardens at the People's Garden Centres.

People come to either of the two educational sites for training and advice from one of the Abalimi employed fieldworkers. At these demonstration gardens, people can access seeds, compost, and advice. To access this, people have to become a member, at the cost of R30 for an individual or R50 for a group, which entitles the members to discounted agri-inputs for one year and to attend a four-day basic agriculture course (the real cost of the four-day training course is R600/farmer, hence the need for a subsidized service).

Abalimi again advocates that crucial to success is that urban farmers (indeed, any farmers anywhere within the modern economy) must have ongoing permanent support, which is part and parcel of the 'extension service' (without this, farmers – particularly emerging ones – will fail). Within their model, this support provides the initial four days of training, on going field support, and then access to scientific services if the fieldworker does not know how to solve a particular problem (that is, the fieldworkers know what expertise is available to help solve a particular problem that they themselves cannot; for example, dealing with unknown pests).

At the demonstration project visited, Mama Mabel Bokolo is the fieldworker-animator and People's Garden Centre operator. She runs the whole thing, with the support of a dedicated trainer. Ma Bokolo signs up the trainees and runs the People's Garden Centre and the trainer also supplies on-site extension services to community gardens that use the People's Garden Centre. She particularly loves providing the training, which is structured in two ways. Firstly, as a starter course of four days, 9am–3pm Monday–Thursday, which enables an urban farmer to achieve subsistence if they have the 100 square metres and persist for the year while accessing support. Secondly, in a more advanced course of eight days, the aim is to help those who are also looking to trade their produce (that is, make financial profit on top of feeding their family).

The third site included the office of Abalimi and also the packing hub for the business-marketing arm of Abalimi, HoH. This business-marketing arm was launched in 2008 and operates as a community-supported agriculture (CSA) unit purchasing fresh produce from the micro-farmers (approximately 70 per cent of these suppliers are women) at a good price, which is then sold via the CSA mechanism to middle-class people who pre-order a weekly box of food. The mechanism thereby connects urban farmers to those who have income sources – a market issue, crucial to success. Every month, Abalimi fieldworkers visit these farmers and make a contract for what produce is needed to be grown to supply HoH, which is bought at a good price. If the produce quality is not good enough, then it is used by farmers to feed their families or is sold across the fence.

Crucially, and disrupting capitalist logics, there is no attempt to squeeze farmers for the best price or maximize profits. This is a socially oriented enterprise, attempting to build a more mutual, reciprocal, and relational economy.

Some key practices and an emergent development model

Particular practices are crucial to the success of this work. The first practice is oriented towards what is called *resource supply*. For example, as already discussed, Abalimi runs two non-profit demonstration gardens that also act as nursery projects in the locations of Nyanga and Khayelitsha. These are called People's Garden Centres and they supply free advice, information, and subsidized gardening inputs such as trees, groundcovers, soil improvers (for example, manure), seed, seedlings, basic tools, windbreaks, and safe pest control remedies.

Secondly, they engage in *training*, whereby up to 1,000 people are trained each year through the four-day basic course already mentioned, along with year-round, on-site, technical follow-up support visits and demonstrations to projects.

Thirdly, a core focus of their practice is *community building*. The rationale for such practice is that the social benefits of organic gardening and micro-farming among the poor are enhanced through activities such as mutual-help work events, where members from different community projects gather and work together on one community project site to accomplish large or difficult tasks. Such collective work is usually accompanied by good food and celebration at the end of the day. Horizontal (farmer to farmer) learning events – where the gardeners and farmers gather to share stories, difficulties, problems, solutions, and achievements among themselves – are also held.

114 DOES COMMUNITY DEVELOPMENT WORK?

Fourthly, Abalimi explicitly focuses on building *partnerships* and *networking*. Within these practices, the organization, through its own partnerships and networks, assists community projects to connect to other opportunities and services that they may require, thereby linking need to resources as effectively and efficiently as possible. For example, a community garden group may wish to start up a sewing group, or obtain support from another service provider.

Finally, but of significance in terms of effectiveness, the organization is focused on useful *research, monitoring,* and *evaluation*. Such practices ensure that Abalimi can continue to 'fine tune' its own development practice, so that community projects become more and more sustainable within a better defined step-by-step process. For example, through careful observation of what actually happens 'on the ground' over 30 years, Abalimi has developed what it calls its 'development theory', which is used to help understand sustainable development of community projects along a clear pathway. Their development theory conceptualizes four phases, understood as survival level, subsistence level, livelihood level, and commercial level. See this depicted pictorially in Figure 8.1.

Distilling the lessons for practice

While this story could be used to discuss dozens of lessons, three main ideas have been distilled for the purposes of this chapter. They include: an action learning approach to community development; 'seeing what the people see' – applying observational skills; and providing ongoing support, training, and organizational development, each discussed below. Before engaging in that discussion, it should also be noted that with regard to the literature

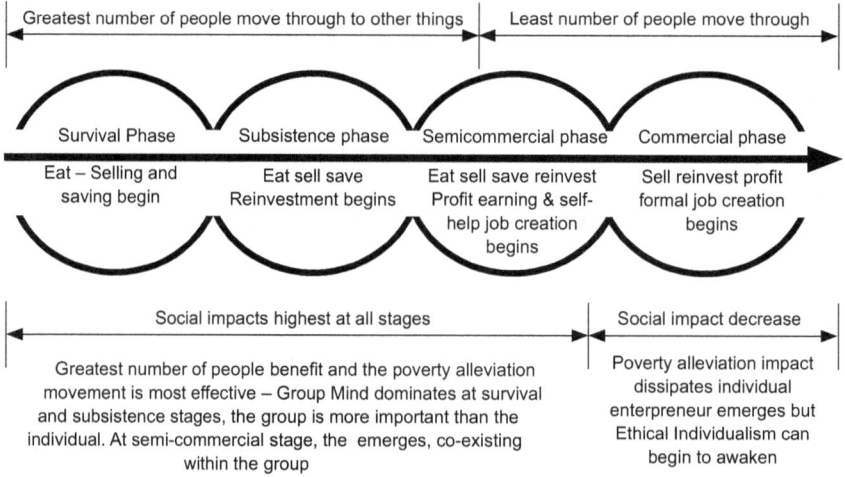

Figure 8.1 The farmer development chain for organic farming projects
Source: originated and developed by Rob Small for Abalimi Bezekhaya and the Farm & Garden National Trust

introduced earlier in the chapter, the Abalimi work could be construed within the Macy and Brown (1998) framework as an example of 'analysis of structural causes and creating of alternative institutions'. The organization has spent many years analysing the causes of urban poverty, trying to make sense of the 'food system' most of us are immersed within, and have created an alternative institution, one that fosters people-centred development processes. These processes also draw on numerous community economic development frameworks harnessing assets (as per the asset-based community development approach) and aiming for sustainable livelihoods (as per the sustainable livelihoods approach, with a thorough analysis again of assets and also potential shocks to the sustainability system). Particular practices relevant for community development are now considered.

An action learning-research approach to community development

While a vision and cooperative leadership create a motivational and intentional edge for people to get things going, an action learning and research approach to the practice ensures that the work is constantly reflected upon, leading to potential new innovations and directions. It is easy for community development work to get 'stuck' in the sense that what works for a while can become dogma – 'the way things are done', so to speak. However, in listening to workers involved at Abalimi and also in reading documents that tell their story, what is striking is their capacity to keep reflecting on their practice in ways that have led to new analyses and new innovations. Here is an organization with more than 30 years of experience, providing a context for deeply reflective work. For example, in the previous section, we shared the development theory that underpins their work, known as the farmer development chain. This chain, while important as a substantive development theory, is more important to a community worker in that it reflects a theory that has emerged *inductively from people* working in the field over many years.

To see what the people see – observational skills

Linked to this inductive, action learning, and action-research approach is the centrality of observational skills. Crucial to the success of this story is the commitment by the community practitioners involved to 'see what the people see' (Lathouras, 2010); that is, to take seriously people's experience of the world and what they aspire to be or do. Taking seriously people's experience of the world requires astute observation skills. However, such skills are not easy to attain for several reasons. For example, Allan Kaplan (2002) writes about the ease with which community or social practitioners fail to conceptualize the difference between observing and interpreting and in that conceptual failure end up interpreting what they 'think they see' in inaccurate ways. Instead, more care needs to be taken to observe what is occurring in a social situation prior to any attempt to interpret. Secondly, many community workers are trained to dismiss what people have to say because training often leads to an attitude of expertise and of 'I know best'. This can result in a setting whereby observation becomes almost superfluous. Thirdly, observing and seeing are incredibly difficult when cleavages such as class, race, and gender are taken into account. Within any given social situation, what a privileged white male community practitioner might see, and then interpret in one way, might well be seen and interpreted in a completely different way by someone who has a totally different lived experience – for example, a poor, black woman.

We are reminded of an insightful story told by Jacob Dlamini in *Native Nostalgia* (2009), reflecting on life in a Johannesburg urban slum. Within the story, the local municipality decided to introduce owls as predators against an epidemic of rats. A good idea, emerging from an analysis built on an introduced scientific understanding of the food chain. But it was an analysis that had no legitimacy with the people and was not based on 'what they see'. In this case, the professional analysis did not take into account the worldview clashes of different sciences. For the local people, owls are linked to witchcraft and they decided to hunt them with more fervour than the rats. The local municipality staff had failed to listen to the people and engage them in an analysis, first 'seeing what they see'.

Within the Abalimi story, the astute observational skills have clearly enabled the community practice to evolve to a level of sophistication where practitioners are able to be responsive to the diverse experiences and desires of the potential and practising urban farmers. For example, the practice takes into account that while the work opens space for poor people to learn how to garden or farm, there is *no pressure* to continue gardening or farming. People can opt in or opt out at any time, depending on where their lives are at and their aspirations are going. Observation also enabled practitioners to quickly see how the formalizing of groups into NPOs, which then chose to form executives, quickly led to control by an elite few, with the emergent practitioner recommendation that groups remain small enough for everyone to participate in plenary decision-making.

Provision of ongoing support, training, and organizational development

From the story, it is clear that ongoing support is crucial to the success of Abalimi. The notion of ongoing support provides a counter-story or counter-analysis to the many short-term orientations of development interventions. Furthermore, the type of support is not limited to training inputs – often known as workshops – but is expanded to include ongoing support around the development of community-based organizations among groups of farmers (should they wish to operate as a group and not stay as backyard gardeners). The attention to the social and organizational formation of groups, in the forms of NPOs or cooperatives, is essential to the work of Abalimi. There is recognition that the technical elements (that is, people learning to grow food) are the easy components of animating a successful movement of urban organic micro-farmers. The more complex elements include the organizational configuration of each group, as discussed earlier, related to the use of executives or not, how decisions are made in plenary, thereby requiring the limiting of group size to about 20, the allocation of cash (either as income or as reinvestment into the garden), and the organizational configuration of the movement itself. This latter component, in the case of Abalimi, is a careful and purposeful mix that includes the urban farmer groups organizing themselves into a voluntary association, called Vukuzenzele Urban Farmers Association; the service system of Abalimi itself (providing technical services and the business marketing arm of HoH); and finally the Farm Garden National Trust, set up to lever corporate and private sponsorship, and also create franchise models so the work can be replicated in other communities. Vukuzenzele in isiXhosa means 'wake up and do it for yourself'.

Conclusion

The energy and enthusiasm encountered in the many visits to this project are still alive to us as researchers. There were familiar faces, which is always a good sign – indicative of people who are loyal to the work. Food was flourishing, markets were being created, and connections woven. Community development practices were also clearly articulated and theories such as 'farmer development chain' were being inductively constructed from reflection in the field – the best kind of theory. The story told within this chapter provides a glimpse into their work and an articulation of some crucial practices relevant to community development. These practices, distilled from the particulars of the story, can be generalized for broader thinking about practice. To work within an action learning / action research frame, to nurture observational skills enabling community facilitators to try and 'see what the people see', and to ensure the community development work provides ongoing mentoring, support, and organizational development (particularly within the meso- and macro-stages of developmental work) are crucial to effective community work. They enhance the possibilities of successful transformational work.

References

Davies M. 2006. *Planet of Slums*. London and New York: Verso.
Dlamini J. 2009. *Native Nostalgia*. South Africa: Jacana Media.
Grobler W.C.J. and Dunga S. 2019. *Analysis of Food Security Status among the Elderly in South Africa*. IISES International Academic Conference, 10 September 2019, Paris.
Kaplan A. 2002. *Development Practitioners and Social Process: Artists of the Invisible*. Chicago and London: Pluto Press.
Lathouras A. 2010. Developmental community work: A method. In Ingamells A., Caniglia F., Lathouras A., Wiseman R. and Westoby P. (eds). *Community Development Stories, Method and Meaning*. Illinois: Common Ground Publishers.

Macy J. and Brown M.Y. 1998. *Coming Back to Life: Practices to Reconnect Our Lives, Our World*. Gabriola Island, BC: New Society Publishers.

Meadows D.H., Meadows D.L., Randers J. and Behrens W. 1972. *Limits to Growth*. New York: Universal Books.

Pieterse E. and Simone A. 2013. *Rogue Urbanism: Emergent African Cities*. Cape Town: UCT Press.

Schumacher E.F. 1974. *Small is Beautiful: Economics as if People Mattered*. London: Abacus.

Statistics South Africa. 2015. *Millennium Development Goals, Country Report, 2015*. Pretoria: Statistics South Africa.

Statistics South Africa. 2017. *Sustainable Development Goals: Indicator Baseline Report*. Pretoria: Statistics South Africa.

Swilling M. and Annecke E. 2012. *Just Transitions: Explorations of Sustainability in an Unfair World*. Cape Town: UCT Press.

CHAPTER 9
Staged place-based community development and the Hantam Community Education Trust

Abstract

Chapter 9 considers the significance of community development and place-based practice within South Africa. The chapter particularly focuses on the case study of the Hantam Community Education Trust, an exemplary piece of emergent place-based community practice located in the rural Karoo area of the Eastern and Northern Cape. The chapter locates its story within the context of the educational crisis of South Africa.

Keywords: stages of community development, time, cooperative leadership, no-advice, start anywhere, go everywhere

Introduction

Peter is driving along a dirt road to visit the Hantam Community Education Trust. It is a dusty drive, some 40 km out from Colesberg, which is 600 km south-west of Johannesburg. He has driven past many small communities, reminding him of the villages he used to work in within Kwa-Zulu Natal from 1994 to 1998. Often, the schools are broken looking, but there are also crowds of young people milling around, kicking up dust. There is a familiar feeling of inner despair in solidarity with the young people who are institutionally marginalized by the ongoing failure of educational reform in South Africa. But Peter keeps his head up; after all, he is visiting the Hantam Community Education Trust, about which we have heard many good stories.

Many commentators consider the crisis in education of young people as the definitive crisis of South Africa. Structurally, the failure of reforming education significantly entrenches marginalization of young black people, but also many other poor people. Modernity's key mechanism of social mobility is thwarted. Within capitalist logics, if people do not have access to financial capital, then cultural capital – gained through education – is the next best thing. In South Africa, many young people lack access to either financial or cultural capital, and therefore their dreams are shattered. It is into this space that the following story speaks, tracing the role of community development catalysing an effective education initiative in South Africa.

However, in digging a bit deeper, beyond the most easily foregrounded education trust, this is a story that is bigger than, or goes beyond, education. Education has here been the catalyst for what is better understood as a staged approach to community development with five stages, which has occurred from the bottom-up, or inside-out, of a locality. That is, the work has been initiated by local people, only supported by professionals or experts. For this reason, the story has met our criteria for a decolonizing approach.

Context

Hantam Community Education Trust is located in the district called Umsobomvu, an area that consists of 28 farms all within a radius of approximately 50 km from the Trust. The work of the Trust focuses primarily on the constituencies of these farms – the labourers, the young people, and even the farmers themselves. As the Trust's credibility has grown, young people are also bussed in from Colesberg, as many parents there consider Hantam to be the best school in the area.

The idea and conversation that sparked the genesis of this project occurred in 1989, as three women of the area came together and decided they wanted to do something. Their initial idea was to form a playgroup and so, with some help from early childhood development experts, some women from the farms were identified by the local population, sent to training, and then given work. The process of identifying women and consolidating the project occurred during a 'community meeting' took place monthly for some time. This regular community meeting was also used as an opportunity to consider a range of other local issues and potential initiatives, such as how to set up community gardens.

Since that initial meeting, and those early days, the Trust has evolved into an 'integrated' rural development initiative that has, among other things, 'provided a school' for well over 6,000 young people in the area. The Trust has also offered bursaries for post-school education, initiated a hospitality training centre that provides professional training, supported and mentored job placements, set up a rural community health strategy (including a pharmacy), and many other things.

The context is not easy. There are endemic issues to do with alcohol abuse (leading to substantial challenges related to foetal alcohol syndrome), HIV-AIDS, farmer–labourer tensions, and economic poverty. The integrated nature of the challenges is well illustrated by the following anecdote, whereby at a community meeting early in 1989 a community spokesperson stood up and said, 'We are not happy with this. We don't like the [play]school!' Asked why, he answered, 'It is all well and good, but where will our children go from here?' Certainly, a reasonable and rational question – in fact a very astute one, demonstrating the complex integrated and interconnected nature of many community and social problems. One could ask the same question having set up a successful school – what next? Dilemmas of employment arise; and then of course foetal alcohol syndrome, namely a health issue, thwarts many efforts to solve educational-economic problems.

It is into such a context that Hantam's integrated work, pioneered via evidence-based educational initiatives, has grown. However, before telling the story in more depth, and also distilling crucial community development practices, we turn to the historical context exploring the linkages between community development and education.

Locating linkages between community development and a staged approach

In many parts of the world, it is easy to discern two strands of theory-practice within the history of evolving community development practices. On the one hand are the more technical approaches that focus on community development as a social-planning or service-delivery practice. For example, this technical approach emerged from the neighbourhood-oriented work in the UK of the 1950s (adapted from Canada's neighbourhood work underpinned by Murray Ross's work). However, the 1950s saw a split occur in the UK, with more progressive elements reorienting community development towards what can be understood as a community and adult education tradition. In many ways, this split still exists around the world, with more institutionally oriented community development continuing to focus on social planning and service delivery, albeit eliciting more community participation, and more 'grassroots' workers focusing on community and adult education.

Revisiting this history, the 1960s saw the emergence of the first UK-based community development programmes focused on localities. The approach was heavily critiqued by those aligned with the progressive impulses of the 1960s. Such impulses were then reinforced by what is often termed the 'radical turn', triggered by numerous publications – but one in particular notable for community development: Paulo Freire's *Pedagogy of the Oppressed*. Also, in the USA, Saul Alinsky's *Rules for Radicals* had already been published, and community organizing took off as an approach that also countered the more 'social planning'-based orientation. Alinsky's work drew on a long lineage of community practice, which could be traced back to Jane Addams' 1880s settlement house tradition, which had a strong emphasis on neighbourhood. Jack Rothman's seminal 1968 article focused on types of community practice, and clearly delineated community development (as a form of social work practice, more focused on community organization), community organizing, and social planning.

Importantly to this story, community development is also predominantly a place-based practice. In this, work that starts as an activity can form into a project, and as projects multiply and integrate, a community organization and/or 'community programme' can emerge, and even the seeds of a social movement. So while this is a story of the education trust, it is more accurately a story of the emergence of an integrated community programme.

The five stages of place-based practice

Effective community development work involves a series of processes that may mature through five important stages. These stages are connected, in the sense that if practitioners omit or neglect the tasks associated with each, problems compound in the next stage and the development process is stunted or even halted. These stages also provide a linkage between micro- and macro-level work, in the sense that while the activity and project stages remain squarely and firmly within the space of relational and group work, the latter three stages involve organizational-level work, or linkages to policy or social movement formation. The stages are portrayed in Table 9.1, and then each is explained in detail.

Stage 1: The activity

An activity stage can begin with an initiative from a practitioner and/or a community member. Whatever its origin, and right from the outset, an activity cycle ought to be debated. There are thousands of questions that can and ought to be asked, such as:

- 'Who is going to benefit if we do this?'
- 'Will we learn something from this activity?'
- 'Is it feasible?' and so on.

Table 9.1 The five stages of place-based work

1. The activity stage	The activity stage is exploratory in nature and the results of that exploration may or may not mature into a project.
2. The project stage	An activity becomes a project when a piece of development work has roots within the community and is considered important enough by the members of the community to make the activity part of their work.
3. The people's organization stage	The third stage occurs when the status of a people's organization (PO) is given. Because the name, membership, and purpose of the project are secure, conflict resolution processes are in place and organizational routines are established.
4. The community programme stage	The fourth community programme stage begins when groups of projects or POs come together, usually brought on by their common interests and the efficiencies that can be achieved by sharing. Groups of programmes may then become a community organization, which moves the development process into the domain of macro-method.
5. The stage of people's movement	The fifth, people's movement stage begins when the members of POs, without leaving their organization, help promote the work by sharing their experience with groups who may be thinking of beginning the journey, or by sharing their ideas as to how they resolved important issues. There is a movement when enough people graduate from the programme not as a client, but as a helper and an associate. This fifth stage opens the participatory process to the wider world of meta-method.

These are important questions, but by far the most important questions in the activity cycle, if the work is to be developmental and not service-oriented, are 'Who wants this activity?' and 'Are those same people who want this activity willing to do the work associated with accomplishing it?'

Exploring answers to these difficult questions is at the core of the activity cycle. In some instances, the practitioner may decide that the development option is not the best way forward, but the idea or need is important enough to seek resources for it. Having decided that, the practitioner might then recommend putting in a submission for funding to employ a practitioner to set up a service, but then the project will be a service delivery and not a participatory project.

Overall, unless these questions are answered, the activity will have difficulty maturing into a participatory community development project. However, this answering is hard work, and development practitioners have learned from bitter experience that the activity phase is shortened at peril. Some ideas seem so good and so right that all sorts of rationalizations take place:

- 'Maybe if we do it for a while, the community members will get the idea?'
- 'Maybe we can talk people into it as we go along?'
- 'Maybe if we employ someone, they will generate interest?'

It is important to recognize that many participatory activities do not need to move to the next stage. They are short, sharp, and to the point, and then have served their purpose. The situation is more difficult when the worker sees that help is desperately needed. It is just so easy to be seduced by fantasies of importance, by the urgency and drama of the moment. Therefore, the decision not to proceed with a participatory project is a hard one to take, and yet the very point of having an activity stage is that such assessments can be done. There is only a limited amount of energy in a community, and if it is to be a participatory development project, then it needs to justify that energy and justify itself as an activity through which we can grow and learn.

Stage 2: The project

The decision to give an activity the status of a project and move to the next stage is very important, for the space between the transition from an activity to a project is a very important exit point. If an activity is given the status of a project, there is a decision by the people involved, and by the host organization, that this project is important in its own right, that it has some strategic significance, and that there will be a commitment of material and human resources – namely, their energy and goodwill. It is possible, but difficult, to exit a participatory project once it is underway. Within the Hantam story this shift became self-evident as people early on in the process wanted more than an ad hoc activity at stage one. They wanted a project.

In a more formal sense, achieving project status means that a bottom-up agenda has been endorsed both by the people of the community and sometimes by a formal community auspice, most commonly a community organization.

With this two-fold approval, there is a convergence of bottom-up energy from the people, with the top-down energy flowing from the approval of the leadership of the community organization. It means that the project has become a legitimate part of a worker's load and the management of the organization has considered it important enough to commit resources to it over a period of time.

When an activity achieves the status of a project, other identifiable attributes are required. The project is often given a name, a people's name, something that means something to the people involved. Too often, community projects are given names that repeat the institutional names of the social or global programme that has provided funding, names that reflect the administrative concerns of government or some donor and not the aspirations of local people. A project would usually have a file that is kept not in the worker's private filing cabinet, but in an accessible place for everybody involved. In the file should be the contact points of all involved and, if they agree, maybe their photographs too, because this helps with recognition and builds linkages. In the file should be a brief record – the storyline of what has happened, including a copy of the initial decisions that authorized action and gave the project its public legitimacy. Inside the file should be a page that outlines the vision, a plan that states the objectives, a timetable of meetings, job descriptions for everyone, and a description of the flow of the work. Also, if it is possible, the file should include a rationale for the project, the insight of analysis that illuminates why this project is important and why the people involved are doing it.

Stage 3: The people's organization

The third stage of participatory development is achieved when a project is given the status of a people's organization. This occurs within this story with the registering of the Hantam Education Trust.

As depicted in Table 9.2, there are, in fact, at least three levels of maturity: moving from self-help groups to community-based organizations, through to 'people's organizations'. Note that we use the term 'community-based organization', because that is how they have been named in practice, but in fact they are more like an organized group in a community than an organization. These three levels of maturity reflect a growing appreciation of who actually benefits from their work. Although the distinction between these levels is of secondary importance, it can help explain the different levels of participation and awareness that these groups demonstrate.

The particular recognition of the maturity of people's organizations is important because practitioners greatly appreciate the contribution they make. One of the most important breakthroughs in participatory development work in the last few decades has been the recognition of the importance of the different levels of maturation – from self-help groups towards people's organizations. Wisdom has also been gained in how to harness the contribution

Table 9.2 Levels of maturity of people's organizations

Organizational type	Focus	Beneficiaries
Self-help group	Self	Individual member: 'This group helps me.'
Community-based organization	Mutual aid	Individual member and group: 'This group helps me and my fellow group members.'
People's organization	Group	Individual member and group and community: 'This group not only helps me and my fellow members but is a contribution to our community.'

of people's organizations appropriately, without converting them into a community organization constituted to service others. One important hallmark of a great participatory development process is the number of people's organizations that are self-sufficient in their own right, focused on their own well-being, so they do not lose their small group-level charter but are networked in a range of strategic partnerships with other groups and organizations.

A people's organization can reach both back and forward from formality to informality, providing both structure and predictability and yet flexibility and responsiveness. On the one hand, people's organizations stabilize work routines that help people avoid constant chaos, making the work purposeful and efficient, making it recognizable so that people can participate. On the other hand, the people's organization is like a living membrane, a recognizable and organized entry point – but permeable enough for even the poorest to enter and take part. Even community organizations, participatory though they may be, if they are to really distinguish themselves from bureaucratic institutions must know how to open the boundaries of their organization and drive their processes from the bottom up. Self-help groups, community-based organizations, and – above all – people's organizations are the means to achieve that important goal.

Stage 4: The community programme

The transition from people's organization to the fourth programme stage presents new opportunities and challenges. There are limits to the size of a project (or people's organization), and they lose efficiency and effectiveness after about 20 members. In a group of 20 members, there are 190 one-on-one relationships and a variety of combinations and permutations of groups within that. Even if members have long-standing relationships with each other, the numbers become too large for participation and there is an inexorable move to hierarchy and representation – arrangements much more suitable for service delivery than participatory development work. When numbers grow, the time comes to set up another project and people's organization, perhaps with a different focus or at a different location. With numbers of projects cooperating, the move from individualized projects to the formation of a community programme has begun.

126 DOES COMMUNITY DEVELOPMENT WORK?

The role of the community development practitioner based in the community organization is a critical one in such transitional times. Development practitioners work with projects and people's organizations if and when necessary – they do not work *for* them. If community members think community development practitioners work for them in a people's organization, there is an immediate move into a service relationship and all sorts of complications flow. The moment the worker takes control, the centre point of activity and decision-making moves to the staff and management committee of the organization, rather than functioning at the level of the project or the people's organization. Such a move signals a change in ownership from the people to the authorities within the community organization. A 'serviced' project becomes much more time consuming for development staff, limiting their capacity to set up the next project.

Stage 5: The people's movement

The people have a most important contribution to make in the fifth stage. Without leaving their own group, people can create and share templates and procedures, standards of practice, and practical wisdom grown from experience in projects and people's organizations. The mutual creation and sharing of these templates and wisdoms from – and between – projects are an important characteristic of the movement and maturation of development work. The sharing and creating process enables what can be understood as a people's movement. In this stage, the people in a participatory programme do not graduate as ex-clients who move on but are instead welcomed as valued friends and colleagues who have a special place in the movement with much to share. At this stage, community development intersects with people and social movement theory and practice. Some of this thinking is considered further in other chapters, but we have also articulated these ideas in other writing (Westoby and Lyons, 2017).

Returning to the story

Having established the legacy of linkages between community development and the five stages of development, we now return to the story of the Hantam Community Education Trust, an exquisite example of how community development approaches can be used to create emergent oases within the context described above.

Building on the initial efforts of the three women who dreamed up the idea of a playgroup and hosted the regular community meetings, energy was harnessed to respond to community-identified issues. Schooling was on the agenda of the community, as per the assertion of the spokesperson recounted earlier. Ideas translated quickly to activity, and then to a project status.

At first, the school was established within the farm buildings that were available, and initially consisted of 60 children and several teachers. The dining room, the garage, and the stable were used as classrooms. Eventually, one of the local farmers donated several hectares of land and this was registered as a school site, providing not only a geographical and identity base, but also a legal basis for raising funds. This represented a shift to a community organization.

An architect designed a school, which was built over a period of the next 15 years, and funds were gradually donated enabling several buildings to be constructed.

The school targets children aged three to 16 years, with the idea that some of the students can then matriculate to boarding schools in Colesberg or Bloemfontein, supported by Trust bursaries. The medium of learning is English, at the request of the parents, and the pedagogy of the school is constructed on good practice researched and taught by the most engaged educational scholars from different parts of the world. The school also has an excellent library, a fully functional computer lab, and a science laboratory. Transport, while provided for the children (seven vehicles), is paid for by parents – but subsidized by the Trust. At the time of our visit, the school had 210 students attending, with the only limits to growth being space and other resources.

The work has expanded beyond formal schooling, thereby moving from community organization to a community programme (stage 4). For example, a farmworkers' apprenticeship programme has been established, aimed mainly at young people who have foetal alcohol syndrome and therefore would find it difficult to work within other contexts. They are able, with support, to learn the skills to be farmhands. Sitting behind this initiative is a philosophy of giving young people a 'realistic chance', thereby not setting people up to fail. Such a philosophy argues that young people with foetal alcohol syndrome would not succeed within many other learning contexts and are in fact easy prey for organized criminals. The realistic alternative of becoming farmhands was therefore established.

Additionally, a hospitality programme has been created in Colesberg where graduating young people can enrol for an 18-month internationally accredited certificate in hospitality. They spend one year learning in the Colesberg-based programme and are then mentored on the job for the next three years, but graduate after six months of this mentoring. They are given their certificate six months into the mentorship phase ensuring that they have to stick with the whole programme for 18 months prior to graduating. For several years, this programme has had a 100 per cent success rate in placing and keeping young people in a job. The graduates are well-sought-after employees.

Furthermore, a health clinic and community pharmacy have been established, servicing the community and particularly young children, focusing on primary health care. This health initiative also incorporates seven community health workers who engage with groups, conducting community education around issues such as HIV, foetal alcohol syndrome, parenting, pre-natal care, and so forth.

More recently, some 'edgy' community work (Kenny, 2011) has involved the seven community workers engaging directly with some of the labourers of the neighbouring farms, currently focusing on four farms. They ask the labourers questions such as, 'What do we expect of our employees?' and conversely, 'What do the farmers expect of us?' This work of questioning is creating a conversational space for labourers to consider transformational options – signifying a potential shift to a social movement stage (stage 5). For example, one story recounted how the process of questioning led to one labourer asking, 'Should we keep beating our wives and kids and drink more alcohol, just because the farmer treats us badly?' It was a crucial question, one reflecting Freire's hope that oppressed people not only be questioned, but also learn to question themselves (Freire and Faundez, 1989), and also one that could kick-start a process of transformation from victim to agent of change.

Finally, and as a way of concluding the story, when interviewed the director affirmed that, 'We've created an enabling environment, but now people have to take responsibility'. The statement reflects the Trust's philosophy of partnership work, recognizing the co-creative efforts required of local people and outsiders and internal and external resources.

Having explicated the story, we now distil some crucial generic lessons for effective community development practice.

Distilling the lessons for practice

While this story could be used to discuss dozens of ideas, and we have used it to represent an example of staged practice, three other main lessons have been distilled for the purposes of this chapter. These are: the element of time in decolonizing community development work; the notion of cooperative leadership and the no-advice 'rule' from experts; and the meme 'start anywhere, go everywhere'.

The element of time in decolonizing community development work

The story told above fills a page or two of text. The reader might be able to sense the rich texture of the work despite this limited account. However, the 'told' story only makes visible traces, or small components, of the real story. It is a chosen story, one that obviously obscures so much. One aspect of the story rendered invisible by such a brief telling is the length of time embedded within the work. It is not obvious at first glance that this story, at the time of writing, provides glimpses into more than 30 years of combined work by uncountable numbers of people. The time element quite literally 'slips away' in the telling – it is rendered invisible by the quick read. Decolonizing community development requires a clear understanding of the time needed for change. Colonization has left a painful, wounded legacy of poverties, and it has been created over a long time. In turn, the decolonization process – depicted earlier in this book with the Fanon framework – takes a long time. There is no 'magic bullet', no 'Prozac pill'.

The crucial point is that most community development that supports decolonizing work takes a great deal of time. Moving from idea to activity, to achieving the status of a project and then people's organization and/or community programme, all shaped by a locality and place, takes a great deal of time. Within this story, the processes, being relationally oriented, required the building of trust, and trust is something earned over time. The endless informal meetings between the women leading the initiative and local leaders and people, supplemented with formal monthly meetings, are a time investment that builds a platform for solid trust. As such, the activity stage that consolidated into a project took months. Clearly, this investment of relational and staged work – taking the time – leads to an emphasis on process over product (albeit 'product' as outcome is also important, and it is best to avoid a binary split between process and product). Within the told story, the product is visible – a school, teaching, a library, a health clinic, and so forth. What is easily submerged is the process work (sometimes colloquially referred to as 'the footwork, the legwork') of meeting people, spending time eliciting their stories, building trust and collegiality, and then working cooperatively together. People spoken to or interviewed as we developed this case study were attentive to process, that of the past, present, and future. This is crucial within effective community development work.

Cooperative leadership and the no-advice 'rule' from experts

If time is one crucial element to community work, then cooperative leadership is another. Within the telling of the story – both by people at Hantam and also in our telling – it is easy to miss the significance of leadership. Sometimes, the binary of people and experts, or people versus experts, obscures the third key player: the leader. Often, what is required is the interaction of all three, but with the people and leaders taking the lead, and experts providing information – and, importantly from a decolonizing perspective, not advice (which we discuss below).

In our experience, leadership is often an unspoken dimension to community development stories because the leaders in community work, unlike leadership within many other kinds of contexts, do not like to 'blow their own trumpet'. They often lead quietly from within, behind, or even beneath. Their leadership is often not heroic leadership. Instead, it is cooperative leadership, or leadership with a 'nudge'. This kind of leadership can be crystallized through the story of initiating the work of the Hantam Community Education Trust.

Technically, the kind of leadership demonstrated in the story is sometimes referred to in the community development literature as cooperative leadership, which can be supported using the '0-1-3' method (Lathouras, 2010; Westoby and Owen, 2010). Within this method, leadership is *initiated* when one person has an idea. However, that one person – with an idea *not yet tested* with others, and thereby not in relationship with anyone else around the idea – has '0'/zero relationships. To act on an idea alone is to ensure that the process will not be community-oriented. It would instead be heroic or entrepreneurial leadership. In contrast, within community leadership, the idea is shared with at least one other person. Consequently, two people then hold the idea, and there is also now a relationship – signified technically as '0-1' – because there is a shift from zero to one relationship. Furthermore, they potentially share the idea with a third person. Three people make for three relationships; again, technically signified as '0-1-3', and here is the initial *building block* of a community process – a minimum of three people and three relationships (Kelly and Burkett, 2008; Kelly and Westoby, 2018). This triad creates the cooperative platform for community-oriented action (see Simmel [via Wolff, 1964: 139ff] on the significance of triads).

Within the Hantam story, we see this process in action, with the account of three women initially coming together, sharing an idea, and then starting an initiative. Of course, they quickly move on technically from 0-1-3 – through talking and consulting with potential beneficiaries, such as the community meetings – and quickly there is a 0-1-3-6-9 (as more individuals get involved, the number of relationships multiplies exponentially). This is a web-weaving process that leads to a leadership ethos where people cooperate and take responsibility in different ways. A minimal triad structure (0-1-3) that evolves into a strong web structure provides for a strong leadership structure, as it should become non- or at least less dependent on any one person (Westoby and Owen, 2010).

At the same time as cooperative leadership gets things going, community development tends to, at times, need the input of experts. Taking Myles Horton's wisdom as our point of departure, we suggest that a decolonizing approach to community development ensures experts are only invited into a process by community members and leaders when it is the right time. And, importantly, they are only invited in to *give information*. That information is then available to community members and leaders to deliberate on and make decisions about their pathway for change. In this way, it is important that experts do not bring advice along with their information, as the addition of advice tends to undermine people's confidence and capacity in making their own decisions. We suggest that experts giving advice is an over-stepping of the 'brief', and therefore the 'rule' is 'no advice'. As such, experts need to be briefed very clearly by the community practitioner that their advice is not welcome, even if community members say 'we want your advice'. Decolonizing community development invites a reorientation towards community members – in dialogue with leaders – making decisions (that are of course now informed by the experts).

'Start anywhere, go everywhere'

A vexed issue in place-based community development is *where you start* – what issue, which people? There are often many issues to be tackled in a place. Community practitioners wonder what the first activity could be or what the initial project should be.

One perspective most clearly articulated by a key informant in the Hantam story goes something like, 'community education is the key, being the catalyst within a holistic model'. This perspective, that there is such a thing as 'a key', suggests that community workers have to identify *the core or root issue* to work on. This perspective represents a particular kind of analytical approach whereby the analysis of the community worker or intervener is crucial. Linked to the previous discussion, such an analytical approach is very persuasive among experts – although it makes sense because, within this frame, it is often assumed that outside experts are needed to help a community, thereby justifying the experts' role. The expertise is focused on using technical tools to analyse the community or social context to identify the root cause of poverty. Groups, or a community, might then be mobilized to act around that identified issue.

In contrast, another perspective – best articulated within Margaret Wheatley and Deborah Freize's book *Walk Out Walk On: A Journey into Communities Daring to Live the Future Now* (2011) – is that the real core issue is to work where people have energy, enthusiasm, vision, and knowledge (as opposed to correct analysis of the root issue at hand). Wheatley and Frieze use the meme 'start anywhere, go everywhere' to hold in a concise manner the wisdom of this way of thinking and working. Again, we suggest that this approach fits more with a decolonizing approach, as it puts people's energy front and centre, disrupting the expert role.

From this perspective, in the case of the Hantam story, the issue was not so much whether 'education' is a core issue, or the root cause of poverty, but that there were three women who had the energy, enthusiasm, and knowledge of how to initiate educational experiments and so that is where they started – and this energy connected to the energy and concerns of the people in the locality. From this perspective, the issue is that the process started where there was energy, a vision, and some skills, neither a convoluted community planning process, nor an abstract analysis of what was the core problem. The point is that three women, working cooperatively (as per the 0-1-3 discussion earlier), started something and from that more work can grow (as per the 'start anywhere, go everywhere' meme).

Again, from this latter viewpoint, it is easier to get work going in a community because experts are not central to the process. Work can start wherever there are the combined inputs of energy, enthusiasm, a vision, and some knowledge.

Conclusion

One participant interviewed explained how hope is the crux of the work's success. From their perspective, if the school does not create a context within which children and young people, along with their parents, can hope – for a better life or, more concretely, paid work – then the community development initiative would collapse quickly. There would be no resonance between hopes and action. Hope as a concept is wonderfully articulated in Freire's *Pedagogy of Hope* (2004), as a concrete process of change. Hope is theorized in a way that differentiates it from 'magical thinking', understood as wishful thinking inspired by dreams alone. For Freire, hope instead requires *concrete praxis*, therefore grounding hope in real possibilities that have emerged from an analysis of options and opportunities.

Such a perspective appeared to us to resonate with the people we talked to at Hantam Community Education Trust. The school did not simply create realizable expectations or dreams. Instead, it elicited both dreams and expectations, and then set out to create concrete pathways and connections, enabling the dreams and expectations to be realized.

The analysis of people encountered indicated that such concrete pathways were made to manifest through the holistic nature of the work, providing linkages between primary school, secondary school, and a possible next step: the hospitality programme, the farmworkers' apprenticeship programme, or bursaries onto tertiary-level education. Educational issues were linked to health and worker rights, and what began as activity and morphed into projects then evolved into a substantial community programme.

Most importantly, the hope was made concrete in a clear process, with stages of work, presented here in a five-fold set. This set involves moving from activity to project, to people's organization, to a community programme, and even a social movement. It is a bottom-up, place-based approach that puts people at the heart of development – yet is linked to, and supported by, community leaders and experts invited in to give appropriate information.

Overall, it is an exemplary story of the stages of emergent place-based community development work, which meets the criteria for effective community development.

References

Alinsky S. 1971. *Rules for Radicals: A Pragmatic Primer for Realistic Radicals*. New York: Random House.

Freire P. 1970/2006. *Pedagogy of the Oppressed*. New York: Continuum.

Freire P. 2004. *Pedagogy of Hope: Reliving Pedagogy of the Oppressed*. New York: Continuum.

Freire P. and Faundez A. 1989. *Learning to Question: A Pedagogy of Liberation*. Geneva: WCC Publications.

Kelly A. and Burkett I. 2008. *People Centred Development: Building the People Centred Approach*. Brisbane, Australia: The Centre for Social Response.

Kelly A. and Westoby P. 2018. *Participatory Development Practice: Using Traditional and Contemporary Frameworks*. Rugby: Practical Action Publishing.

Kenny S. 2011. Towards unsettling community development. *Community Development Journal* 46 (suppl 1):i7–i19.

Lathouras A. 2010. Developmental community work: A method. In Ingamells A., Caniglia F., Lathouras A., Wiseman R. and Westoby P. (eds). *Community Development Stories, Method and Meaning*. Illinois: Common Ground Publishers.

Rothman J. 1968. Three models of community organisation practice. In *Social Work Practice*. Rothman, J, Erlich, L. and Tropman, J.E. (eds) New York: Columbia University Press.

Westoby P. and Lyons K. 2017. The place of social learning and social movement in transformative learning: A case study of sustainability schools in Uganda. *Journal of Transformative Education* 15(3):223–240.

Westoby P. and Owen J. 2010. The sociality and geometry of community development practice. *Community Development Journal* 45(1):58–74.

Wheatley M. and Frieze D. 2011. *Walk Out Walk On: A Journey into Communities Daring to Live the Future Now*. San Francisco: Berrett-Koehler Publishers Inc.

Wolff K.H. (ed.). 1964. *The Sociology of Georg Simmel*. New York: Free Press.

CHAPTER 10
From marginalization to destiny: Anger, violence, and community protest in South Africa

Abstract

Chapter 10 tells the story of how discontent and anger have erupted in the post-apartheid nation and have resulted in ongoing community protests currently endemic in South Africa. The chapter not only elaborates on the reasons for these community and service-delivery protests, but also explores and explains how community voice, anger, violence, and protest are and should be an integral part of making sense of community development approaches.

Keywords: community protests, service-delivery protests, community anger, community violence, citizen-led community development

Introduction

There is serious discontent and dissatisfaction among the poorest of the poor in post-apartheid South Africa. The focus of this chapter is to tell the story of how local marginalized communities are reclaiming their futures through civil strife against an often non-responsive and under performing government of the day. At the time of writing, South Africa had experienced some 237 community protests during 2018 as a result of what some called the politics of discontent (Bond and Mottiar, 2012 ; Savides, 2019). Since 2004, there have been hundreds of local protests throughout South Africa, currently one of the most unequal societies in the world. These protests have increased in number and incidence, but also in intensity, becoming more violent and more destructive.

Also, at the time of writing in March 2019, as Lucius was driving home from the Vanderbijlpark Campus of the North-West University in Gauteng, on the radio alone there were seven reports of serious riots (three in Gauteng, one in KwaZulu-Natal, one in the North West Province, and two in the Western Cape), with some severe impacts on key traffic flow.

This chapter explores the key dynamics of these community protests and their multiple intended and unintended consequences. It also reflects both on where this civil strife leaves South Africa's so-called developmental local government, and the implications for a reconstructed community development,

http://dx.doi.org/10.3362/9781788531320.010

renewed by the decolonial turn and responsive to community anger and violence.

The chapter uses a meta-analysis by drawing together different documentary and literature sources to present an exploration of the current knowledge, views, trends of service delivery, and community and social protests as well as civil strife in South Africa. A literature search among all scholarly and peer-reviewed articles from 2004 to 2018 on the online database EBSCOHost was completed.

Background and context

Often, the question is asked why and how South Africa moved from the negotiated miracle of the creation of a rainbow nation (a negotiated constitutional democracy with heaps of promise) to a cauldron of a country riddled with community and service-delivery protests.[1] The signs of dissent against prevailing power relations were obvious over many years. Since 2004, there have been hundreds of local community protests throughout South Africa. The South African media reports daily on popular protests in poorer townships around the country, with some protests leading to extensive property damage, burning of tyres, and violent confrontations with police – reminiscent of anti-apartheid struggle days (Goebel, 2011; Wasserman et al., 2018). There is serious discontent among the poor in post-apartheid South Africa. According to Peter Alexander (2012) and Sethulego Matebesi (2017), two million people per year are taking to the streets to protest about land and housing issues, poor public service delivery, authoritarian governance, corruption, as well as non-responsive and non-functional governance. According to Municipal IQ (2019), there were 237 protests in South African municipalities during 2018. This was the highest number of local protests ever recorded since the dawn of democracy in 1994, and up from a mere 10 recorded protests in 2004 (Municipal IQ, 2019). Reasons that are cited include an economy that remains in recession, the highest ever national debt, many state-owned enterprises on the verge of bankruptcy, severe breakdowns in municipal service delivery, and unemployment running rampant. Patrick Bond and Shauna Mottiar (2012) indicate that the South Africa of today is indeed more economically unequal, ecologically degraded, socially desperate, indebted, and corrupt than what Nelson Mandela's first democratic government had inherited 18 years earlier.

With the end of the Zuma regime in mid-February 2018, South Africa entered a new phase. In turn, new aspirations and hopes arose that South Africa would now become a true developmental state as opposed to a 'captured state'.[2] A key question for students of grassroots development and social movements is whether the so-called dawn of yet another 'new South Africa' will result in fewer community-based protests and a more content citizenry. Not so. In fact, just three months into Cyril Ramphosa's presidency and a national spirit of 'Ramaphoria', there was a renewed flurry of community protests and, as already indicated, 2018 became the year with the highest ever recorded number of protests. So much so that Ramaphosa had to return two days earlier from the Commonwealth Summit in the United Kingdom on 20 April 2018 to address some areas in the North West Province of South Africa that were experiencing many community protests.

Despite the improving quantity and quality of services provided, Allison Goebel (2011) suggests that mass protests in poor communities in South Africa are not only about slow delivery of services, housing, and roads, but also often reveal frustration at government corruption, elite capture of wealth and opportunities (see note 2), and the criminalization and political exclusion of the poor. For many marginalized communities, protest is a form of communication to express their frustration.

The dynamics of community protests in South Africa

A series of local community protests (also commonly referred to as service-related or service-delivery protests) erupted in a number of municipalities in South Africa during 2004 and 2005 (Botes et al., 2008a) and continue at the time of writing. Since 2004, progressively more local communities have started to protest against the government's apparent inability to provide adequate services, including water, electricity, housing, roads, and sanitation (Botes et al., 2008b; Marais et al., 2008; Matebesi, 2017; Matebesi and Botes, 2011). These protests take place not only because of the perceived slow pace of service delivery, but also often due to poor quality of services and the practices of patronage and exclusion associated with their delivery. However, Alexander et al. (2013) – in a study of 2,100 reported protests drawing on interviews with some 250 key participants – caution against ascribing the root causes of such protests in South Africa exclusively to 'service delivery' issues. They argue that to do so risks underestimating the importance of protesters' other grievances, including representation, corruption, nepotism, dishonesty, government unresponsiveness, police violence, poverty, jobs, and crime. Alexander et al. therefore suggest that the term 'community protests' should be taken to reflect a genuine rebellion by South Africa's poor (see also Alexander and Pfaffe, 2014: 1; Habib, 2013).

Figure 10.1 clearly depicts the increasing trend in the number of community protests in South Africa. Since 2004, the contours of the protests have been transformed by changes in the tactics used by protesters. In essence, the historical protest landscape of South Africa could be divided into three periods, which are: no protests (1994–2003); civilized protests (2004–2009); and violent protests (2010–recently) (Botes, 2018). Indeed, societal instability has increased dramatically since the democratization of South Africa. Importantly, for this chapter right now, we are in a historical period where violence seems to be the order of the day. The scale of, and capacity for, violence, devastation, and death have escalated to previously unimaginable levels. There were 2,020 protests between 2011 and 2013, where 43 protesters died because of police action (Van Schie, 2014). The extent and intensity of these protests

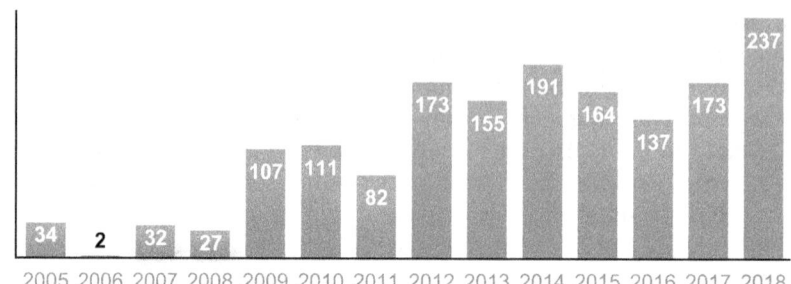

Figure 10.1 Major service-delivery protests, by year (2004–2018)
Source: Municipal IQ Municipal Hotspots Monitor[3]

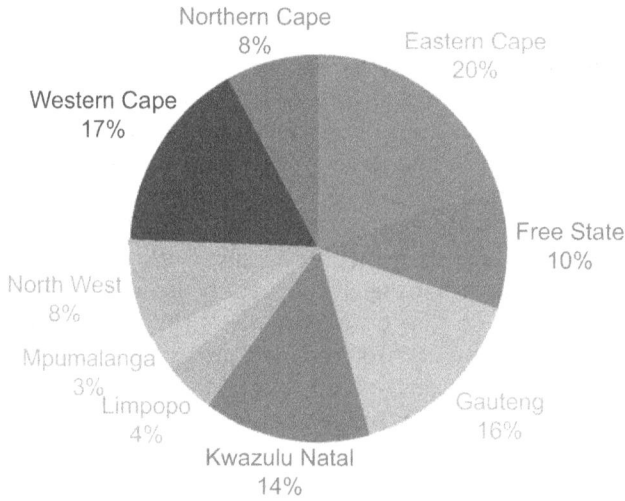

Figure 10.2 Service-delivery protests by province, 2018
Source: Municipal IQ Municipal Hotspots Monitor

dramatically increased to almost 16 protests per month in 2012 and 39 protests per month in 2013, many of which turned violent, resulting in huge social and financial costs. Of the 155 service-delivery protests recorded in South Africa in 2013, 71.6 per cent were violent (Van Schie, 2014).

The geographic distribution of the community protests is quite evident in Figure 10.2, with the highest incidence of protests in the Eastern Cape, Western Cape, and Gauteng. Gauteng has 'improved' and shifted to third place during 2018. It was the leading province in terms of proportion of recorded protests until 2017. When the local population as a proportion of the total South African population is taken into account, the Northern Cape, Eastern Cape, Free State, Western Cape, and North West all have a higher share of the protests when compared to the remaining provinces.

As mentioned, Alexander (2014) has divided social protests into three categories: peaceful, disruptive, and violent. A protest is deemed violent when people are injured or property is damaged. Significantly, his research found that by the time protests turned violent, communities had often exhausted peaceful methods of raising concerns, lobbying, and claims-making. This raises significant questions for community development. Is a peaceful approach to community practice adequate when engaging a non-responsive state? In turn, what are the consequences of turning to violence?

Almost half (46 per cent) of all community protests during July 2012 occurred in informal settlements,[4] and yet, only 12 per cent of South Africans live in informal dwellings. This illustrates the desperation experienced by those communities living on the peripheries and margins of society. Because of this concentration of despondent people, the government of the day should have a more targeted approach to upgrading informal settlements. This is consistent with many protests on the African continent where the urban masses at the margins of society, particularly young men from the urban fringes, form the backbone of protests (see Philipps, 2016). A measure of the threats they pose can be seen in a *Government Gazette* announcement in 2012 that municipal councillors must be insured against risk, because service-delivery protests put their lives and property in danger (Botha, 2012: 1). These developments show that South Africa appears to be moving towards a new phase, where accepted governance channels that facilitate negotiation are either jettisoned or are seen to be failing, with violence-backed demands and protests becoming the accepted mode of bargaining (Cull, 2012). This seems to be borne out in the following quotes from protest leaders, gathered from the fieldwork of the sociologist Sethulego Matebesi (2013) in the Northern Cape Province:

> We don't have the luxury of public facilities here ... Our only weapon, as destructive as it may seem to outsiders, was to forcefully shut down schools. You may call it intimidation, but we call it community power (Leader: Cassel Village Residents' Forum).

> We never planned any violent strategy. We have exhausted all public spaces of dialogue and they all failed us. The community and not us [leaders] decided to shut down schools. Well, in any case, violence seems to be the only language our government understands (Leader: Residents' Forum).

Why are South Africans protesting?

Our analyses suggest several reasons as to why community protests occur in South Africa. These are:

- Protest as a manifestation of lack of political trust and quest for political accountability.

- Protest as an urge for 'development as freedom' and restoring human dignity.
- Protest due to poor service delivery.
- Protest because of financial and economic hardship.
- Protest due to lack of consultation and participation in public service delivery.
- Protest as resistance to the commodification of life.

Protest as manifestation of lack of political trust and quest for political accountability

Social stress and instability often emerge from feelings of non-recognition and discontent. This links up with the fact that in many communities, community protests are a result of the non-responsive attitudes and culture of self-interest of the power elite (politicians and public officials). Many key politicians and officials seem to be self-serving, defying the essence of Mandela's legacy in pursuit of socio-economic justice. Social protests are mostly linked to uncaring, self-serving, and corrupt leaders (Alexander, 2014). This seems to follow trends globally of a growing distrust of government by citizens, fuelling all sorts of populism (Matebesi, 2017).

Many researchers have indicated that social protests are largely prevalent because of the growing unresponsiveness of government and lack of accountability of those in key positions (both bureaucrats and politicians) in local government.[5] Corruption, broken promises, unresponsive management at local and provincial level, and evidence of incompetence, especially among the leadership of the local sphere of government, feature as a secondary category of key concerns raised by protesters, jointly totalling 17 per cent of grievances (Alexander et al., 2013: 11; Karamoko, 2011: 31–32). This view on the aetiology of service-delivery protests is to regard it as emerging from grassroots mobilizations that seek to enhance the accountability of political elites to the country's citizens – again, the goal is legitimate. Service-delivery protests could be seen as reflecting communities' efforts to engage with and challenge an unfavourable and inequitable balance of power.

Given the notion that the state actually often works against the public agenda, it is not surprising that evidence suggests that the level of trust and perceived accountability pertaining to the sphere of public authority is very low in South Africa (Netswara and Phago, 2013). In fact, Adam Habib (2013: 70–71) depicted protest in this very way during the launch of his book, *South Africa's Suspended Revolution*:

> The fundamental deficit in our society is accountability, and unless we build an inclusive society in which poor people are as included as the rich people and the middle class, we are in a real danger of losing the plot.

In 2009, a similar perspective was articulated by 220 branches of the National Tax Payers Union, which has a presence in towns across 49 different municipalities. Declaring disputes with their respective municipalities, members have withheld their local government tax payment (Mouton, 2013). Here, we see that the key issue is not so much about specific services, but about if and how a truly responsive and accountable local government is possible. Clearly, the bridging of interests between distinct and sometimes alienated constituencies is not an easy endeavour, but it is essential for the building of more responsive governments with true civil *servants*, that is, bureaucrats and state-employed workers and professionals who seek to ensure that ordinary citizens and community members are properly served.

Therefore, it is evident that many of the community protests in South Africa are inspired by unmet promises and the limited capacity of a young democracy to deliver on people's hopes and aspirations. Protests are articulations of people's voices of discontent and dissatisfaction (see Good Governance Learning Network, 2011) According to Marianne Merten (2018), roughly a third (87) of South Africa's municipalities are dysfunctional and 137 municipalities have huge debt burdens, with very small budgets for capital and infrastructure expenditure.[6]

The bridging of interests between distinct and sometimes alienated constituencies is not an easy endeavour, but it is essential for the building of more responsive governments with true civil *servants*. For this to happen, there must also be a fundamental shift in the distribution of wealth in South African society, with a conscious and deliberate commitment that the economy be run in the interests of the poor. Ward councillors are at the centre of a crisis of representation, and those power differentials are mirrored by the gaps in earnings between poorer citizens and their putative representatives. For example, part-time councillors in a large municipality now receive a basic salary of R34,674 per month (*Government Gazette*, 2015: 12), more than 25 times as much as the older person's grant, a disparity that widens the social gap between them and most unemployed residents.

The evidence seems to suggest that South Africa's communities are in crisis due to a lack of service delivery and bad governance. The ideals of a developmental state with participatory governance and good service delivery are not possible where bad or no governance is the order of the day (see Botes, 2018).

Protest as urge to restore human dignity

Many commentators are quite clear that the root cause of the social service-delivery protests in post-apartheid South Africa is not so much poverty, but rather people's experiences of inequality and relative deprivation (Amtaika, 2013; Habib, 2013; Pillay et al., 2013). In other words, people are dissatisfied when they compare their own quality of life and their economic and social opportunities with those of better-off communities and households. Alongside these alienating experiences of human inequality and deprivation, the realization often lingers that the state and its structures do not care at all or do not care enough about people's dignity.

Clearly, South Africa's most disadvantaged are more vulnerable because of poor service delivery. The most marginalized and poorest of the poor are already struggling for survival and yet, compounding their marginalization, they are under even more stress to maintain a dignified life if the few services they rely on from the government are not forthcoming. The impact of poor service delivery is definitely more detrimental for poorer communities, with very little savings and financial leverage to improve their living conditions and lack of agency to mobilize a local government to provide these services. It is clear from recent research (Chikulo, 2013; Death, 2016; Philipps, 2016) that community protests in South Africa are manifestations of counter-conduct out of desperation, with the aim to achieve freedom and human dignity through development. Protests are here to stay and should be considered as *legitimate forms* of civil strife against non-responsive and underperforming local governments. This is crucial to understand as we rethink community development. Clearly, the goals of community protest are legitimate.

Protest as an act of discontent about poor service delivery

It is notable that the continued escalation of service-delivery protests occurs despite the fact that there is now a democratic system in South Africa (Matebesi and Botes, 2017), and that the government has an impressive record of service delivery in quantitative terms. A total of 2.8 million starter houses have been built in South Africa over the past 20 years, 78.4 per cent of all households are connected to the power grid (58.2 per cent in 1994), 92.7 per cent of all households have access to piped water (61.7 per cent in 1994), and 60.6 per cent have access to sanitation (Sehlatswe, 2014; Statistics South Africa, 2017). This is a mammoth achievement for a so-called developmental state. South Africa is also one of the few states in Africa with an extensive social grant system: more than 18 million people receive social grants from the state (for child support, foster care, pension, disability, etc.). However, although there has been progress in alleviating absolute poverty in South Africa, the overall picture is not encouraging. Unemployment has not declined; inequality – as measured by the Gini coefficient[7] – has increased; education for those who need it most if they are to work their way out of poverty has declined; many urban areas have not been upgraded; and the housing backlog is still enormous (see Habib, 2013; Whisson, 2012).

In the words of a spokesperson from Abahlali base Mjondolo,[8] a shackdwellers' association in KwaZulu-Natal:

> Waiting for 'delivery' will not liberate us from our life sentence ... Sometimes 'delivery' does not come ... When 'delivery' does come, it often makes things worse by forcing us into government shacks that are worse than the shacks we have built ourselves, and which are in human dumping grounds far outside the cities ... 'Delivery' can be a

way of formalizing our exclusion from society ... But we have not only been sentenced to permanent physical exclusion from society and its cities, schools, electricity, refuse removal and sewerage systems ... Our life sentence has also removed us from the discussions that take place in society. Inasmuch as the government need to deliver services, they cannot do that without engagement or direct engagement ... If people were engaged and consulted about development, then people become a vital tool in their own development and such developments will also be owned at a community level (Matebesi, 2013).

Protest because of financial and economic hardship

In an economic analysis of the micro-foundations of direct political action in pre- and post-democratized South Africa, Bedasso (2014: 13–14) indicated how the political action agenda and protest action have shifted from racial-political to economic and class issues in recent years. The most consistent patterns in the predictions of direct political action can be summarized as a strong increase in the effect of unfolding largely economic expectations. According to Bedasso (2014: 6), economic issues – defined by jobs, economic reasons, and the economy in general – determine the protest agenda. During the high protest years, up to 85 per cent of the protests have economic issues as the underlying fuelling factors. Clearly, there is a case – particularly within a rural, regional, and informal settlement context – that the major fault line of dissent is now class, replacing race in post-democratic South Africa.

The now famous 'full-loaf' interview adequately describes how financial hardship is the fuel for many a social protest in South Africa. The quote comes from a community protest leader in KwaZulu-Natal during the upsurge of service-delivery protests in 2011:

> [W]e have to be out of the order that oppresses us ... We have to rebel ... Everyone must have the full loaf of bread that each person needs to live well ... Service delivery is just trying to keep the people happy with one slice of bread when in fact a person needs the whole loaf ... It is the same with human rights ... Having the human right to a house is not the same as having a house ... Of course if you don't have any bread then you must struggle for that one slice. But our struggle does not stop there ... After you have won one slice you struggle for the next slice up until you have the whole loaf ... Only then can you relax. Our struggle is not only for service delivery or human rights ... Our struggle is for the full loaf. It is important that this is clear to everybody (Mnikelo Ndabankulo, leader of the protest movement in KwaZulu-Natal in Goebel, 2011).

When protests are correlated on a quarterly basis with GDP, it seems that an increase in service-delivery protests correlates with economic retraction. Furthermore, rising unemployment levels also correlate with an increase in service-delivery protests (Municipal IQ, 2019). Karen Heese, economist at Municipal IQ, notes:

> The dual economic pressures of a recessionary environment and rising unemployment seem to be feeding into service delivery protests. Over the course of 2018, a growing number of protest grievances included the demand for municipalities to create employment opportunities, or unhappiness with how these were allocated. It can be concluded that it is crucially important for reinvigorated, and equitable economic growth to mitigate the social and financial pressures manifested in many service delivery protests (Municipal IQ, 2019).

Protest due to lack of consultation and participation

Irrespective of the type of protest, the main concern has been that 'service delivery' provided through a top-down approach is not acceptable. Instead, residents are interested in 'public service'. It is argued that with 'public service' there is a meaningful incorporation of citizens' choices and aspirations from 'the bottom'. Put differently, consultation and public participation in South Africa have not reached a level that satisfies communities (see Netswara and Phago, 2013). Often, state-led service-delivery development runs the inherent risk of being nothing more than socially engineered, externally designed programmes, plans, and projects where communities are co-opted in if they are lucky, or coerced in if they are less fortunate. As we demonstrate in Chapter 12, exploring state-led community development and cooperative formation, this kind of social engineering is a kind of neo-colonial activity, not working *with* communities. As a result, citizens are now demanding a bottom-up approach in development processes. Grassroots protest has therefore become the only viable platform for expressing concerns. Genuine, and we emphasize *genuine*, participatory development in local matters is therefore a *sine qua non* for meaningful community development, particularly one reconstructed and renewed in response to the decolonial turn.

Protests as resistance to the commodification of life

From 2008 to 2015, the average tariff increase of electricity by South Africa's main electricity supplier was 20.8 per cent per annum (Moolman, 2017), three times more than the average inflation rate (6.4 per cent) for the same period! Many people experience the commercialization of municipal services as highly problematic. Bond and Mottiar (2012: 284-285) put it eloquently:

> the rash of 'service delivery protests' in South Africa reflects the distorted character of 'growth' that South Africa witnessed after adopting neoliberal macroeconomic and micro-development policies following the demise of apartheid in 1994. In the sense of a Polanyian double movement, it can be argued that protests represent resistance to the

commodification of life – e.g. commercialization of municipal services – and to rising poverty and inequality in the country's slums. The global financial meltdown in 2007–09 amplified and extended the existing, inherited internal contradictions, as more than one million formal sector jobs were lost, the highest rate in any major country aside from Spain.

Discussion

We suggest that the civil strife against non-responsive local government and their often poor-quality and slow-paced service delivery is a manifestation of what we explored in Chapter 5, as the reconstruction tradition of community development. Reminiscent of Gandhi, Steve Biko, and Es'kia Mphahlele, this tradition involves community leaders, community workers, and residents forging analyses together and engaging in acts of resistance. They are not spontaneous acts of resistance, but often strategic and tactical efforts for community and social change. What is clear, though, contrary to Gandhi, is that many of these community protests are turning to violence. As per our Chapter 6 exploration of Frantz Fanon, a figure often accused of advocating violence, we therefore consider the role of anger and violence as a reconstructed community development. Before doing this, we briefly consider the consequences of community protests, for this ensures a reflection not only on the legitimate goals of community-level violent protest, but also the means. Are these protests effective?

What are the consequences or effects of these community protests?

Firstly, these community protests have huge financial costs for South Africa's economy. Directly, because of physical damage to infrastructure that needs to be repaired with a limited tax basis, but also because of strikes, intimidation, and lawlessness that interfere negatively with the productive capacity of South Africa's economy. The negative impact of these social protests is also indirect, affecting the economic standing of South Africa by contributing to investor flight because of the socio-political instability and lack of confidence in the country as a destination for investors. Therefore, South Africa, from an orthodox economic development model, does not succeed in drawing the substantial foreign direct investment necessary for maintaining reasonable levels of economic growth to support sustainable human development. Secondly, there are huge social costs. Community protests often are very divisive in communities, threatening the cohesive fibre of neighbourhoods, and come with huge social sacrifices for the protesting communities. Thirdly, such protests could indicate that people are becoming disheartened in their belief about a democratic political dispensation that can deliver for them. The unintended consequence of this continued civil strife is that there is huge erosion of the political legitimacy and ability to deliver the public good necessary to live a decent life in South Africa, which may result, in the words of Mhkize (2015), in a 'democratic crisis for South Africa', and in the words of Lesley Connolly (2013: 93):

> pockets of fragility were creeping into South Africa and the state was no longer able to meet the needs of the people. In a new democracy, increasing fragility is dangerous, as it could spread to increased violence and protest, which could ultimately destabilize the country and the region as a whole.

On a more positive note, there is a question about whether these community protests lead to any successes and changes for the better. Alluding to the core question of this book, are they effective? According to Steven Friedman (2012), grassroots protests do yield results such as the shack-dweller movement's (Abahlali base Mjondolo) ability to act independently of political parties and the provision of taps and toilets. There are also other major gains for communities who embark on civil strife against their local and provincial government. For example, Matebesi (2017) noted how rural roads were provided after eight-month-long community protests in the Northern Cape.

A local government that is responsive to the plight of local communities

The main question for those concerned about a responsive state is how local government can play a more proactive role in improving services to local communities while also improving their community engagement (state–citizen engagement) efforts. Such efforts include keeping communities informed, involving communities more in decision-making, and reducing the incidence of disruptive and violent protests. In turn, what are the conditions for local government to be considered as avenues for participatory governance?

With the end of the Zuma regime in mid-February 2018, South Africa entered a new phase, and aspirations and hopes were rising that the nation would now become a more developmental state as opposed to a captured state.⁹ It would appear that the so-called developmental state will only happen once municipalities become useful vehicles of participatory governance and move from just *making plans* to delivering public goods. Friedman (2012) reminded us that people are seeking public services, not service delivery. Local governments could only be typified as participatory if communities and their livelihoods matter to both the politicians and the public servants. The change from Zuma to Ramaphosa alone will not bring an end to community protests. People need to see tangible improvement in their local living spaces and their lived experiences. Analyses suggest that only once people see a genuine effort from their local government and perceive local-level politicians and bureaucrats to be responsive – seeing them fill the potholes, provide serviced land, deal with the sewerage running in the street, collect the mountains of garbage, repair street lights not working for months, appoint qualified, skilled, and caring managers, do proper financial management and stop corruption, stop political infighting, and enhance community engagement – will communities stop protesting. In the words of Mhkize (2015: 13):

> The South African government needs to create, widen, enhance and harness spaces for public participation in development initiatives so that its citizens can regard themselves as the architects of their own development and future.

According to Connolly (2013), one needs to undertake state-building measures that will re-legitimize the state–society contract – meaning that society's expectations of the state are in balance with what the state can provide to the people. Participatory democracy should be widened and consolidated in an attempt to stop further protests from taking place.

Reconstructing community development in light of anger and violence

If what Connolly says is true, that there is a need for such state-building measures and a re-legitimizing of the state–society contract, what role can community development offer? We suggest that, pragmatically, there are many possibilities for community development workers to play *a facilitative role* between communities and municipal officials and politicians. As catalysts of local-level change, as 'boundary-crossers', community development workers could ensure that development plans to improve the services to the poorest of the poor are indeed better designed and implemented.

However, from a more radical perspective, as per our earlier mention of the social reconstruction tradition of Gandhi and Biko, and alluding to Fanon's thinking on violence, clearly community development workers could 'sit at the table' with those community leaders and citizens who are strategizing and developing tactics for community protests. Community development is *for* community service-delivery protest. It is not the job of community development workers to try and control or manage protest energy, but to instead discern what is unfolding within a community, and accompany mobilizers in their strategizing and tactic development. It is tempting for community development practitioners to be 'agents of the state', pouring water on the anger and violence of people suffering marginalization. Thinking about both anger and violence, we first suggest that a reconstructed community development, responsive to the anger, which is indicative of people not being heard, instead supports a praxis that includes action, reflection, and, importantly, *emotion*. Anger is a legitimate expression of human dignity. A decolonized community development includes a role for anger and emotion, generally disrupting any old tendencies to separate the mind-body-feeling functions.

But what of violence? Žižek (2008), in his meditation on violence, suggests that it is all too easy to focus on the visible 'subjective' violence – in this story, of the visible community-level protest violence. However, Žižek argues that focusing on this visible subjective violence masks a social system that is deeply violent in the way many citizens live without social hope. Therefore, community development practitioners taking the decolonial turn seriously should not only focus on visible 'subjective' violence, but deeper structural violence – which Žižek calls 'objective violence'. Clearly, such frameworks of analysis are not going to be welcomed by many policy-makers, nor by community development practitioners averse to violence. Aligning Žižek's analysis to Fanon's recognition that sometimes violence is necessary for the colonized, we suggest that: 1) South African structures of society are violent and citizens are simply learning to survive within this context; and 2) violence is a better strategy than apathy or victimization. Gandhi suggested that acting violently is better than doing nothing, while clearly advocating for nonviolent action. Our sense is that community development practitioners might *prefer nonviolence,* and can bring that strategy to the table. If they have credibility with grassroots leaders and organizers, they might be able to persuade already frustrated constituents to choose nonviolence. However, solidarity is still needed if communities choose violence.

Conclusion: A reconstructed community development

The jury is out on whether South Africa's poor will continue to revolt and rebel amidst their contexts of marginalization with limited hope of improvement in life opportunities and quality. The energy of this revolt and rebellion is certainly a summons to the power elite that community protests are manifestations and articulations of people's voices 'from below' and indeed a rebellion of the poor (Habib, 2013; Alexander, 2014). These community protests resemble rallying cries for basic dignity and economic freedom from responsive citizens. They will not go away. However, the positive outcome of civil strife and community protest is that ordinary people are creating their own future in taking their destiny into their hands – perhaps the best kind of citizen-led community development. Such citizen-led community development also summons professional community development workers to navigate their 'dilemmatic space' or 'in and against the state' (Westoby and Botes, 2013) with an eye on being mainly 'for the people'. The energy of the marginalized in these communities is indicative of the generative potential of community development accompanying people who have opted against victimhood, and for either nonviolence or violence.

Ultimately, the story of community-led service-delivery protests affirms the need for a reconstructed community development tradition that embraces an activist role and epitomizes active resistance, positioning against the power elite in society.

Note

1. The concepts community protests, social protests, service-delivery protests, and local protests will be used interchangeably.

2. Transparency International, the anti-corruption watchdog, defines state capture as 'a situation where powerful individuals, institutions, companies or groups within or outside a country use corruption to shape a nation's policies, legal environment and economy to benefit their own private interests' (Pilling, 2017: 1).
3. Methodology: Municipal IQ's Hotspots Monitor database tracks protests staged by community members (identified with a particular ward/s) against a municipality, as recorded by the media (or other public domain sources such as SAPS press releases). Such protesters raise issues that are the responsibility or perceived responsibility of local government (such as councillor accountability, the quality and pace of basic service delivery, and, in metro areas, housing). These protests may be violent (impinging on the freedom of movement or property of others, including the state) or peaceful, but there is a clear dissatisfaction with the management of a municipality. Not included are issues falling outside of local government's service-delivery mandate, such as demarcation, industrial relation disputes, or clear party political issues (including candidate lists). Where protests are sustained over several days or weeks, these are recorded as a single entry, with qualitative details updated on the database.
4. Informal settlements refer to those neighbourhoods that consist predominantly of non-formal houses (houses of corrugated iron, old discarded material, etc.) and often lack many other neighbourhood amenities, such as roads, storm-water drainage and water-borne sanitation.
5. In a study on female-headed households to illustrate the gendered nature of people's struggles in post-apartheid South Africa, most interview respondents from townships in Msunduzi (Pietermaritzburg, KwaZulu-Natal) said that their local officials neither listened to their concerns nor responded to problems in their communities. This has led to cynicism and lack of confidence in local governance: 'They act like they are listening but nothing happens' (see Goebel, 2011).
6. According to a damning report by South Africa's Auditor-General, 128 of the 275 municipalities are in financial trouble. Only 33 of the 275 (13 per cent) municipalities received unqualified audits in 2018 and irregular expenditure increased with 75 per cent from R16.2 billion to R28.4 billion (Coetzee, 2018: 6). These figures had largely stayed the same since 2016 when also only 33 of the 285 municipalities received 'clean' audits (Govender, 2016: 25).
7. South Africa is ranked the second most unequal society in the world next to Lesotho. The Gini coefficient is currently at 0.625 (Central Intelligence Agency, 2018), an indication of continued high inequality partly borne out of South Africa's apartheid past, but also the result of high unemployment and dismal primary and secondary education with accompanying high unequal distribution of incomes, resources, and opportunities (Chitiga-Mabugu, 2014).
8. AbM is a shack-dwellers' movement that emerged from Durban's Kennedy Road informal settlements. AbM fights for the constitutional rights of the poor to housing, services, and a dignified life out of poverty. AbM most notably won a case in the Constitutional Court challenging the so-called 'Slums Act' (Elimination and Prevention of Re-emergence

of Slums Act) brought in by the government of KwaZulu-Natal in 2007, which was found to be unconstitutional in its provisions to clear 'slums' through forced evictions. The Slums Act also contradicted the Unlawful Occupation of Land Act No 19 of 1998, which protects people from illegal eviction (see Goebel, 2011).
9. Well-known chief economist of Standard Bank Goolam Ballim (2018) calculated that the Zuma era (end of an error) cost South Africa one trillion rand due to mismanagement, corruption, and lack of leadership. The estimation of Merten (2019) is closer to 1.5 trillion rand. An economist from UCT (4 May 2018) indicated that it would take at least a generation, 12 to 20 years, to escape the devastating impact of Zuma's state capture years. This could have added one million jobs to the labour market and sustained at least five million people (if we accept that the average household size for South Africa is five people). Then there are also millions of indirect costs that have hit the average South African in terms of the financial downgrade to junk status of South Africa and the very weak economy with a weak rand.

References

Alexander P. 2012. Protests and police statistics: Some commentary. *Amandla Magazine,* 28 March.

Alexander P. 2014. Media briefing on South Africa community protests. *Mail & Guardian,* 12 February, 2012.

Alexander P. and Pfaffe P. 2014. Social relationships to the means and ends of protest in South Africa's ongoing rebellion of the poor: The Balfour insurrections. *Social Movements Studies* 13(2):204–221.

Alexander P., Runciman C. and Ngwane T. 2013. Growing civil unrest shows yearning for accountability, *Business Day.* 27 December 2013.

Amtaika A. 2013. *Local Government in South Africa since 1994: Leadership, Democracy, Development and Service Delivery in a Post-apartheid Era.* Durham, NC: Carolina Academic Press.

Ballim G. 2018. Political uncertainty and the impact on business and the regional economy. Standard Bank.

Bedasso B. 2014. *A Dream Deferred: The Micro-foundations of Direct Political Action in Pre- and Post-Democratization South Africa, Economic Research Southern Africa.* Working Paper 483. Pretoria: National Treasury.

Bond P. and Mottiar S. 2013. Movements, protests and a massacre in South Africa. *Journal of Contemporary African Studies* 31(2):283–302.

Botes L. 2018. South Africa's landscape of social protests: A way forward for local government? *African Journal of Public Affairs* 10(4):241–256.

Botes L., Lenka M., Marais L., Matebesi Z. and Sigenu K. 2008a. *The Cauldron of Local Protests: Reasons, Impacts and Lessons Learnt,* Bloemfontein: University of the Free State, Centre for Development Support.

Botes L., Lenka M., Marais L., Matebesi Z. and Sigenu K. 2008b. *The New Struggle: Service Delivery-related Unrests in South Africa.* Bloemfontein: University of the Free State, Centre for Development Support.

Botha J. 2012. Councillors must get risk cover against service delivery outrage. *Witness.* 27 December 2012.

Central Intelligence Agency. 2018. *Gini-Index: The World Fact Book.*
Chikulo, B.C. 2013. Developmental local governance and service delivery in South Africa: Progress, achievements and challenges. *Journal of Social Development in Africa* 28(1):35–64.
Chitiga-Mabugu, M. 2014. Special Issue: Redistribution for equitable development in SA, *Development Southern Africa* 31(2):195–196.
Coetzee G. 2018. VS, NK se mense kan nie langer versaak word. *Volksblad.* 24 May 2018.
Connolly L. 2013. Fragility and the state: Post-apartheid South Africa and the state-society contract in the 21st century. *Africa Journal on Conflict Resolution* 13(2):87–111.
Cull, P. 2012. Violence-backed demands become bargaining tool. *The Herald.* 1 December 2012.
Death C. 2016. Counter-conducts as a mode of resistance: Ways of 'not being like that' in South Africa. *Global Society* 30(2):201–217.
Friedman S. 2012. Beyond the fringe? South African social movements and the politics of redistribution. *Review of African Political Economy* 39 (131):85–100.
Goebel A. 2011. 'Our struggle is for the full loaf': Protests, social welfare and gendered citizenship in South Africa. *Journal of Southern African Studies* 37(2):369–388.
Good Governance Learning Network (GGLN). 2011. *Recognising Community Voices and Dissatisfaction: A Civil Society Perspective on Local Governance in South Africa.* Cape Town: GGLN.
Govender I.J. 2016. Monitoring and evaluating service delivery as a wicked problem in South Africa. *Journal of Human Ecology* 55(1–2):21–34.
Government Gazette. No 38886, Department of Cooperative Governance and Traditional Affairs, Renumeration of Public Office Bearers. 7 June 2015.
Habib A. 2013. *South Africa's Suspended Revolution: Hopes and Prospects.* Johannesburg: Wits University.
Karamoko J. 2011. *Community Protests in South Africa: Trends, Analysis and Explanations (Report 2).* Belville: Community Law Centre.
Marais L., Matebesi S.Z., Mthombeni M., Botes L. and Grieshaber D. 2008. Municipal unrest in the Free State (South Africa): A new form of social movement? *Politeia* 27(2):51–69.
Matebesi S. 2013. Social protest and the social fabric: The case of Kuruman and Sannieshof. Presentation at the Small Towns Symposium at the University of the Free State, South Africa, 7 November.
Matebesi S. 2017. *Civil Strife against Local Governance: Dynamics of Community Protests in Contemporary South Africa.* Berlin: Barbara Budrich.
Matebesi S. and Botes L. 2011. Khutsong cross-boundary protests: The triumph and failure of participatory governance? *Politeia* 30(1):51–69.
Matebesi S. and Botes L. 2017. Party identification and service delivery protests in the Eastern Cape and Northern Cape, South Africa. *African Sociological Review* 21(2):81–99.
Merten M. 2018. Budget votes debate: MPs hurry to unblock government bottlenecks before parliamentary recess. *Daily Maverick.* 18 May 2018.
Merten M. 2019. State capture wipes out a third of SA's R4.9 trillion GDP – never mind lost trust, confidence and opportunity. *Daily Maverick,* 1 March 2019.

Mhkize M.C. 2015. Is SA's 20 years of democracy in crisis? Examining the impact of unrest indicators in local protests in the post-apartheid SA. *African Security Review* 24(2):190–206.

Mouton S. 2013. Lack of water service delivery angers all. *The Herald*. 17 September 2013.

Moolman S. 2017. 350% increase in a decade: how expensive is electricity in South Africa compared to other countries? htpps://www.poweroptimal.com/350-increase-decade-expensive-electricity-south-africa-compared-countries [Accessed on 25 May 2020].

Municipal IQ 2019. Available at: www.municipaliq.co.za.

Netswara F.G. and Phago K.G. 2013. How popular protests influence public discourse and public accountability – revisiting the theory of public spheres in South Africa. *Politeia* 32(1):24–39.

Philipps J. 2016. Crystallising contention: Social movements, protests and riots in African Studies. *Review of African Political Economy* 43(150):592–607.

Pillay U., Hagg G. and Nyamnjoh F. 2013. *State of the Nation South Africa (2012–2013)*. Cape Town: HSRC.

Pilling D. 2017. How corruption became state capture in South Africa. *Financial Times*, 4 October 2017, p.1.

Savides M. 2019. More protests in 2018 than in any of the previous 13 years ... and it could get worse. Times Live. 16 January 2019

Sehlatswe B. 2014. *Reflecting on Twenty Years of Democracy*. Pretoria: South Africa Institute of Race Relations.

Statistics South Africa. 2017. *Sustainable Development Goals: Indicator Baseline Report*. Pretoria: Statistics South Africa.

UCT Economist. 2018. Personal communication. 4 May 2018.

Van Schie K. 2014. Protesters willing to die for their causes. *Star*. 13 February 2014.

Wasserman H., Chuma W. and Bosch T. 2018. Print media coverage of service delivery protests: A Content Analysis. *African Studies* 77(1):145–156.

Westoby P. and Botes L. 2013. I work with the community, not the parties! The political and practical dilemmas of South Africa's state employed community development workers. *British Journal of Social Work* 43(7):1294–1311.

Whisson M. 2012. Violent protests: Listen to message in fire and stones. *The Herald*. 4 October 2012.

Žižek S. 2008. *Violence*. London: Profile Books.

CHAPTER 11
Informal housing and community development: A historical and human rights approach

Abstract

Chapter 11 takes a different turn in illustrating why and how a historical approach, in this case the low-cost housing landscape of South Africa, is a sine qua non *for community development work practice. This then sets the scene for arguing for the importance of working within a social justice and rights-based approach in dealing with low-cost housing issues in community development.*

Keywords: low-cost housing, housing in South Africa, rights-based housing, social housing, informal housing, human rights, informal settlements.

Introduction

It is common sense that the housing issue is about much more than merely addressing the physical need for shelter. Housing is a multi-dimensional concern and has socio-economic impacts on people, places, and economies. Therefore, in any attempt to study housing, the focus should not so much be on 'what housing is' (the physical dimensions) but 'what housing does' (the functional value and its meaning for people) (Turner, 1976). Appropriate housing for the poor is therefore a vital aspect of community development.

As such, housing and community development are the focus of this chapter. Departing from the pattern of other chapters in Part III, we do not so much offer a story of practice, but instead tell a story of housing policy that shapes community-level experience of housing that is historical. In doing this, we foreground the 'practice' of doing historical analysis for community practitioners. Disrupting the idea that practice is something done in the field, within communities, we highlight how practice includes analysis and theorizing.

Drawing on this historical analysis, we then explain some key elements of a rights-based approach to housing, drawing on the idea of 'the right to the city', put forward by Marie Huchzermeyer (2011).

At a recent workshop, a 'property' developer introduced himself by saying 'I am building houses for the state'. With these seven words, he illustrated the essence of a state-driven housing development agenda, so dominant in pre- and post-apartheid South Africa. Contractor-driven service-delivery models that provide low-cost housing are eminent in the South African housing landscape. As a response, a good question would be: 'Should houses be built *for* and *with* the people?' Or even better: 'Should people not have been encouraged to build houses for themselves (self-help housing), and the state and developers provide an enabling environment for self-help and people's housing to thrive?'

It is worth being reminded of the now famous dictum of John Turner (1976) that *housing is a verb and not a noun*. The logic stemming from this simple announcement is that housing is not something a government or a contractor should give as a hand-out to so-called passive beneficiaries. The involvement of ordinary citizens as equals with rights, and not mere benefactors, is vital for building sustainable settlements and encouraging participatory settlement formation. Turner argued strongly that if the poor could be given security of tenure and a plot of land in a favourable location, progressive improvement would transform the 'squatter shack' into a respectable house and the 'slum' into a more formal neighbourhood. So, for him, a shack is a *house in process* and therefore housing should be seen as a process, and people should have the freedom to build and have the right to dweller control.

Low-cost and informal housing in South Africa

In the past 40 years, the theme of urban policies to ameliorate what is known as 'shelter poverty' has generated a considerable body of scholarly writing on what is now called sustainable settlements. In low-income housing policies, there are many terms, such as 'progressive housing', 'conventional housing', 'public housing provision', 'site-and-service initiatives', '*in-situ* upgrading', 'self-help housing', and 'contractor-driven housing'.

In studying housing provision in South Africa, four approaches have dominated (Manomano et al., 2016). These include the rights-based approach, the basic needs approach, the social development approach, and the bottom-up approach. At least two of these approaches remind us of the frameworks discussed in Chapter 6.

Informal settlements and informal houses as perceived spaces of unwanted squalor

Informal living is still viewed as largely negative, associated with more crime and a lower quality of life. As such, the eradication of slum/informal settlements was a key goal in the Millennium Development Goals (Statistics South Africa, 2015), and such a goal is still embedded within the ethos of the aims and targets of the Sustainable Development Goals. For example, they refer to the 'upgrading of slums' (to be specific, Target 11.1 states that by 2030 they will 'ensure access for all to adequate, safe and affordable housing and basic services and upgrade slums'). Yet, 12.2 per cent of South Africans currently reside in informal settlements, despite some three million state-subsidized houses that were provided during the past 25 years of democratic rule in South Africa (Huchzermeyer, 2011; Statistics South Africa, 2017a).

Informal settlements are often viewed as criminalized spaces, and their residents are regularly criminalized by association. At best, some of the informal settlements are left alone by the authorities; at worst, they are harassed by police, and bulldozed and/or evicted. By definition, most informal settlers are, or were, illegal in both the occupation of land and the formation of non-standard structures. Writing within the Brazilian context, Teresa Pires do Rio Caldeira explains that, 'excluded from the universe of the proper, [informal settlements] are symbolically constituted as spaces of crime, spaces of anomalous, polluting, and dangerous qualities' (Caldeira, 2000: 79). She goes on to argue that '[p]redictably, inhabitants of such spaces are also conceived of as marginal. The list of prejudices against them is endless' (Caldeira, 2000: 79). This criminalization of marginalized communities shapes the notion that informal settlements are spaces of crime: 'It is commonly alleged that an anti-establishment, or oppositional, culture prevails in slum areas, which is broadly supportive of all kinds of illegal activities' (Caldeira, 2000: 76).

Globally, this criminalization of informal settlements has led to the justification of aggressive state-led practices of their eradication from cities, rationalized in 'developmental terms'. In South Africa, Huchzermeyer (2011: 57) reveals the increasing use of private security to effect eradication, control growth, and manage informal settlements. Beall and Goodfellow (2014: 21) classify forced slum clearances as a form of civic conflict, which they argue 'ultimately result[s] from the state's failure to cope in the face of specifically urban issues such as the provision of adequate housing'. Huchzermeyer (2011), in her thought-provoking title *Cities with 'Slums': From Informal Settlement Eradication to a Right to the City in Africa*, makes the point that if human-centred and sustainable development is taken seriously, then informal housing and less formal neighbourhoods will always be part of the housing solution of South Africa. As such, informal housing should not, per se, be defined as a problem. This again returns us to the Turner dictum cited earlier: that low-cost housing is a verb and not a noun. Arguing that a shack is a *house in process* – with the accompanying policy and programme goal being incremental upgrading from informal to formal – is clearly the way to go. However, global market capitalism constantly shouting the mantra of the necessity for urban competitiveness does not bode well for a global acceptance and change in favour and in support of informal settlements. Because of these global pressures of dominant forces, emphasizing cities as the engines of economic growth, governments of the day yield too easily to wishing away informal housing by either ignoring it or eradicating it.

According to Huchzermeyer (2011), there needs to be a shift in favour of cities with slums; that is, from informal settlement eradication to a right to the city in Africa. This echoes the words of Hernando de Soto (1989), who presented an image of informality as 'heroic entrepreneurship'.

The reality of informal living in contemporary South Africa

Nearly 70 per cent of 56 million South Africans currently live in cities and towns, compared to only 50 per cent in 1994, making South Africa the most urbanized country on the African continent (Centre for Development and Enterprise, 2019). Of these South Africans, some 17 per cent live in informal structures, also referred to as shacks, in informal settlements (which some refer to as slums or squatter camps). According to Statistics South Africa (2017b), 12.2 per cent of the urban South African population live in informal dwelling units. This makes for a total of 1,962,800 households in informal dwellings (Lemanski, 2009), while Kamna Patel (2016) estimates the formal housing shortage as high as 2.2 million housing units. This makes the urge for sustainable settlements very pertinent. Rapid urbanization in South Africa goes hand in hand with the growth of informal housing on a large scale. This unusual growth in informal housing appears to have taken the form of backyard shacks in established townships and free-standing shacks in squatter settlements. The significance of backyard shacks became apparent with the release of the 2011 population census data. This found that the number of households living in backyards increased by 55 per cent from 460,000 to 713,000 over the previous decade, while the number living in free-standing shacks decreased by 126,900 to 1,249,800. However, the issue has been neglected by government policy (Lemanski, 2009). It does not feature in the 2009 National Housing Code and was dismissed in the Presidential Delivery Agreement for Sustainable Human Settlements: 'Whilst informal rental is an accommodation provider, these units are illegal, do not conform to minimum standards and thus cannot be accounted for in this document' (The Presidency, 2010: 43). Backyards were ignored in the current housing minister's key policy statement for her five-year term in office (Sisulu, 2014).

South Africa's housing and settlement policies should therefore focus on both aspects of urban informality, which is important for household wellbeing (e.g. better provision and access to services), and for the efficient functioning of urban areas. The burning question remains: how can urban settlements be better managed to become platforms of hope and opportunity and not traps of despair and poverty? The research of Ivan Turok and Jackie Borel-Saladin (2016) in Gauteng finds that people are slightly better off in backyards than in free-standing shacks elsewhere, although the wider benefits for urban areas are equivocal. In some respects, backyard shacks are a stopgap for poor households desperate for somewhere to live. In other respects, they represent a kind of prototype solution to the urban housing crisis. The government could do more to improve basic dwelling conditions and to relieve the extra pressure on local services.

South Africa has made housing a cornerstone of its social development policies (Jay and Bowen, 2011). Almost three million so-called Reconstruction and Development Programme houses have been built since 1994, which is indeed a mammoth achievement. However, there remains significant dissatisfaction expressed by the residents of the housing schemes, particularly with regard to the quality of the houses. In turn, there is serious discontent among those who are on housing waiting lists, but who have not yet benefited from a state-subsidized house due to lack of progress on delivery. Many community protests could be linked to discontent with housing-related matters. According to Patrick Bond and Shauna Mottiar (2013: 285):

> In townships, there were many more houses built annually with state subsidies in the post-apartheid period, compared to the last decade of apartheid, yet they were typically half as large, and constructed with flimsier materials than during apartheid; located even further from jobs and community amenities; characterized by disconnections of water and electricity; with lower-grade state services including rare rubbish collection, inhumane sanitation, dirt roads and inadequate storm-water drainage.

The other big threat to people living in informal settlements is the lack of secure tenure, leaving many thousands of South Africans very vulnerable in the unenviable position of having a precarious livelihood. In many of South Africa's less formal settlements, there have been outbursts of anger and dissatisfaction with the lack of decent housing, and an accompanying aggression produced by overcrowding. Housing and essential basic services are regularly cited as the key motivations driving protests (Karamoko, 2011). Inadequate housing tops the list of grievances for South Africans (21 per cent), followed by lack of access to clean water and electricity (11 per cent each) and then sanitation (9 per cent) (Botes, 2018; Karamoko, 2011: 32). In the Chapter 10 of this book, we discussed community protests as a manifestation of community development in detail. This has often led to the invasion of vacant land (mostly public land owned by a local municipality or the provincial government but in some cases also private land), which, in turn, is usually followed by forced removals and demolition of informal structures, followed by waves of resistance and protest. In most cases, such processes conclude with some concessions and compromises by the authorities to provide greater tenure security, followed by undertakings to provide serviced land with water, sanitation, electricity, and solid waste removal.

Housing and human settlements prior to 1991

In providing an overview of the evolution of low-income housing policy, it is clear that there is a dominance of state-driven conventional housing schemes in low-income housing provision in South Africa's urban areas. Coming from a historical perspective, four phases can be identified in the evolution of South African state interventions in the urban arena.

The first phase (1900–1920) is associated with *public health and disease control*. Legislation in favour of slum control was an outgrowth of rising concern among public health officials and urban managers that unsegregated, overcrowded, and unsanitary black African neighbourhoods posed a threat to white health and safety. According to the aims of this approach, housing could be declared not fit for human habitation, the occupants removed, and the buildings demolished (Maylam, 1995).

The second phase of legislation (1921–1950) was more directly concerned with *achieving urban control*. Black Africans had to live in declared locations. This was difficult to achieve and enforce due to a lack of available alternative accommodation for those the government wished to remove. Besides racist motivations, policies of urban segregation and forced removals also served capitalist interests with the intention of creating space for business development. Urban control measures were therefore borne into the class struggle (Botes, 1999).

The third phase (1951–1986) can generally be described as the *apartheid phase*, which was in many respects a consolidation and streamlining of previous urban policies. Until the abolition of influx control and spatial apartheid laws such as the Group Areas Act, the South African urban landscape was enormously transformed on the basis of racially segregated cities and the application of a multitude of urban policy controls. These forms of urban policy controls were aimed at preventing the settling of black people in white urban South Africa or at 'de-blackening' some of the existing white areas by forcing Africans to relocate in so-called 'homelands' (Botes, 1999). Until the mid-1980s, the international experience in housing had little influence on housing policies in South Africa because the state focused on planning for apartheid.

The last and fourth period (1987–1990) can be regarded as the *neo-apartheid phase*. During this and the post-1990 phase, housing moved to the centre stage of social and political order. The Urban Foundation (an NGO formed by socially responsible 'big businesses') lobbied extensively for influx control to be lifted. This centrepiece of apartheid was abandoned in 1986. However, there were still several attempts to legislate what was called 'orderly urbanization', which made urban residents dependent on housing availability. This was not effectively implemented, but shows how the housing problem has been closely associated with urban governance. The Urban Foundation once again played a pioneering and facilitating role to resolve the housing crisis, albeit while being subjected to significant critique. The minimal provision of shelter was considered efficient for the urban poor. This resulted in site-and-service schemes and informal settlement upgrading. During this period, attention was given to providing security of tenure and access to housing for low-income households, while the futility of eradicating informal settlements was also acknowledged. As such, in some government circles, there was recognition that households and owners would feel secure in making housing investments only when they were safe from eviction and harassment. Various researchers (Botes, 1999; Ntema et al., 2018) have indicated that legalized tenure plays the most important role in giving people the confidence to upgrade and improve their houses. This emphasis on ownership enhances both social security and the social value of the individual household.

Prior to the release of Nelson Mandela in 1990, the South African government's approach towards informal housing shifted from coercive measures and anti-urbanization policies to allowing informal urbanization to take place. After 1990, the government adopted a supportive role in which the upgrading of informal settlements through conventional and progressive housing was promoted. In the last years of the apartheid regime, informal settlements mushroomed in many of the large urban areas of South Africa, as the people 'invaded' and settled on vacant land.

Housing and human settlements post-1991

The post-1991 phase can also be divided into five phases. The first phase, 1991–1993, could be described as the *gradual dismantling of apartheid* urban policies. Organizations such as the newly created National Housing Forum, Planact, and the Independent Development Trust played an important role in this regard (Botes, 1999).

The second *post-apartheid phase* (from 1994–1995) is characterized by the institutionalization of a non-racial framework to design and implement new housing policies. This was demonstrated by the creation of a formal structure called the National Housing Board and the creation of a Ministry of Housing (with the late Joe Slovo, also leader of the South African Communist Party, as first housing minister) (Botes, 1999).

The third phase was initiated with the birth of the *capital subsidy scheme*. Introduced by the Housing White Paper released in 1995, it was one of the first post-apartheid policy responses to the housing challenges faced by South African communities. According to Amisi et al. (2018), the policy emphasized three key things: ownership, a focus on the poor (only households with incomes below R3,500 per month were able to access the subsidy), and a fixed-amount capital subsidy. The original capital subsidy amount in 1995 was R15,000 for those households with the lowest incomes. (In 1995, the USD:R exchange rate was 1:3 and about 1:14 at the time of writing in April 2019.)

In 2004, a fourth phase started with a revised policy, titled 'Breaking New Ground: A Comprehensive Housing Plan for the Development of Integrated Sustainable Human Settlements'. This has retained the above three elements while re-emphasizing informal settlement upgrading and rental accommodation, and drawing attention to the need to establish sustainable settlements and to develop the property market (Amisi et al., 2018; Ntema et al., 2018). This laid the foundation for a new approach to informal settlement upgrading. Essentially, the new policy was more flexible and acknowledged the informal settlements as being here to stay. During this phase, there was also a major shift away from producing vast numbers of houses towards the creation of human settlements.

This culminated in the fifth and current phase, aligned to the National Housing Code of 2009. The South African Housing Subsidy Programme has delivered approximately four million housing opportunities (subsidized houses and site-and-services) in slightly more than 20 years, mostly by providing a capital subsidy and home ownership to households at the lower end of the market. By then, the Department of Housing had also had a meaningful and thought-provoking name change to the Department of Human Settlements.

Tomlinson (1998) sees the capital subsidy scheme policy as a trade-off between market-driven and state-driven forces, and Gilbert (2002) suggests the policy landscape can be understood as a case of 'scan globally, reinvent locally'. At the same time, the National Housing Code, guiding housing policy, has been criticized for its dominant neoliberal elements (Huchzermeyer, 2011; Todes, 2006; Venter et al., 2015).

From Table 11.1, it is clear that three key drivers for achieving sustainable settlements since 1994 were the Informal Settlement Upgrading Programme, the National Housing Programmes, and the Integrated National Development Programme. Two themes that run through these programmes are 'community' and 'service delivery'.

After a thorough literature review, Tatenda Manomano et al. (2016) found that most housing problems in South Africa are caused by corruption and poor management, and go on to cite the following specific issues: housing is too small for occupation; poor housing material; poor location of housing projects; lack of stakeholders and beneficiary involvement; urbanization and unemployment; and misuse of houses by beneficiaries. These challenges were recorded amidst a mammoth drive by the African Nation Congress-led government making inroads into the housing backlog in South Africa.

Shifting from the historical analysis, this chapter now turns to a consideration of several key issues linked to a rights-based approach to affordable housing. Many of the themes that follow will illustrate how acknowledging and safeguarding the socio-economic and livelihood rights of people living informally and often on the precipice of society in very precarious conditions should be key in community development workers' understanding of these contexts. In interacting with this precariat class (those with no or limited shelter security), having a rights-based approach to their housing and settlement needs, creating spaces for negotiated urban renewal, allowing for feminist perspectives, and turning around stigmatization and prejudice against informal living are essential to making inroads in housing the poor.

The golden thread and underlying context for a rights-based approach to housing is marginalized people's struggle for human decency and being taken care of by a responsive state. One could even allude here to an ethics of care and decency, the building blocks of social justice and a rights-based approach to affordable housing.

The right to decent housing

To what extent have South African communities been involved in opposing aggressive state-led attempts to eradicate informal houses? It was because of the now famous 'Grootboom' case in South Africa's Constitutional Court that

Table 11.1 Key national programmes in housing provision and creating sustainable settlements

National programme	Responsible department	Key objectives of the programme
Integrated Residential Development Programme (2009)	Department of Human Settlements	• Primary implementation tool for integrated housing • Offering access to amenities, services, and economic opportunities in well-located housing developments • Prioritizes housing for various income groups and mixed land uses • Seeks to eliminate peripheral human settlement development • Mixed land-use development with consideration of employment opportunities • Incorporates community participation into the planning and management of integrated developments
National Housing Programmes (2009)	Department of Human Settlements	• Support residential property market development • Development of social housing for low-income households • Lower- and medium-density housing development with various typologies (single stand, double-storey buildings, row houses) • Include Finance Linked Individual Subsidized Programme, Community Residential Units, and Breaking New Ground units, among others • Foster partnerships between the community, developers, and government in housing delivery
Informal Settlement Upgrading Programme (2009)	Department of Human Settlements	• Guides the upgrade and formalization of informal settlements that are situated within areas of potential, including the provision of engineering services (water, sanitation, electricity) • Informal housing is replaced by formal housing structures • Emphasizes the importance of community participation in the process of planning and managing the formalization of human settlements, constituting an integrated process

Source: Department of Human Settlements, 2009, 2010; South African Government, 2018

the need for housing was declared as a socio-economic right. The respondents in the court case had been evicted from their informal homes situated on private land earmarked for formal low-cost housing. They applied to a High Court for an order requiring the government to provide them with adequate basic shelter or housing until they obtained permanent accommodation. The High Court held that, in terms of the constitution:

> the State was obliged to provide rudimentary shelter to children and their parents on demand if the parents were unable to shelter their children; that this obligation existed independently of and in addition to the obligation to take reasonable legislative and other measures in

terms of the Constitution; and that the State was bound to provide this rudimentary shelter irrespective of the availability of resources. The appellants were accordingly ordered by the High Court to provide those among respondents who were children, as well as their parents, with shelter (Government of the Republic of South Africa, 2001).

Because of this now famous Grootboom case and other cases, the South African Constitutional Court's housing rights jurisprudence is more developed than any other social and economic right contained in the South African Constitution. The Grootboom case confirmed the constitutional right to housing in the spatial planning politics in post-apartheid South Africa. The court's extensive attention to housing rights is partly explained by the profound trauma of forced removals and evictions during the apartheid era (see Williams, 2014).

A gendered perspective on housing

Kirsty McLean and Lilian Chenwi (2009: 517) make the point that due to their greater vulnerability compared to men, women's rights to access adequate housing have been undermined for years, and still are. As they aptly put it:

> the systemic constraints which poor women face and which undermine their full enjoyment of the right to access adequate housing: namely, their greater vulnerability, when inadequately housed, to gender-based violence; their particular vulnerability to forced eviction; and the disproportionate burden they bear to provide childcare.

If one considers this systematic and systemic disadvantage of women – which infringes on their need for shelter – we also need to consider women's marginalization, accommodate women's difference, and encourage greater participation of women in decision-making in housing and settlement matters. Using a capabilities and substantive equality approach to socio-economic rights could go a long way to catering for the housing rights of women and living up to the title of McLean and Chenwi's 2009 article: 'A woman's home is her castle'.

Urban renewal, but always within a negotiated and participatory context

In 2001, then President Mbeki announced the Urban Renewal Programme (URP), a 10-year initiative to address poverty and underdevelopment in targeted areas (predominantly township areas). We know that townships were spatially engineered by the architects of apartheid and were exclusionary by design. The URP was designed to focus on eight major townships to pilot integrated area-based renewal to address the malaise of poverty and crime and promote integrated spatial development. The research of Ronnie Donaldson et al. (2013) indicated that the most successful urban settlement and renewal programmes were informed by explicit and negotiated frameworks that required buy-in and common vision from community members, their local leaders, government officials (at national, provincial, and local level), and contractors. South Africa's current housing drive, through so-called mega-cities, with the aim of providing settlements of at least 10,000 housing units per city, leaves little room for imagining the role of communities other than through formal 'body corporates' or housing associations. One is tempted to conclude that this may give very little space for participatory urban reform. In many of these mega-housing drives, the private developer comes with private land to the table, leaving the state with little space to allow community leaders to negotiate for self-help housing and embracing elements of incremental housing. From the early 1990s, low-cost housing in South Africa became predominantly state-led and contractor-driven, leaving little space for people's housing. However, the fact that more than one out of 10 South African households are also providing their own housing, albeit in an informal manner, is further proof of community resilience and of poor people securing their own livelihoods. This is again a confirmation of the double story of South Africa explained in Chapter 3 – of suffering, poverty, and distress on the one hand and, on the other hand, the story of ordinary people's resilience, agency, and action.

In parallel to these interlinked development imperatives are the big challenges captured in the Sustainable Development Goals, ranging from food insecurity, climate change, political instability, growing inequalities, and vast discrepancies between the rich and the poor. In facing these challenges head-on, it is important to build and maintain more sustainable settlements. In this reflection on low-cost housing, the housing debate should indeed shift from housing for the poor to housing with the poor, and eventually housing by the poor.

Views from the bottom-up: Do shack dwellers see the way we see?

Emphasizing once more the importance of listening to the voices of those from the margins, the earlier work of Coetzee (2003), *Life on the Margin: Listening to the Squatters,* charts important early ground. All good practice starts with deep listening. As such, John Ntema et al. (2018) studied the perceptions of residents in the informal settlement of Freedom Square that has, since 1990, been upgraded to a formal settlement in Mangaung, Bloemfontein. Four surveys (1990, 1993, 2008, and 2014) were analysed to depict people's attitudes towards informal settlement upgrading and their housing-related experiences. The following key findings were noted:

> Firstly, informal settlement upgrading is a step towards ensuring the housing rights of black people in urban South Africa. Secondly, spatial infilling and locational advantage continue to play valuable roles. Thirdly, dweller control, in terms of which residents themselves are

able to design extensions to their houses, remains important. Residents who have built their own houses experience higher levels of satisfaction than those whose houses were built by government contractors. Some respondents expect the government to 'fix' their homes, suggesting a lingering view that these houses belong to the government. Fourthly, social cohesion among community members is proving to be more important than access to a stand, despite the fact that the ratings related to social cohesion had apparently declined since residents first settled in Freedom Square. However, the point is that the memory of the struggle to obtain a stand or house is fading as time passes. Fifthly, urban management remains an important long-term requirement. Upgrading should mean continued investment in the physical infrastructure and the living environment. Lastly, elements of informality persist in the area. It remains a reality that elements of both formality and informality coexist in upgraded settlements (Ntema et al., 2018: 15–16).

In a question posed by Ian Jay and Paul Bowen (2011) as to what residents value in South African low-cost housing schemes, nine distinct themes were identified: comfort, cost, environment, facilities, local economy, safety, security, social, and space. These markers of urban living, we argue, could form a good framework for a rights-based approach to housing and community development.

Self-help housing vs contractor-driven housing

Research by Lochner Marais et al. (2003) provided a comparison between houses delivered by means of the People's Housing Process (self-help) in Thabong, Welkom (self-help), and housing delivered by means of a contractor (contractor-driven) in Freedom Square, Mangaung-Bloemfontein (contractor-driven) – both townships being in the two urban centres of the Free State. It was found that the settlement with self-help housing units (Thabong), on average, had more rooms than in the contractor-driven settlement of Freedom Square. People in the self-help housing units were also more satisfied with various aspects of the houses, were more involved in the building process, and had also invested significantly more of their own resources in their housing provision than households within the contractor-driven housing context. Despite these findings, it seems that community-driven housing provision and people's housing (self-help) have declined during the past decade in South Africa (see Zonke and Matsiliza, 2015).

Discussion

What this chapter is telling us, as community development workers, is that we need to understand the historical context of an informal settlement and how the people of a specific settlement have exercised their rights to demand a decent living, to be able to work and facilitate meaningfully within contexts of informal living. In this, the lived experiences of individual families and their livelihoods with needs, assets, and capabilities as well as the rights to a life in the city are vital components to engage with as development workers.

The dilemma in evaluating housing interventions and programmes in South Africa is that the state largely works with a linear theory of change. Ntema et al. (2018) indicate that this one pathway of change, mainly a market-oriented approach to asset building, makes the impact of the provision of low-cost housing indeed a challenge. Many assets develop outside the formal market process, which go unaccounted for. This is a further illustration of how difficult it is to measure success in low-cost housing provision, and relates to some of the issues addressed in the effectiveness questions posed in Chapter 4, where development evaluation was discussed.

In many other domains or sectors, such as the affordable housing sector, we do not see so much juxtaposition between social justice versus market competition, democracy versus neoliberalism, and participatory citizenship versus government intervention. These all have implications for people's lived experience and whether their 'rights to the city' are not only tolerated but supported. For Jay and Bowen (2011), the dilemma of low-cost housing lies in the achievement of a balance between large-scale development to meet policy goals and targets, versus the specific needs of individuals. This opens up notions of how human decency and human dignity could stand up against the profit-driven agenda of the market and the power-driven 'formal is acceptable' agenda of the state and its political and fiscal apparatus. To create safe, resilient, and sustainable settlements (according to the UN's Sustainable Development Agenda), indeed, should allow ordinary citizens to live out their insurgent citizenship and facilitate bottom-up participation in many decisions. This could impact on their livelihoods, and form important building blocks for creating sustainable settlements and thus granting these marginalized communities their full rights to a city and all the socio-economic benefits and responsibilities that come with it. Where a housing agenda of the state should open up is the notion that the state could at best provide an enabling environment to co-create with the communities it serves. This implies a multi-pronged approach in housing provision, where self-help housing, social housing, and contractor-driven housing are all embarked upon. This multi-pronged and flexible approach to affordable housing, we argue, is perhaps the best attempt at securing the rights of very precarious communities and helping them to build sustainable settlements.

Conclusion

This chapter is about how the stories of struggles for sustainable livelihoods in addressing the need for human shelter could be transferred to practices of possibilities. A reconstructed approach to community development and informal housing needs a historical and human rights approach, albeit we also recognize that a decolonizing perspective complicates things even further (raising questions about whose land the housing is being built on). The chapter considered firstly a historical policy overview, ensuring community development practitioners understand the historical perspective; and then, secondly, discussed a rights-based approach to affordable housing in building human settlements, thereby foregrounding 'rights to the city'. Adding a decolonizing perspective would also foreground the fact that the housing is being built on stolen land.

Where authorities are not predominantly pursuing comply and control policies, but creating a climate of enabling environments, progressive and incremental housing could thrive. In this community, development workers should understand the historic context of specific informal settlements, but should also constantly be aware of marginalized people's right to the city. Embracing the human dignity of informal settlers is perhaps the first step in creating a culture of care and an ethic of human decency, so important for community development work with a social justice agenda in South Africa's deprived urban areas.

References

Amisi M.M., Marais L. and Cloete J.S. 2018. The appropriateness of a realist review for evaluating the South African housing subsidy scheme. *South African Journal of Science* 114(11/12):53–61.

Beall J. and Goodfellow T. 2014. Conflict and post-war transition in African cities. In Parnell S. and Pieterse E. (eds). *Africa's Urban Revolution*. London: Zed Books.

Bond P. and Mottiar S. 2012. Movements, protests and a massacre in South Africa. *Journal of Contemporary African Studies* 39(2):283–302.

Botes L. 2018. South Africa's landscape of social protests: A way forward for local government? *African Journal of Public Affairs* 10(4):241–256.

Botes L.J.S. 1999. Community participation in the upgrading of informal settlements: theoretical and practical guidelines. Unpublished PhD thesis, Bloemfontein: University of the Free State.

Coetzee J.K. 2003. *Life on the Margin: Listening to the Squatters*. Grahamstown: Rhodes University.

Caldeira T. 2000. *City of Walls: Crime, Segregation, and Citizenship in São Paolo*. Los Angeles: University of California Press.

Centre for Development and Enterprise. 2019. *Creating Cities of Hope*. Johannesburg.

Department of Human Settlements. 2009. *Upgrading of Informal Settlement Programme*, Pretoria: Department of Human Settlements.

Department of Human Settlements. 2010. *National Housing Policy and Subsidy Programmes*, Pretoria: Department of Human Settlements.

De Soto H. 1989. *The Other Path: The Invisible Revolution in the Third World*. London: Taurus.

Donaldson R., Du Plessis D., Spocter M. and Massey R. 2013. The South African area-based urban renewal programme: Experiences from Cape Town. *Journal for Housing and the Built Environment* 28:629–638.

Gilbert A. 2002. 'Scan globally; reinvent locally': Reflecting on the origins of South Africa's capital subsidy housing policy. *Urban Studies* 39(10):1911–1933.

Government of the Republic of South Africa, 2001. Constitutional Court Case: *Government of the Republic of South Africa and Others vs Irene Grootboom and Others* (CCT11/00) [2000]. ZACC 19; 2001 (1) SA 46; 2000 (11) BCLR 1169 (4 October 2000).

Huchzermeyer M. 2011. *Cities with 'Slums': From Informal Settlement Eradication to a Right to the City in Africa*. Cape Town: UCT Press.

Jay I. and Bowen P. 2011. What residents value in low-cost housing schemes: Some South African concepts. *Building Research and Information* 39(6):574–588.

Karamoko, J. 2011. *Community Protests in South Africa: Trends, Analysis and Explanations (Report 2)*, Belville: Community Law Centre.

Lemanski C. 2009. Augmented informality: South Africa's backyard dwellings as a by-product of formal housing policies, *Habitat International* 33:472–484.

Manomano T., Tanga P. and Tanyi P. 2016. Housing problems and programs in South Africa. *Journal for Sociology and Social Anthropology* 7(2):111–117.

Maylam P. 1995. Explaining the apartheid city: 20 years of South African urban historiography. *Journal of Southern African Studies* 21(1):19–38.

Marais L., Van Rensburg N. and Botes L. 2003. An empirical comparison of self-help housing and contractor driven housing: Evidence from Thabong (Welkom) and Mangaung (Bloemfontein). *Urban Forum* 14(4):347–365.

McLean K. and Chenwi L. 2009. 'A woman's home is her castle?' Poor women and housing inadequacy in South Africa. *South African Journal on Human Rights* 25(3):517–545.

Ntema J., Massey R., Marais L., Cloete J. and Lenka M. 2018. Informal settlement upgrading in South Africa: Beneficiaries' perceptions over nearly twenty-five years. *Journal of Urbanism: International Research on Placemaking and Urban Sustainability* 11(4):460–479

Patel K. 2016. Sowing the seeds of conflict? Low income housing delivery, community participation and inclusive citizenship in South Africa. *Urban Studies* 53(13):2738–2757.

The Presidency. 2010. *Outcome and Delivery Agreement: Sustainable Human Settlements*. Pretoria: The Presidency.

Sisulu L. 2014. Budget speech by the Minister of Human Settlements 15 July. Available at: http://housingfinanceafrica.org/documents/minister-sisulus-housing-budget-speech-15-july-2014/ [Accessed 29 July 2014].

South African Government. 2018. Human settlements programmes and projects. Available at: www.gov.za/about-government/government-programmes/sustainable-human-settlements-breaking-new-ground [Accessed 13 May 2020].

Statistics South Africa. 2015. Millennium Development Goals, *Country Report, 2015*. Pretoria: Statistics South Africa.

Statistics South Africa. 2017a. *Sustainable Development Goals: Indicator Baseline Report*. Pretoria: Statistics South Africa.

Statistics South Africa. 2017b. *General Household Survey*. Pretoria: Statistics South Africa.

Todes A. 2006. Urban spatial policy. In Pillay U., Tomlinson R. and Du Toit J. (eds). *Democracy and Delivery Urban Policy*. Cape Town: HSRC Press.

Tomlinson M.R. 1998. South Africa's new housing policy: An assessment of the first two years, 1994–1996. *International Journal of Urban and Regional Research* 22(1):137–146.

Turner J. 1976. *Housing by People: Towards Autonomy in Building*. London: Marion Boyars.

Turok I. and Borel-Saladin J. 2016. Backyard shacks, informality and the urban housing crisis in South Africa: Stopgap or prototype solution? *Housing Studies* 31(4):384–409.

Venter A., Marais L., Hoekstra J. and Cloete J. 2015. Reinterpreting SA housing policy through welfare state theory. *Housing, Theory and Society* 32(3):346–366.

Williams L.A. 2014. The right to housing in South Africa: An evolving jurisprudence. *Columbia Human Rights Law Review* 45(3):817–843.

Zonke N. and Matsiliza N. 2015. Community participation in housing development trends – a selected case of Khayelitsha township, Cape Town South Africa. *Africa Insight* 45(2):86–100.

CHAPTER 12

'Seeing like a state' and neo-colonial cooperative development within South Africa

Abstract

Chapter 12 considers our investigation into the interaction between supply-oriented, state-led community development and cooperative formation. Cooperative formation is a crucial element of the South African national development plan and has been well integrated into the national community development programmes. The chapter considers the challenges of state-led strategies such as cooperative formation, particularly when linked to a supply-oriented chain, and foregrounds the problematics of neo-colonial approaches to community development.

Keywords: cooperatives, 'seeing like a state', state-led, statecraft, emotional labour, neo-colonial

Introduction

This chapter focuses on the interplay of community development practice in relation to cooperative development, a South African national priority. We bring a critical perspective, subjecting this state-led community development programme to a decolonizing disruption.

South Africa has both a national (Department of Trade and Industry, 2012) and provincial (for example, Economic Development Chief Directorate, 2012) focus on cooperative development and how they can be fostered through state-led community development programmes, so it seems timely to learn from, and reimagine possibilities in light of, what has been occurring during the past few years.

Background/context

The context of this story is our inquiry into two national community development programmes – the Community Development Worker Programme and the Community Development Practitioner Programme – and the national focus on cooperative development as a crucial component of the livelihood development strategy.

Of contextual significance to this chapter is the important place of cooperative development within the goals of South Africa's post-apartheid developmental state. This is evidenced in the development of the 2004 Cooperative Development Policy the 2005 Cooperatives Act, the announcement in May 2012 by South Africa's Department of Trade and Industry that it would increase support for cooperatives in the country by establishing a Cooperatives Development Agency and Tribunal, and the development of an Integrated Strategy on the Promotion and Development of Cooperatives (2012).

This is not to say that cooperatives have not previously been utilized within South Africa – during the apartheid era, cooperative development was one strategy for Afrikaner economic empowerment (Satgar and Williams, 2011: 218) – but it is to say that there is a renewed interest. In the pre-apartheid era, the state created enabling conditions for such white cooperative development through financial, regulatory, and technical support (Satgar and Williams, 2011: 218). In a sense, pre- and post-apartheid cooperative development mirror one another in that they have been designed with a racialized dimension, although clearly pre-apartheid development focused on the minority Afrikaner population and the post-apartheid era, under the guise of black economic empowerment, is focused on the majority black population.

'Seeing like a state' and cooperative formation

We unpack this story conceptually by examining how state-employed community workers are caught within a lens that James Scott's seminal work called 'seeing like a state' (1998). At the core of this approach, which itself builds on a long lineage of thought (see, for example, Schumacher, 1974), is the idea that large-scale state planning, without real attention to organic local knowledge and needs identification, can be quite catastrophic. While arguing within this chapter that the South African state's plans for cooperative development are in no way catastrophic, the experience so far appears to be quite damaging to the potential future of a cooperative movement, and also to the lives of people who become members of cooperatives, but with little understanding of cooperative capacities, or knowledge of the cooperative and mutuality tradition.

The research also locates itself within the practice of cooperative formation as a sub-component of the social economy (Amin, 2009). This body of literature therefore contextualizes cooperatives as a particular prioritized South African community economic development strategy. There is a long lineage of research and literature around cooperative formation and development, including the early seminal work of Robert Owen, *A New View of Society* (1813) or Bernstein's *Evolutionary Socialism: The Economic Capacity of Co-operative Associations* (1907). Examples of more recent work would include Yair Levi and Howard Litwin (1986), Wilson Majee and Ann Hoyt (2010), and John Restakis (2010). Niekerk (1988) is a particular South African example, with his early work providing a foundation for a more recent flourish of studies – ranging from those conducted by more progressive organizations such as the Johannesburg-based Cooperative and Policy Alternative Centre (COPAC) (Satgar, 2007; Satgar and Williams, 2008, 2011) through to more economically orthodox organizations such as the South African Foundation, an association of South Africa's largest corporations (Philip, 2007).

This inquiry brings these literatures together, focusing on how community development workers employed by the state (therefore deployed within a social guidance tradition and 'seeing like a state') are forming cooperatives as part of a national sustainable livelihood strategy, and an economic transformation aspiration.

There are boundless contradictions for any state-employed community worker. Drawing on a global body of research, particular dilemmas within the interaction between community development and cooperative development have been highlighted by Levi (1986). While arguing that there is high potential complementarity between community development and cooperative formation, he identifies the particular dilemmas of what he calls the 'process orientation versus task accomplishment dilemma' and also the 'structural change versus service delivery dilemma' (Levi, 1986: 4). For Levi, how community development and cooperative formation engage with each of those two dilemmas then leads to four possible outcomes. His analysis provides a model that is a useful departure point for analysing the more recent South African experience, and can best be summarized in the form of Table 12.1, with the four possible outcomes named within the four lower-right-hand quadrants.

The combination of the process-focus and structural-change emphasis would for many be the ideal type, drawing on both community development's relational and gradualist practices (process-focused) and the cooperative's mutuality tradition (Restakis, 2010), which is rooted in emancipatory hopes rather than simply job-creation aspirations.

Findings

While many themes emerged from the inquiry, we foreground four, which are: 1) state-led community workers as catalysts for cooperative development; 2) a dilemma of statecraft – working within instrumental contexts; 3) the emotional work required of the practitioner; and finally, 4) confusing the participatory process. The first theme is reported with appreciative awareness that the interviews, site visits, and workshops we conducted led to the telling of many hopeful stories of cooperative development. The latter three themes are more critical.

State-led community workers as catalysts for cooperative development

Many of the interviewees reported that community development workers (CDWs) and community development practitioners (CDPs) – working with the help of some technical experts – were able to support the formation of

Table 12.1 Relationship between community development and cooperative formation

Cooperative formation emphasis on:	Community development emphasis on	
	Process focus	Task accomplishment focus
Structural change	Potential for mature self-sustaining cooperatives aimed at structural change that reduces social and economic inequality and democratizes workplaces	Ambitious/premature self-management aimed at increasing democratization of workplace but failing to institutionalize cooperative principles and practices
Service delivery	Potential for mature self-management of cooperative with limited structural change, albeit providing limited income and/or benefits to members	Premature self-management with limited change, unable to either democratize workplace successfully or deliver any sustainable income/benefits to members

cooperatives. For example, the following worker talks about how their work has led to cooperative formation:

> We've also met with [the Small Enterprise Development Agency (SEDA)] to register as a cooperative – with about 16 young people. Initially we called all the community members and we identified different social groups. We asked at the community meeting which social group do we want to focus on for the [community-based planning (CBP)]. All the community agreed to focus on the youth. So youth came for three days to CBP. Then we called another community meeting to provide feedback that the outcome was an agreement to form the cooperative. ... I will continue to support this cooperative in linking to training institutions (to learn to make bricks ...). Also, these young people are frustrated; and I as a CDP to be accommodating – show there is hope and life. You need to really listen and give advice. You need to resolve conflict so they don't split, but remain in the organization (community development worker).

This story explains how a community-based planning process, a social technique used within the Department of Social Development (DSD) among its community development practitioners, led to the participants identifying young people as particularly vulnerable to unemployment. Subsequent engagement with a cohort of young people led to 16 of them joining up to what was then registered as a cooperative enterprise. According to the CDP, there are still plenty of issues of support needed – from the 'hard' business technical skills, to the 'soft' relational ones, such as dealing with conflict among members.

What is clear is that the state has taken a lead in the process: firstly, with state-employed community practitioners as crucial catalysts of a community planning exercise; secondly, in ongoing engagement with the identified group of young people; and finally, in supporting the young people to liaise with the relevant government departments to access support. This reported success is reinforced by an excerpt of a second story:

> Before a project starts – for example, someone comes with an idea – we firstly analyse and shape up the idea – do the feasibility study (SEDA might help us) – and we, as DSD, identify the stakeholders who can be of use. Then we start the process above. The person who had the idea will usually be appointed as a mentor of the beneficiaries (community development practitioner).

The story again illustrates the complex array of state stakeholders involved in making a cooperative work. After the community practitioner identifies a person who has a workable idea for an enterprise, they then bring together government stakeholders to consider each of their contributions. Every cooperative visited within this inquiry could have told the same story. A state employee supported them in getting started and then also connected them to other state agencies for particular help. One of the CDWs shared their analysis:

> A great achievement is that we have conscientized our community about how government works. People, in the past, have been marching, protesting, but now they know they live in a democracy and need to negotiate. Also a big achievement is we have involved our communities in local economic development, in terms of cooperatives – you can go to any number of communities in the Free State and you'll find in each municipality co-ops that are working – some funded, others not and behind each and every cooperative you'll find a CDW. They would have been involved at the beginning (community development worker).

It is a confident statement that behind each and every cooperative there will be the work of a community development worker, indicative of the central catalytic role of both community development and the state in cooperative formation within South Africa. Such stories are illustrative of the importance of cooperatives within both community-based planning exercises led by the state and more relational work, whereby a state-employed community worker meets someone with an idea and the energy to potentially form a cooperative. Within both stories, there are accounts of several crucial government stakeholders that then play an ongoing supportive role. The architecture of a particular kind of statecraft is set in place.

However, such an account of cooperative development represents only one story in the multiple narratives available. Many cooperatives have been established with the support of the state, and on one level visits to several were inspiring; on another level, this inquiry indicates that there were substantial challenges, such that the architecture of statecraft in relation to cooperative formation might be cracking.

Working within instrumental contexts: A dilemma of statecraft

Such cracks can be illuminated by reporting on a number of crucial dilemmas facing community workers. While there were several positive stories, many community workers also talked about the challenge of whether to focus on the real sustainability of community cooperatives or on the requirement of reporting to the programme managers in the form of 'outputs'. During interviews and observations, what emerged was a very clear analysis that can best be summed up in the following comment:

> When people approach us to start a cooperative, and we support them, the enterprises usually work and are sustainable. But, when we, because we are under pressure to 'produce' several cooperatives per year for the programme, and we push people to start a cooperative, they usually fail (participant in focus group).

Another participant also describes the problem:

> In the municipality there is a unit called local economic development and when you look at the problem of CDW reporting, the one that gives me most points is when I form a cooperative with women, youth ... but it is much harder to form a co-op, it is easier with a smaller group of two people or so. In co-ops usually you have up to 20 people, so it is a good number for the reporting, but hard to sustain (community development worker).

Or on an equally critical note, the same participant explained how:

> Each year every CDW must submit 12 cooperatives set up by community. I can do that, but the problem is I can't tell good stories about that. For several reasons, they have not continued – I have tried and failed – because of finance and training – I also do not know how to start and sustain a cooperative.

Within these narratives, echoed in almost all the interviews and informal discussions, are insights into crucial issues related to the instrumental pressures to form cooperatives as a numerical imperative. Cooperatives are considered particularly useful because if, for example, there are 20 members of a cooperative, then it can be reported that 20 jobs have been created. Cooperative formation is then subjected to the instrumental and political needs of the state and ruling political party, which has staked its legitimacy upon 'jobs, jobs, and jobs'.

Returning to the last narrative, the pressure to deliver 12 cooperatives within a year, each with a potential 20 members equalling 20 jobs, can deliver the *appearance* of 240 jobs. This is an appealing prospect for a government needing to 'create jobs' among populations that could be described as surplus to the central formal economy. One worker interviewed, responsible for registering cooperatives, explained that he was registering more than

20 cooperatives per month, but also lamented the ongoing collapse of many of them.

The comments above also provide an insight into the dilemma that kept appearing when interviewing workers. Do community workers focus primarily on the sustainability of community initiatives, or do they focus on the survival of themselves as workers and of their programme? They sense that their managers are really only interested in reports that affirm outputs, rather than outcomes and impact. Upward accountability and audit culture become the key drivers, and downward accountabilities to communities become shadowy.

Managing the emotional work of practice

Clearly the reporting and accounting requirements lead to a real sense of disappointment for community workers over the constant failure of cooperatives. This would indicate the need for significant emotional labour by the state-employed community development workers or practitioners to survive in their jobs. How does a worker keep managing the disappointment of seeing cooperatives form and then fail, because they are not yet sustainable?

This disappointment was at times also amplified as workers experienced real despair. They did not want to add another layer of failure onto the experiences of the poor – but they felt that they had little choice. One participant told a story of an initiative that unravelled. The story also provides an insight into the emotional work required:

> I worked with a group of young people – saying you can't wait for a job – don't depend on someone else. I inform them to make a business plan together as a group, a company ... Then they started, they called me for their meetings. I had to teach them accounting. The problem I encountered was when a few didn't do anything, and then the fights started. The group dynamics become a problem if there is no communication – I told them there is no boss – you are all employees and employers, as a cooperative ... It didn't do any good, and then I feel bad that I failed them. I find I have to draw a line and only hold their hands for a small time, and then leave them because there is so much to do (community development worker).

The telling statement is within the very final line – 'leave them because there is so much to do'. The imperative to 'deliver' or at least account for development outputs in terms of quantity becomes more important than attending to – nurturing – sustainable development processes that lead to quality-of-life outcomes. The practitioner is aware that the tension and resultant way of resolving the tension lead to a feeling of failure: 'I failed them'. But the worker seems unable to navigate the dilemma or tension in a way that is acceptable to themselves (as a reflective practitioner), the young people (clearly needing some ongoing support in the development initiative), and managers. Such a finding is indicative of the many narratives of community workers. The emotional work required to stay engaged with their community practice is intensified by the organizational and institutional pressures.

A second significant finding in terms of the emotional labour required of workers can be discussed in terms of the dilemma of failing to 'transform mindsets of the people'. Many interviewees indicated that state-employed community workers agreed with the 'official' government analysis that people had historically been over-reliant on government hand-outs or government-funded projects. The official analysis, explained on several occasions, was that forming cooperatives is a way of transforming people's attitudes towards the state, engineering a shift towards self-reliance drawing on business-oriented models of development and away from dependence. However, all the workers engaged within this research lamented that with cooperative formation 'on the ground', the main shift had been from government hand-outs in the form of government-funded projects to an expectation by community members of the government providing contracts to the cooperatives. These contracts would occur through either social procurement and/or providing ongoing grants to the cooperatives to ensure salaries could be maintained in the form of stipends.

With these ongoing forms of 'hand-out', or what we think of as supply-oriented development, this failure to transform mindsets was experienced by community workers as frustrating. Many community workers shared how they were tired because, as someone put it, 'people here are lazy, they believe government must do it', or, 'when things get difficult people just give up'. It is an expression of frustration and also a move towards a 'blame the victim' mentality, so easy to do when things are not working.

Some workers had an astute analysis that most people were forming cooperatives not because they really had a vision, but 'because they were hungry', which enabled the workers to engage with care and humility, but the emotional work of seeing constant failure and lack of a mindset transformation appeared to be undermining worker motivation.

Confusing the participatory process

Another significant finding from the interviews concerned how the political and instrumental needs of the state led to confusion about how to catalyse cooperative formation, or any social economy activity, using a participatory process (Kelly and Westoby, 2018). The ideological commitment to a collective economic enterprise confused the participatory process, imposing onto people a previously designed strategy. Taking into account the work of Nobel Prize-winning economist Elinor Ostrom and her colleagues Amy Poteete and Marco Janssen (Poteete et al., 2010), it would seem that the conditions for successful collective action (in their research referring to managing the commons; in this research referring to formation of cooperative enterprises) are not in place. One community development worker talked about the endemic failure of cooperatives, stating that: 'Every community development worker is meant to produce the outcome of one cooperative per ward. Yet they are all failing.'

In some cases, practitioner analysis of these failures linked them to capacity issues; for example, a lack of financial literacy among cooperative members and the government officials supporting the cooperative endeavours. However, the main problem seemed to be a misunderstanding of the delicate nature of nurturing collective action. In reflections on the cooperative enterprises, the assumption embedded within either the community development programme methodology and/or the community development work approach appeared to often undermine participatory community practice.

In a nutshell, we would describe the problem as confusion about 'collective from below' versus 'collective from above'. Within the former, collective action is an emergent property of the participatory work of building a group (which takes time) and the group together consciously choosing a collective structure, such as a cooperative, with some consciousness of the requirements of being a co-operator.

Some CDPs and CDWs understand this. For example, the same participant previously quoted stated: 'If you tell people to set up a cooperative then you have a problem because they don't have a passion. But sometimes people come to us and say we want to set one up. This is a key – whether the co-op has come from people or not' (community development worker).

'Collective from above' implies an assumption or ideological belief that people can and will work together if there is an incentive, bypassing the participatory work of group-building. The CDW quoted above refers to this as 'telling people to set up a cooperative'. The motivation for setting up the cooperative then is primarily state-led (or supply-oriented) rather than community- or member-led. Or to ground the analysis further within the research, when members were asked, 'Why did you set up a cooperative?' the reply in every case, with the exception of one person (the director of the financial services cooperative), was an approximation of, 'Because the government told us to set up cooperatives, and that if we did they would provide grants'. Funding became the driving force, and not community-led initiatives. The consequence of this was that only a handful of members or even community workers involved understood anything at all about the cooperative and mutuality tradition. As already discussed, the pressure appeared to be pragmatic, instrumental, and political, with the ideology underpinning the use of cooperatives being two-fold: firstly, that collective action is better than individual; and, secondly, that collective action using cooperatives would shift people's mindsets from government-funded projects to self-reliant businesses.

In contrast, often, collective 'from below' is either organic or requires careful and discerning work of bringing people together, ensuring the 'co-op has come from the people'. Certainly, as the previously mentioned work of Poteete et al. (2010) has clarified, putting in place the careful conditions for effective collective work is crucial for success – to bypass this is to ensure failure – echoing what many community development workers within this inquiry were lamenting.

Discussion: A neo-colonial intervention?

Some crucial issues arise from the findings of this chapter. Firstly, findings indicate that, like comments made by prominent cooperative-sector organization COPAC, there is a potential problem with an approach to cooperative development that is oriented towards the 'top-down' logics (that is, building a sector, rather than enabling a movement). Drawing on Levi's model of community development and cooperative formation interaction, the two South African national community development programmes, located within the constraints of an instrumentally oriented statecraft, are focused on task accomplishment and service delivery. The lack of attention to the participatory process, or simply the lack of time available, combined with workers' lack of understanding of the long lineage of the cooperative mutuality tradition, appears to be undermining gradualist, participatory, and process-oriented work that might lead to stable and mature cooperatives.

Secondly, the narratives also indicate that cooperative formation is framed as job creation – that is, captured within the service-delivery part of the dilemma mentioned above. Cooperatives are simply seen as one legal vehicle alongside others within a broader job-creation and small and medium-sized enterprise (SMSE) strategy. Within this inquiry, there was never a mention of the importance of participatory work towards cooperatives within a mutuality or social economy tradition, or the significance of cooperatives as a humanizing form of economic enterprise (Restakis, 2010). The motivation to form cooperatives appears to have become captive to some contradictory logics between, on the one hand, particular 'neoliberal logics' (oriented to self-help and market-oriented business) and, on the other hand, an intended progressive focus on social state intervention that targets populations who have had few previous roles or places within the formal economy (see Ferguson, 2009). Cooperatives as a post-structural genuine alternative vehicle of social and structural change (McMichael, 2010), de-centring capitalist logics, appear to have been thwarted within the South African context.

Thirdly, community development workers are very conscious of what Hoggert et al. (2009) talked about as the 'dilemmatic space' of their practice – they are more than aware that there is a contradiction between the imperatives of the state – to 'deliver' and create livelihoods versus the realities 'on the ground' of actual practice. They have been trained to 'see like a state' (Scott, 1998), but are also able to see the problem of the state strategy *in situ*. Community workers are conscious of the contradictions that emerge as forms of new public management are imposed on both their work and their reporting processes. Many of them are very aware that cooperatives are seen as a way of creating numerous jobs and are therefore very attractive to the state looking to do just that. Furthermore, one significant consequence of this dilemmatic space is the emotional work required of state-employed community workers. Returning to the findings reported upon, it is clear that several of the workers interviewed and accompanied into the field struggled with the emotional guilt and frustration of setting up cooperatives, knowing they were bound to fail due to inadequate inputs such as education, training, and market access. Such disappointment was further amplified into despair for some workers, thereby contributing to a moral problem among workers as they struggled to integrate their sense of professional hopes with political and bureaucratic requirements.

Finally, findings indicated that a crucial element of community development, one related to the hopes for process orientation and structural change (Levi, 1986), is being undermined by what we call a neo-colonial approach. By this, we imply that the state is preoccupied primarily with its own agendas and puts pressure on those community workers/practitioners deployed to deliver outputs. It appears that this kind of preoccupation ensures an unravelling of a community process: group relationships are not strong enough, analysis has not been considered deeply enough, an individual is too domineering, or groups are not stable. In turn, to move too slowly could mean that momentum is lost, or actions and activities become too localized and unable to connect with broader movements tackling international or national forces. What is clear from the findings is that there is little space for such a discerning approach to method. A neo-colonial approach to intervention eschews the possibility of such discernment. Work is driven more by instrumental pressures to achieve outcomes, rather than working from the 'inside-out' of a community based on their energies and ideas.

Conclusion

In conclusion, it could be argued that, from a more macro-level perspective, one of the dilemmas of the community workers is that most core 'developmental processes' of South Africa are being worked out within the class-based struggles represented by centres of power. Here, mainstream development can be seen as South African workers struggle for their fair share of the surplus generated by the capitalist development trajectory of one of the BRICS nations. In contrast, most community development work occurs at the margins, among what has been previously described as surplus people. Attempts to generate economic or livelihood activity within this peripheral position continues to be highly problematic. The state sees the need to 'generate jobs' – the government's legitimacy rests heavily on its ability to be successful in this endeavour. Seeing like a state, then, leads to grand plans and hopes for strategies such as cooperative development, located as a subsector of SMSEs and Black Economic Empowerment. However, as per Scott's original work (1998), this research confirms the dangers of community workers seeing like a state.

With this in mind, the question is left: how do South African state-employed community workers and practitioners – tasked to develop cooperatives within their state-led work, thereby 'seeing like a state' – conduct their practices with community members, who have not yet learned the skilful art, craft, and practice of cooperation (Sennett, 2012) (that is, have not yet developed the capabilities to be co-operators)? Surely, investment in supporting the cooperative movement to run processes of community-based education and learning around this mutuality tradition would pay more long-term dividends than attempting to 'fast-track' cooperative formation as a job-creation strategy. The interaction between community development practice and cooperative formation requires an additional input of longer-term community-based education, stretching Levi's model to a three-fold set of practices: 1) cooperative formation; 2) community development; and 3) community-based education. Without the latter, there is a good chance the other two processes will fail. This has implications for rethinking how to develop cooperatives and also for policy within South Africa.

Finally, in relation to policy implications, the main required reform emerging from this inquiry is an investment in community-based education processes that *create a demand* for cooperatives from communities – a demand generated because their role in developing a healthy social economy is understood. This stands in contrast to the current emphasis on what can be characterized as an investment in *supply-oriented development*, whereby the state provides grants as a means of incentivizing the formation of cooperatives.

References

Amin A. 2009. *Social Economy: International Perspectives on Economic Solidarity*. London and New York: Zed Books.

Bernstein E. 1907. *Evolutionary Socialism: The Economic Capacity of Co-operative Associations*. The Independent Labour Party.

Department of Social Development. (n.d.). *Promoting Sustainable Livelihoods Through Social Development Cooperatives*. Republic of South Africa: Department of Social Development.

Department of Social Development. (n.d.). *Integrated Service Delivery Model: Towards Improved Social Services*. Republic of South Africa: Department of Social Development.

Department of Trade and Industry. 2012. *Integrated Strategy on the Promotion and Development of Cooperatives*. Pretoria: Department of Trade and Industry.

Ferguson J. 2009. The uses of neoliberalism. *Antipode*, 41(S1):166–184.

Hoggert P., Mayo M. and Miller C. 2009. *The Dilemmas of Development Practice*. Bristol: The Policy Press.

Kelly A. and Westoby P. 2018. *Participatory Development Practice: Using Traditional and Contemporary Frameworks*. Rugby: Practical Action Publishing.

Levi Y. 1986. Community-cooperative relationships. In Levi Y and Litwin H. (eds). *Community and Cooperatives in Participatory Development*. Aldershot: Gower.

Levi Y. and Litwin H. (eds). 1986. *Community and Cooperatives in Participatory Development*. Aldershot: Gower.

McMichael P. 2010. *Contested Development*. London and New York: Routledge.
Majee W. and Hoyt A. 2010. Are worker-owned cooperatives the brewing pots for social capital? *Community Development*, 41(4):417–430.
Niekerk J.A.S. 1988. *Co-operative Theory and Practice*. South Africa: South African Agricultural Union.
Owen R. 1813. *A New View of Society: Essays on the Formation of Human Character*. London.
Philip K. 2007. A reality check: Worker coops in South Africa. *Labour Bulletin*, 31(1) March/April.
Poteete A., Janssen M. and Ostrom E. 2010. *Working Together: Collective Action, the Commons, and Multiple Methods in Practice*. Princeton and Oxford: Princeton University Press.
Restakis J. 2010. *Humanising the Economy: Co-operatives in the Age of Capital*. Canada: New Society Publishers.
Satgar V. 2007. *The State of the South African Cooperative Sector*. Johannesburg: COPAC.
Satgar V. and Williams M. 2008. *The Passion of the People: Successful Cooperative Experience in Africa*. Johannesburg: COPAC.
Satgar V. and Williams M. 2011. The worker cooperative alternative in South Africa. In Daniel J., Naidoo P., Pillay D. and Southall R. (eds). *New South Africa Review 2: New Paths, Old Compromises?* Johannesburg: WITS University Press.
Scott J. 1998. *Seeing Like a State*. New Haven: Yale University Press.
Schumacher E.F. 1974. *Small is Beautiful: Economics as if People Mattered*. London: Abacus.
Sennett R. 2012. *Together: The Rituals, Pleasures and Politics of Cooperation*. London and New York: Penguin Press Group.

CHAPTER 13
Interlude: In dialogue with Es'kia – the decolonial turn

Abstract

Chapter 13 (the Interlude), 'In dialogue with Es'kia', focuses on the community development process from a decolonizing perspective. The chapter departs from the dialogical encounter with people in the field, and instead reflects on an encounter and analysis of a piece of text about community development from the writings of South African exile and activist Es'kia Mphahlele.

Keywords: decolonial turn, Es'kia Mphahlele

Introduction

In the case of many good things in life, you tend to stumble on them rather than find them through wilful effort. This happened with the discovery of Es'kia Mphahlele's work. Peter, indulging in one of his most pleasurable activities, browsing through a bookshop, was attracted to a beautiful-looking hardback book titled *Es'kia* (Mphahlele, 2002a). It was the photo of the thoughtful and somewhat pained man on the front cover that caught his initial attention. Flicking through the pages, he quickly recognized that here was a man of extraordinary breadth and depth: an exile who had returned to South Africa and, having seen the old South Africa, was now writing on the verge of birthing the new.

And then, lo and behold, Peter found some essays titled 'Community Development' (Mphahlele 2002b, c). Animated by turning the pages, there was recognition that a gem, a treasure, had been discovered.

During the next months of careful reading – mostly on the author's thinking about education and literature, but also his musings on social consciousness – community development wisdom was discovered. In thinking about this book, we realized a whole chapter based on this wisdom would be useful: simple and practical wisdom about the processes of community development that applied both deconstructive and decolonizing perspectives.

So we have chosen to engage with each section of a particular text carefully and supplement it with other material from our own inquiry. The reflection has been organized into several sections, with the Es'kia text indented. The text used is *Es'kia* (Mphahlele, 1992: 188–190).

Reflection

Prior to the first section of the text reproduced here, Es'kia had spent some time writing on the African family and its gradual dissolution through apartheid policies and capitalist development modes. For Es'kia, the individual and families are the foundation of community, but he then explicitly moves on to reflect on the nature of community and how to start community projects. The following part of the text is very careful to argue that someone with an idea for community development should enlist others who share the same interests and vision. He is also very forthright in resisting an abstract form of democracy that can sometimes be used to strangle the kind of community vision and energy that could be unleashed in organic processes. Read carefully:

> You organize a project, for instance, enlisting support of some members of the community who share your interests and vision. I find it necessary to emphasise the origins of an idea that eventually becomes the property of the community at large. Out of sheer obsession with democracy as an idea – an abstraction – some self-appointed political faction will often insist that a group of persons who want to translate an individual's idea into a concrete programme first seeks its permission to do so. The faction's purpose is undoubtedly to assert its own political supremacy, real or imagined.

Es'kia is arguing against gatekeepers or powerbrokers determining what initiatives can be started within communities, even in the name of 'democratically elected' gatekeepers. It mirrors the findings and discussion in our chapter on neo-colonialism and cooperative formation in South Africa – where are the origins of an idea? As the Chinese say, 'how something starts determines how it'll finish' (put less politely, 'shit in, shit out'). If the work does not start with the ideas of the people, then it will never gain momentum that is sustainable and embedded within the complex ecology of community life. The first premise of a reconstructed approach to community development insists on this integrity of the original idea.

The spirit of the text is that anyone, with an idea and energy, if they can enlist some others who share the same idea and energy, can start an initiative. Our inquiry and experience concur and add that effective community development practice dreams of such initiatives flourishing from many parts of the community. One of the crucial roles of a community worker is to sow seeds within communities, spreading ideas carefully – usually through sharing stories – which are then taken up by some community members, watered within their imagination and shared with others. Some of those stories, like seeds, take root and, in flourishing, give birth to actual activities or initiatives.

This movement, from an individually inspired idea to a group of people who share an idea, is critical. Again, Es'kia discusses the importance of this:

> And yet the natural path is actually for a project first to take root, driven by a small group of persons who then solicit further ideas from those

members of the community whose real strengths are known at a practical level, rather than conferred by 'democratic' elections. It is not difficult to imagine that a committee may be democratically elected but still turn out to be a mix of crooked, indolent, self-seeking but highly articulate, popular figures who happen to be politically 'correct'. A time may come when a project deems it proper, because it has developed strong legs, so to speak, to exercise controlled democracy in selecting a board of management. The most important prerequisite is that its goals be inspired by the highest ideals that we have come to associate with community development. There may be similar, diverse projects in the community, even variations of a particular one. Collectively all these cultivate an awareness among members of the community of, shall we say, Gugulethu or Langa or Nyanga; an awareness of their own needs and capacity (or lack of it) to deal with their immediate socio-economic problems. Still collectively, the projects stimulate self-help, self-realization and can even lead to the creation of a community chest.

Building on the previous reflection, there are a couple of extra important points to make here. Es'kia first recognizes the ecological or organic nature of powerful community praxis. When the right person, with a vision and energy, finds others who share that vision, or through osmosis come to share it, then things happen. It resonates with Margaret Wheatley's meme, 'start anywhere, go everywhere' (Wheatley and Frieze, 2011: 91). Democratic processes are perceived to be somewhat instrumental, easily manipulated by the powerful, captured by potentially 'crooked' people. From the perspective articulated within this book, we would like to draw on Es'kia's wisdom, but also add to it, arguing that a framework that holds Es'kia's wisdom but extends it requires an understanding of both mezzo (meso)-level group and macro-level organizational work, ordered in the best way. The organic nature of community work occurs most powerfully at mezzo-level group processes, with several people choosing to come together around a shared vision that morphs into a shared task or process (Kelly and Westoby, 2018: 89–120). However, as that small group engages with the wider 'community', then the process might need to be transformed *from* organic, relational, and informal group work *to* a more structured, democratic initiative with transparent governance structures in place.

Secondly, Es'kia's comments focus the reader on the notion of 'highest ideals' linking community development work to what we referred to in the Introduction as having a clear vision and values. Clearly, this aspiration is worthy of deep respect and any community development practitioner dreams of it. However, in the cut and thrust of the real world, many people get involved in community processes due to 'interests' rather than 'ideal ethical commitments'. The rhetoric might be ethical, but under pressure, most espoused ethics are shown to be interests. This is not to imply withdrawal due to a cynical perspective, but simply to highlight some of the real challenges in supporting processes of dialogue, discussion, disruption, and debate about the kinds of ideals and ideas informing a community development process. Es'kia goes on:

> Now, brutal realities exist in our townships that cripple many self-help ventures and excellent ideas for community development at birth. These realities are related to sectional political divisions. It becomes immediately imperative for us to consider the first item on the agenda for community development as 'community organization towards a unified vision of the road ahead'. Here we could discuss concrete practical strategies for the resolution of sectarian political conflicts. We may even devote several meetings to such a topic. Even if we find the constitution of the group to be one-sided, the agenda must go on. We must simply appreciate that we have to go through a process of evolution, discussion and interaction being a part of it.

Salient comments from someone who clearly had observed and experienced the realities of community life, and particularly the organizational dimension – previously discussed as macro-level work (Kelly and Westoby, 2018). The structuring of community initiatives or projects into organizational forms is a fraught process. Commentators such as Paul Henderson and David Thomas (2005) have examined the complex issues at stake when a group of people consider moving into a formal organizational form. Es'kia identifies one of the inevitable elements – politics, and the potential to undermine any clear unified vision. One of the challenges in community development is negotiating or navigating between the potential centrifugal tendencies of differing perspectives, divergent analyses, and degenerative conflict versus the potential centripetal tendencies to seek 'unity within diversity' (Freire, 1970: 57) and work towards a common goal. In other writings, we have called this 'seeking a narrative thread' – that is, a common analysis and vision that can generate collective energy (Westoby and Kaplan, 2013). It is not easy, particularly when some people are often intent on holding to their own agendas rather than exploring the possibility of a common agenda. Es'kia goes further in his analysis of the challenge exploring how:

> Some of the major difficulties in African urban community organization in South Africa are: the fact of political strife among black, self-generated or incited by a third force; poverty and/or survival consumer economics; and the overarching fact that we are strangers in urban life, even though several of us may be third-generation inhabitants. There is also that part of urban life that does not express us in the fullest sense of the phrase. I mean we did not choose to live in these ghettos, but were dumped here. Had we created our own urban environment in the first place we would be proud and ready to mobilise our human resources, in spite of underdeveloped economics, because our commitment to such an environment would have been above reproach.

> The cosmopolitan nature of our urban townships is forever changing, as new inhabitants enter and shantytowns, which may sooner or later become permanent, spring up. We are generally slow to volunteer services in welfare and educational work. It may be argued that volunteering community service is a typically middle class way of extending oneself, for people who have surplus time and a relatively comfortable income. That may be. But must this mean that such development has to wait until a middle class evolves?

His analysis includes a historical approach, trying to understand some of the consequences of forced removal, the non-voluntaristic nature of rural to urban drift, and the lack of a community ethos within urban geographies. His analysis underpins an ethos of trying to 'see what the people see' (Lathouras, 2010), integrating a realistic picture of the challenges that beset urban communities that are marginal to the mainstream. As per Biko's decolonizing analysis, there are cultural and consciousness issues to do with loss of pride, which undermine motivation. And for Es'kia, there are also other material and structural dynamics at play as people move in and out of geographic spaces undermining the possibilities of people, over time, building trusting relationships that can then be the foundation of effective community development work. Lacking connection and commitment to the spaces and places that people inhabit, people are reticent to make it their base, giving of themselves to service and involvement. As such, a decolonizing perspective would also acknowledge Indigenous peoples linked to their spaces and places, landscapes and stories. In turn, there needs to be a particularly deep respect for the elders that know such land, landscape, and stories intimately. Es'kia contrasts this urban challenge with a perspective of rurality, arguing that:

> In the rural areas communities are more homogeneous, and people are good listeners and will hear you out if you have a proposition for community organization and development. But you have to be a 'native' son or daughter, or something close to that, in a matter of speaking. They don't easily take to perceived 'outsiders' initiating a project, although we must admit that rejection is not absolute: one simply has to work harder to be accepted. I am optimistic, too, that this is a passing phase, inasmuch as the whole rural landscape is rapidly changing.

His perspective is not necessarily overtly dualistic in arguing that community development is hard in urban settings and easy within the rural context. The above comments provide a sharp analysis of the insider/outsider dynamics of rural communities, arguing that it is very hard to initiate community processes as outsiders.

As quoted in the Introduction to this book, Neville Alexander's reflections on ways forward for the New South Africa (2013: 199) conclude that:

> Besides the ongoing political and economic class struggles in which we are willy-nilly involved, and by means of which we attempt to

create and consolidate more democratic space in the short to medium term, we have to go back to the community development tasks ... we have to rebuild our communities and our neighbourhoods by means of establishing, as far as possible on a voluntary basis, all manner of community projects that bring visible short-term benefit to the people and that initiate at the same time the trajectories of fundamental social transformation.

Alexander offers an analysis of a way forward. Es'kia offers 'practice wisdom' on how such community development work might emerge, particularly exploring the significance of a particular kind of leadership. For Es'kia, leadership is crucial in catalysing the community development process. Effective leadership, holding to an ethos of community work, starts through building awareness. Es'kia offers the following signposts on this kind of work:

May I make the following remarks concerning the origins of community awareness:

1. Both in urban and rural areas there will be individuals who have an extra-ordinarily heightened and passionate concern for people: they identify problems, and a problem-solving cause is relatively easier to get across to one's audience than a mere brainwave that brings people together purely for the sake of fellowship. It is to the credit of our women that they have initiated self-help projects in their communities, and are still serving in positions of leadership and as the general membership of other establishments.
2. Initiators or pioneers of community projects display an instinct for priorities in any catalogue of social causes; they also display a restlessness born of the idea that fired their imagination in the first place.
3. They are knowledgeable about contacts with civics, educational agencies, funding establishments and mass media. I'm talking here mostly about natural leaders, among them teachers, nurses, doctors, lawyers, social workers, trade unionists, artisans and so on. Generally, people who are sensitized about human concerns because their occupations bring them close to people.
4. There is a need for us to form study groups in our communities that can be a resource for initiators of projects intended to serve them.
5. We should harness the energies of survival support groups, such as burial and benefit societies, so as to cultivate among them a social conscience and consciousness that go beyond basic survival. They could use the interest on their group savings for worthy causes.

Some of the characteristics identified in these signposts include 'heightened and passionate concern for people', 'an instinct for priorities', 'sensitized about human concerns ... [they are] close to the people', 'able to initiate "study groups" as a resource for energizing collective action', and 'harness[ing]' existing resources'. In many ways, Es'kia has put together the wisdom of a reconstructed approach to community development arguing essentially for: endogenous-led development (local people as leaders of change processes), assets and people-oriented approaches, and community-based education similar to contemporary REFLECT processes to catalyse thinking, reflection, and collective analysis.

Having provided these insights into how to raise community awareness as a crucial element of the community development process that takes decolonization seriously, Es'kia then uncannily tackles what can be considered a most contemporary challenge for community workers. In essence, he considers the question: what is the role of community development in relation to the state? Or, put another way, what is the relationship between self-help approaches and rights/advocacy approaches? In his own language, he discusses how:

> I am always deeply moved by rural and semi-rural village communities that collect money from their lean savings to build a school. By contrast I have heard urbanites, among them highly placed political activists who should know better, say they are not going to involve themselves with non-government organizations engaged in providing alternative and non-formal education. The reason they give is that this is a State responsibility.
>
> I do not deny this. But what if the State has abdicated its responsibility? What guarantees do we have that future governments will want to build most of the schools we want? Furthermore, I would not want to entrust a people's welfare and education wholly to State-run institutions. Let governments give community projects money, yes; but leave us to manage them. Governments have made a mess of things by monitoring welfare, health and educational services to stagnation. It is in these institutions where the educator, social worker and health worker can give community enterprise a human dimension. It is here that self-help initiatives can train us to speak for ourselves, and experiment with and develop our own ideas, instead of responding to government policy. It is here that we, as [Council for Black Education and Research], work towards the development of the whole personality, and not only skills and assimilation of social, political and economic theories. It is here that we create a learning environment of our own, where we have a fighting chance to promote the humanistic qualities of education ...
>
> A community is often what we make of it. It realizes its status as such through the alignment of individual and group interests, concerns, anxieties, aspirations and goals, into a unified purpose.

His perspective is clear, not requiring much comment. Like Alexander (2013), Es'kia does not see service delivery by the state as the best way forward (not to suggest that good service delivery is not crucial). Es'kia identifies the task of the community development practitioner to, while waiting and even pressuring the state to work with the community in delivering services (in this story, schools), get on with the task at hand. Communities are capable of creating, often with the help and support of outsiders (non-government or government), projects and programmes that need to be established. To only wait for the state can ensure that feelings of stagnation, anger, and frustration become debilitating. While waiting, Es'kia suggests that people and communities self-activate or, using some more contemporary thinking, co-create new initiatives. Furthermore, he argues that there are clear benefits in getting on with the tasks at hand – to do with building self-confidence, learning new skills, and creating something ourselves. In a sense, such practice embodies what Alexander calls 'building a new historical community' (2013: 186).

Conclusion

Es'kia has offered simple practical wisdom for community development practitioners that certainly adds to our call for a community development reconstructed in the light of the decolonial turn. He could go further, but we hope our book has managed to do that. Es'kia's wisdom often insists on subtle yet significant shifts in the way a community worker approaches people in a community – how they seed, yet wait for the original ideas to come from that seeding. It is a practice of deep respect and accompanying – one we have said several times is crucial for community development. The applied wisdom requires substantial patience – observing and understanding local dynamics to do with value-led leadership, who 'walks the talk', who is willing to take action despite the lack of state interest. In some way, this represents an Indigenous way of knowing – watching carefully as people learn humble yet potent practice. It is wisdom that sits alongside the well-read works of Biko and Fanon, which together call for a decolonizing of the mind as well as practical initiatives that bring material and structural change.

Written for another time, the ideas still resonate with contemporary contexts. Things have changed – yet also they have not. Drawing on other literature to illuminate or extend Es'kia's thinking provides a reflection on practice that we hope can help community development workers navigate this complex field.

References

Alexander N. 2013. *Thoughts on the New South Africa*. Auckland Park, South Africa: Jacana Press.
Freire P. 1970/2006. *Pedagogy of the Oppressed*. New York: Continuum.
Henderson P. and Thomas D. 2005. *Skills in Neighbourhood Work*, 3rd edn. London: Routledge.
Kelly, A. and Westoby, P. 2018. *Participatory Development Practice: Using Traditional and Contemporary Frameworks*. Rugby: Practical Action Publishing.
Lathouras A. 2010. Developmental community work – a method. In Ingamells A., Caniglia F., Lathouras A., Wiseman R. and Westoby P. (eds). *Community*

Development Stories, Method and Meaning. Illinois: Common Ground Publishers.

Mphahlele E. 1992. *Es'kia.* South Africa: Kwela Books in association with Stainbank and Associates.

Mphahlele E. 2002a. *Es'kia.* South Africa: Kwela Books in association with Stainbank and Associates.

Mphahlele E. 2002b. Community development for self-knowledge, self-realisation and collective empowerment – 1992. In Mphahlele, *Es'kia.* South Africa: Kwela Books in association with Stainbank and Associates.

Mphahlele E. 2002c. Education as community development – 1990. In Mphahlele, *Es'kia.* South Africa: Kwela Books in association with Stainbank and Associates.

Wheatley M. and Frieze D. 2011. *Walk Out Walk On: A Journey into Communities Daring to Live the Future Now.* San Francisco: Berrett-Koehler Publishers Inc.

Westoby P. and Kaplan A. 2013. Foregrounding practice – reaching for a responsive and ecological approach to community development: A conversational inquiry into the dialogical and developmental frameworks of community development. *Community Development Journal* 49(2):214–227.

CHAPTER 14
In conclusion: Promissory reflections

Abstract

Chapter 14 (the Conclusion), brings all the practices together from the stories in this book and interprets their meaning, more or less foregrounding our key framework for what makes community development work within post-structural, deconstructive, and decolonizing perspectives.

Keywords: reconstructed community development, the decolonial turn, effectiveness, the quality of practitioner, hauntology of justice, the shadow of effectiveness

At the heart of this book are ideas and stories. In our experience, stories invoke imagination, which, in turn, opens up new possibilities; therefore, part of the title is 'stories and possibilities'. In turn, ideas are crucial as disruptions into the 'taken for granted', the 'assumed', or the 'common sense' (usually a euphemism for non-thought or non-reflective thinking). Ideas require critical thinking – never seeing the world as is, but as new possibilities.

However, our ideas and dreams are not of *any kind* of ideas or possibilities, but reconstructed ones, engaged with the contemporary realities of South Africa, and linked to the more emancipatory traditions of community development. We have invited a reimagining of community development, understood as 'reconstructed' as a way of emphasizing the never-ending, ongoing need for this renewal.

This reconstruction, or reimagining, is a response to the endless need for renewal of community development haunted by the Derridean ghost of justice. This haunting and renewal require a dance with the originary concepts of community development's past, yet need to be ever responsive to the call of evolving and shifting context and new issues. We have suggested one of the big calls is the decolonial turn and our ideas of reconstructed community development have engaged foremost with this.

Although not only this, because as practitioners and scholars we are also committed to effectiveness. 'Does community development work?' sits as the shadowy question situated alongside that call to haunting justice. Two calls to renewal, then. Effective, yet responsive to the deep colonial injustices that still lie as fault lines across South African society, entangled in globalizing forces and fissures too.

Aligned to the post-structural perspective, there is certainly *no one way* of reconstructing community development, no obvious path that is responsive to the shadowy calls for effectiveness and haunting justice. However, we have offered some ideas which in this conclusion we call 'promissory reflections'. In doing this, our conclusion finishes with a sense of the work that is indicative of something to come, 'full of promise'. But before we get to this, let us recap some of the book.

What is it we have said?

We have hopefully backed up our proposition in the Introduction that the MIT professor had things very wrong. Of course, community development is effective. Not that it changes the world, yet it clearly changes the world *for some*. Not that it is effective in overcoming all forms of poverty or structural inequality nor historical wrong-doings, yet it is effective in producing some changes in people's lives. The key criteria for change are that people have more power in their lives, more options; that they become unstuck in whatever kind of poverty has been constraining their lives; that they have more control over the resources and decisions affecting their lives; that the marginalized gain some control over their own affairs to face an environment that is usually unsympathetic to their plight; and ultimately that those who've suffered colonial wrong-doings have had some justice – often linked to the return of stolen land. In this sense, community development has given people more freedom. This has happened to many people involved in community development as both a citizen-led and professional project.

We grounded this research in letting the reader know 'where we are coming from', making our positionality transparent. This kind of open, transparent statement of our values and histories is part of the call. We also offered some signposts for how we understand community development from a reading of traditions and frameworks informing South African community development. Chapters 5 and 6 offered a social reconstructionist tradition, as per Gandhi, Steve Biko, and Es'kia Mphahlele, as well as a framework emerging from a particular reading of Frantz Fanon's work.

Importantly, we also signposted a framework for thinking about effectiveness, evidence, and evaluation, and made the case for experimentalism and developmental evaluation. This aligns with a decolonizing approach, crossing the criteria line for working *with* communities, *from the inside-out*, but also *critically*, and from within an *ecological and systems approach*. The *critical* summons the community development practitioner to hold an emancipatory vision of society, a future-yet-to-come, to use a term of Jacques Derrida.

Part III provided stories and encounters in community development that met some of the decolonization criteria. As such, these stories:

- were committed to undoing at least one element of domination culture (class, race, gender, and so forth);

- were engaged with a tough substantive issue facing South Africa and linked to community development and decolonial aspirations, for example, education, land, housing;
- demonstrated use of engaged and critical thinking and reflection in the praxis;
- utilized community development orthodoxies as per relational practices and collective change;
- demonstrated worker/practitioner reflexivity in terms of their own positionality (who they are; how their histories shaped practice) and their everyday practices (they were able to do double-loop reflection, questioning assumptions) and accountabilities to Indigenous/First Nation peoples;
- recognized that people, groups, and communities had a right to their own story, their own definition of what was going (not what a community development practitioner or other decided was going on);
- were indicative of working with people from the 'inside-out' based on the particularity of a place and context; and
- suggest that there probably always will be tension between the actual development project and the ideal version of it. This tension between 'delivery' and 'democracy' is central in development work.

However, what has been learned, and what are the promissory reflections? For all the hard work implied in reconstructing community development, there is a great promise and dream that we hope is also alive within what we have written.

Promise (1) Reconstructed community development and the decolonial turn

A reconstructed community development within South Africa needs to be alive to the call of the decolonial turn. There are still many debates and discussions going on about what the decolonial turn means within all sorts of contexts, from higher education to race relations generally. The debate has hardly started within South African community development. We hope this book opens up that debate in a fresh way.

At risk of repeating ourselves, summing up the implications of a decolonizing perspective, again consider these words from Loretta Pyles (2019: 183):

> The famous quotation from Lilla Watson, (an Indigenous Australian artist, activist and academic), 'If you have come here to help me, you are wasting your time. But if you have come because your liberation is bound up with mine, then let us work together', points not only to all of our shared fates but to a disruption of the often-rigid line between helper and helped.

In this spirit, one of the key messages from our inquiry is that a reconstructed community development needs to remove any traces of helping and instead push towards the idea and practice of 'accompanying'. At the same time, this accompanying insists on a mutual process of decolonizing – the colonizer and the colonized – which cuts across the cleavages of race, gender, class, ability, sexuality, and so forth, but also the (constructed) professional and people divide. Each person's liberation is interlinked with the other, including practitioner and people being engaged. In turn, such an approach disrupts intervention based on externally imposed models, and instead – to risk repeating ourselves – means working with a group or community from the 'inside-out' – that is, working with people's energies, ideas, motivations, analyses. This implies a commitment to co-creation in all aspects of a developmental process. At the same time this so-called liberation is disruptive, particularly to settlers. It's not an easy reconciliation. A decolonizing approach to community development not only disrupts professional–people relations, but also settler/oppressed relations, and this disruption will often focus around issues of land. Disruption is part of the journey, and is really at the heart and soul of a reconstructed community development that is responsive to the decolonial turn.

Decolonizing community development then requires an ever-present reflexivity to be spectral, alongside the shadowy question of effectiveness and the haunting call for justice – hence a third spectre.

Promise (2) Reconstructed community development and effectiveness

This call to reconstruction, renewal, and the decolonial turn in no way implies a lack of rigour around questions and practices related to effectiveness. Practitioners do not want to waste their time, nor do people want their time wasted by practitioners. Nor should public money be wasted in any investment that cannot evidence some kind of transformational effect. However, we have dug into the complexities of thinking about, and therefore being able to see, 'effect'. We have offered some criteria for reimagining effect.

In doing this, we first suggested that often change, or 'development', is invisible, and this invisibility needs to at least be acknowledged. Sometimes we should know that we do not know. Looking for effect means bringing a rigour to *seeing* this invisibility, which is often subtle, otherwise we are at risk of imposing on a social situation something other than what is unfolding. In turn, this requires the community development practitioner to cultivate their capacity to 'see' and 'listen'. The measure of effectiveness is then substantially linked to the measure of a practitioner – what are their observational and listening muscles like?

Secondly, philosophically and practically, this means to understand effectiveness phenomenologically from the *inside-out*. As already mentioned, this implies working *with* what is going on within a person, group, community, or locality, supporting what it wants to become (not what 'we' want it/them to become). For example, in our experience, for many Indigenous groups this 'inside-out' means people want their stolen land back. What we are suggesting also aligns with more experimental and developmental evaluation approaches. Effectiveness, then, can be measured by whether a person, group, community, or locality has found its pathway for change, as defined by itself – or at least through dialogue or in disruptive engagement with others. In turn, again, the quality of the practitioner will be crucial, and discerned by the kinds of metaphors or gestures used in their practice. For example, linking to the earlier point, is the practitioner using the language or gesture of helping, accompanying, solidarity, and co-mutual liberation?

Thirdly, this inside-out approach to reconstructing community development does insist on a complexity-systems approach, recognizing the ever-changing realities of living social phenomena. Any reductionist approaches to thinking about effect and effectiveness will flounder in terms of the genuine transformation that comes from an accurate reading of the social phenomenon and fabric that community development work is a part of.

Fourthly, critically, from a decolonizing perspective, there are also signposts that enable practitioners to see the possibilities that are significant. Building on the previous discussions, the normative ultimate aim of community development is that people gain more power – the essence of empowerment. That is, to have more possibilities in their lives, to feel like they are not stuck, trapped. Clearly, community development implies a collective or social solidarity approach to enabling people to gain more power. Community development is also about responding to the various calls of justice, from the socio-political through to the epistemological-linguistic. And as has been said a few times, power in its materiality will often be linked to the quest to return stolen land.

As such, from a decolonizing perspective, this gaining of power, or more possibilities, can include many pathways – always 'from the inside-out', but often economic, social, cultural, and political. Those are the pathways of change that many individuals, groups, communities, and localities want to walk. And those pathways will be disruptive, painful, requiring relinquishing of power by many, returning what has been stolen. However, adding other wisdoms that come from the decolonial turn, this materiality needs to also include the spiritual, psychological, linguistic, and epistemological/philosophical. Fanon, Biko, and so many others have taught this. It is to imply the possibilities of bell hooks' pedagogy of healing, leading to wholeness as well as overcoming domination.

Promise (3) Reconstructed community development: The practitioner and practices

Clearly, the discussion implies a great deal for the everyday practices of the practitioner, and the quality of the practitioner as well. To have an 'idea' or 'intention' about what to do in supporting a decolonized reconstruction of community development is one thing. To be able to 'do it' – to practise it – is another. For the idea is not the action. From there our third promise: the actual practices, the 'doing with intention'.

Our key lesson is, firstly, that the quality of the community development practitioner is paramount. You cannot just teach people techniques or tools. We need practitioners with particular qualities. People 'smell' the qualities within a practitioner – authenticity or utility, helping or accompanying, kind or mean, alive to the work, or in a state of decay/dead, not caring. Decolonizing the work, reconstructing our community development, needs to focus on infusing practitioners with the kinds of qualities that are enlivening to communities.

Secondly, effective community development practitioners understand the 'practice' of community development – that is, they understand 'the idea' of what they are doing. They are not just ordering tasks or utilizing methods. They are ordering tasks and methods with a *clear understanding* of their intention and within a value framework. Clearly, as per our inquiry into a decolonial perspective, these intentions are to do with solidarity (which must, in turn, be decolonized), and collective social change. Community development practitioners need to be clear about their intention, the ideas behind what they do. We hope this book offers some clarity around possibilities, acknowledging the diversity of the post-structural (it is not a case of 'one-size-fits-all').

Thirdly, the effective community development practitioner is skilled in community development's *specific practices*. We have identified and discussed many through the stories of Part III, but also suggest they are mostly learned 'on the job', as tacit knowledge, and also through reflexive mentoring, reflection, education, and accountability. We again specifically add 'reflexive' in the cocktail of necessities, signposting the need to not only reflect on whether practitioners 'walk their talk' (espoused versus actual practice), but also the assumptions behind what is done. Without specific community development capabilities and reflexivity, practitioners are 'flying in the wind' or, perhaps more aptly, 'pissing in the wind'. We summarize some of these key practices as:

- Staged, place-based, and emergent.
- Historically oriented and rights-based.
- An ethos of accompanying, horizontal learning and structuring.
- Using action learning and action research.
- Not expert-led, but 'start anywhere, go everywhere' (where the people have energy and want to go).
- Nurturing cooperative leadership and ensuring a no-advice 'rule' from experts.
- Acknowledging anger, protest, and violence, and working 'with' communities in such hard spaces.
- Recognizing the emotional labour of community practitioners.
- Avoiding and navigating within neo-colonial state interventions, particularly when working within instrumental contexts.

Fourthly, effective community development needs community workers who are adept in other kinds of fields (or can at least work really closely with those who are): *generic fields,* such as communication, anthropology, and social analysis (to mention a few); and *technical fields,* depending on the sphere of work immersed in – housing, land reform, education, agriculture, and so forth. Each of the stories recounted in Part III illustrates the need to not only be proficient in practice, but also to attend to the field being engaged, which requires a historical analysis and policy and programme literacy.

Finally, clearly, the community development practitioner, even 'equipped' with practices, is working within a *complex context* that includes several other domains. These domains, which profoundly impact on questions of effectiveness, include: the actual 'community development programme', the organizational context hosting the programme; the donor agenda, assuming there is a donor; and, of course, the situational contexts of the place the work is occurring in, along with the policy context that shapes many things. Effectiveness inevitably is then linked to issues of congruency between each domain; for example, the logic within the community development programme and the way policy is either thwarting or supporting the goals of a programme or/and a practitioner. In many ways, this fifth element of what makes for effectiveness – congruency – is the hardest to predict.

In conclusion: The haunting of justice and the shadow of evidence

The ultimate purpose of the book is to disrupt development thinking in order to reimagine and reconstruct community development in South Africa. The book therefore foregrounds the historic legacy of community development work in South Africa, including contemporary traditions and frameworks, and also reinvigorates deliberation that should reach beyond the boundaries of academia to consider what it means to plan, implement, and evaluate the effectiveness of community development in South Africa. This planning, implementing, and evaluating are indicative of the shadowy question or quest for evidence and effectiveness. We hope that the question or quest has been problematized enough such that practitioners, managers, programmers, and policy-makers do not make simple mistakes, reducing community development to the banal – but not so problematized as to not offer practical possibilities.

It would be a given now that in South Africa there is a crucial need for the reconstruction of community development, not as a renewed technical project (responding to positivist pushes, managerial imperatives, and audit culture), but as an ethical intervention into the context of South Africa's historic polarization. Such polarization entangled with issues of land, race, class, gender, ethnicity, sexual orientation, intergenerationality, geography and space, disability, and histories, invites the haunting whisper of justice – ever present, never finished. Justice is always just beyond us, because we can do better. Therefore, always the call for renewal. To settle for what is, or to say 'we're doing okay, good enough', is to miss that ghost, the haunting.

Instead, community development intervention, haunted by the call to justice, aims to add to other methodologies of social change – political movements, mass social movements, legal challenges, public education – to shape a new, more inclusive, just, and socially cohesive society. For this reason, the search in answering the question, 'does community development work?' opens up an inquiry into the significance, meaning, and value of community development in South Africa in this historic moment. Perhaps the MIT professor should have said that community development should and could 'work' better.

This book will hopefully help towards a richer comprehension of South Africa's reality or, as Jonathan Jacobs says, 'matters of normative significance' (Jacobs, 2009: 27). Essentially, the richer comprehension of reality leads to the ability to distinguish what is interesting and what is genuinely important.

References

Jacobs J. 2009. The humanities and the recovery of the real world. *Arts and Humanities in Higher Education* 8:26–40.

Pyles L. 2019. Ethics and transformative community organising in the neoliberal U.S. context. In Banks S. and Westoby P. (eds). *Ethics, Equity and Community Development*. Bristol, UK: Policy Press.

Index

Page numbers in *italics* refer to figures and tables.

Abahlali/Abahlali base Mjondolo (shack-dwellers' association) 69–70, 97, 142–3, 146
Abalimi Home and Community Garden Initiative 107, 108–9, 111–13
   action learning-research approach 115
   key practices and emergent development model 113–14
   lessons for practice 114–15
   observational skills 115–16
   ongoing support, training, and organizational development 116–17
   social-solidarity economy 109–11
   summary and conclusion 117
accompanying the community 101–2
accountability
   political 140–1
   reciprocal 55
   upward 52–3, 175
action learning-research approach 115
activity stage of place-based practice 122–3
African National Congress (ANC) 17, 69, 72, 160
agora ('assembly'), concept of 97
agro-ecology 95–6, 100, 104
Alexander, N. 4, 5, 20, 187–8, 190
Alexander, P. 136, 139, 140
   et al. 19, 137, 140
   and Pfaffe, P. 69
Alinsky, S. 66, 69, 121
analytical frameworks 6–9
anger *see* community protests; service-delivery protests
anti-fracking movement 70
asset-based community development (ABCD) 80

backyard shacks 156
Bauman, Z. 20, 35, 97
Biko, S. 21–2, 42, 43, 70–1, 72–3, 145, 147, 187
Black Consciousness Movement 70–1, 72–3
Bokolo, M.M. 112–13
Bond, P. and Mottiar, S. 136, 144–5, 157
Botes, L. 19–20, 69, 137, 157, 158, 159
   et al. 69, 137
   Matebesi, S. and 98–9, 142
   and Van Rensburg, D. 53

Caldeira, T., Pires do Rio 155
Campfens, H. 65, 66
capital subsidy scheme/housing subsidies 159–60
Chambers, R. 81
citizen-led community development 148
civil servants 141
civil society 97
civil society organizations 100, 101
   see also non-governmental organizations (NGOs)
co-creation
   community–state relations 103–4
   developmental evaluation 56
co-design and implementation 57
co-motion 101–2
Coalition Against Water Privatisation and Johannesburg Water 70
colonial concepts/traces 8, 21
colonizing-decolonizing cycle 86–8
commodification of life, protests concerning 144–5
'community', role of 5
community awareness, origins of 188–9
Community Development Practitioner Programme 68, 81
   see also cooperative development
community development practitioners
   personal practice frameworks 88–9
   professional development stages 77–8
   professionalization 8, 24–5, 36
   qualities 197–9
Community Development Resource Association (CDRA) 78, 81–3
   Barefoot Guide 71
Community Development Worker Programme *see* cooperative development
community healing 40
community programme stage of place-based practice 125–6
community protests 135–6
   background and context 136–7
   consequences/effects of 145–6
   dynamics of 137–9
   failure of participatory governance 98–9
   reasons for 19–20, 98–9, 139–45, 157
   reconstructing community development 147–8

community protests (*contd.*)
   responsive local government 146–7
   summary and conclusion 148
Community Works Programme 68
community–state relations, co-creative approach of 103–4
community-based planning (CBP) 84–5, 172
community-led development 79–80
comparative framework 7
complexity perspective 56
conflict transformation framework 39–41
Connolly, L. 146, 147
consultation and participation, protests concerning 144
contractor-driven vs self-help housing 164
cooperative development 169
   background and context 169–70
   emotional labour 175–6
   participatory process 176–7
   relationship between community development and *172*
   'seeing like a state' and 170–1
   state-led community workers as catalysts 171–3
   statecraft dilemma 174–5
   summary and conclusions 178–80
cooperative leadership 129–30
criminalization of informal/marginalized communities 155

De Beer, F. and Swanepoel, H. 21
de Toqueville, A. 97
decolonial turn (Es'kia Mphahlele) 183
   reflection 184–90
   summary and conclusion 190
decolonial turn and reconstructed community development 195–6
decolonizing perspective 2–6, 7–8, 34–6, 194–5, 197
decolonizing practice framework 85–8
decolonizing work, time element in 128–9
deconstructive perspective 2–6, 31–4
deep vs shallow normativity 61–2
democracy, reflections on 184–5
democratizing local government 98–9
democratizing project 96–8
Denzin, N. 52, 53, 54–5
Department of Agriculture 94–5
Department of Cooperative Government and Traditional Affairs 68
Department of Rural Development and Land Reform 95
Department of Social Development *see* National Department of Social Development (NDSD)
Derrida, J. 2, 31, 32–4, 36, 44, 96, 193, 194
developmental evaluation 55–7
dialogical and relational inquiries, criteria for 41
Dlamini, J. 17, 69, 116

economic community development *see* Abalimi Home and Community Garden Initiative
education/training
   Abalimi Home and Community Garden Initiative 109, 113, 116–17
   and mentoring 35–6, 89
   and professionalization 24–5
   social learning tradition 67, 70–1
   see also Hantam Community Education Trust
effectiveness 47–8
   analytical framework 8–9
   challenge and approaches 49–50
   conventional evaluation 52–3
   criteria for thinking about 'effect' 57
   experimentalism and evaluation 54–7
   organizational and personal practice frameworks 89
   phenomenological understanding of 50–1
   and reconstructed community development 196–7
   and uncertainty 51–2
emotional labour 175–6
Escobar, A. 29, 30–1
Es'kia see decolonial turn (Es'kia Mphahlele)
essentializing vs traditions 62
Esteva, G. 101–2
evidence
   conventional evaluation of effectiveness and 52–3
   politics of 9, 53–4
   shadow of 199–200
experimentalism 54–5
experts, no-advice 'rule' from 129–30

failure
   and emotional labour 175–6
   and learning process 53
Fanon, F. 7, 72–3, 78, 79, 145, 147
   decolonizing practice framework 85–8
farming *see* Abalimi Home and Community Garden Initiative; Hantam Community Education Trust; Southern Cape Land Committee (SCLC)
Federation of Urban Poor (FEDUP) 70
feedback mechanisms 56
financial and economic hardship, protests concerning 143–4
foetal alcohol syndrome 120–1, 127
food security 108–9, 110, 111
frameworks
   analytical 6–9
   conflict transformation 39–41
   double story 17–20, 163
   see also practice frameworks
Freire, P. 3, 35, 42, 67, 70–1, 83, 86, 101, 103, 121, 128, 131–2, 186
'full-loaf' interview 143

Gandhi 21, 63–4, 71–2, 145, 147, 148
garden centres 109, 112–13
gendered perspective on housing 162
Gini coefficient 18, 142
Goebel, A. 136, 137, 143
Grail Centre 83, 84
'Grootboom' case 160–2
guidelines in traditions 64–5

Habermas, J. 53
Habib, A. 140, 148
Hammersley, M. 52
Hantam Community Education Trust 119, 120–1
  crisis of education 119–20
  initiatives 126–8
  lessons for practice 128–31
  place-based practice 121
  stages of place-based practice 122–6
  summary and conclusion 131–2
hauntology of justice 2, 32, 33, 36, 96, 193, 194, 199–200
Heese, K. 144
hooks, b. 3, 35–6, 42, 43
Hope, A. and Timmel, S. 70–1, 83–4
horizonal learning 102
hospitality education programme 127
housing *see* informal housing and settlements
Huchzermeyer, M. 153, 155
Human Development Index (HDI) 18
human dignity, protests concerning 141–2
Human Rights Commission 3, 34

ideas and ideals, reflection on 184–7
Ife, J. 77, 88
impact effectiveness, ideology of 51–2
inequality 18, 141–2
informal housing and settlements 153–4
  gendered perspective 162
  negotiated and participatory urban renewal 162–3
  perception of 154–5
  post-1991 policies 159–60, *161*
  pre-1991 policies 157–9
  reality of 156–7
  residents' surveys 163–4
  right to decent housing 160–1
  self-help vs contractor-driven housing 164
  social movement and protests 69–70, 139, 142–3, 146, 157
  summary and conclusion 164–6
Ingamells, A.
  and Johnson, P. 54–5
  Westoby, P. and 88, 89
'inside-out' approach 41, 55, 57, 196–7
institutionalist/instrumentalist approaches *see* technical/institutionalist approaches
International Association of Community Development 37

Jay, I. and Bowen, P. 164, 165
Jullien, F. 50–1

Kaplan, A. 30, 37, 50, 83, 115
  Westoby, P. and 38, 89, 186
Kelly, A. and Westoby, P. 5, 176, 185, 186
Khanya 84–5, 100
Khoi-San 3, 34

land issue 3
  see also Southern Cape Land Committee (SCLC)
leadership 188
  cooperative 129–30
Levi, Y. 171, 178, 179, 180
local government
  democratizing 98–9
  responsive 146–7
low-cost housing *see* informal housing and settlements
Luthuli, A. 72

McLean, K. and Chenwi, L. 162
McMichael, P. 20, 29, 30–1, 178
Macy, J. and Brown, M.Y. 111, 115
Mandela, N. 72, 136
marginalized people 20–1, 109, 155
  see also community protests
Matebesi, S. 136, 139, 140, 142–3, 146
  and Botes, L. 98–9, 142
Max-Neef, M. 5, 39
Mbeki, T. 68
mentoring 35–6, 89
methodology 9–10
Mhkize, Z. 146, 147
micro-macro articulation 5, 20–1, 85
Millennium Development Goals 154
Motlanthe Report (2017) 18–19
Movement for Community-Led Development (MCLD) 79–80
Mpahlele, E. 72
  see also decolonial turn (Es'kia Mpahlele)
multidisciplinary approach 7
Municipal IQ 136, *138*, 143–4

National Community Development Programme 22, 23, 68
National Department of Social Development (NDSD) 22, 23, 24–5, 68, 81
National Housing Code (2009) 159–60
National Income Dynamics Study 18
'native nostalia' 17, 69, 116
Ndabankulo, M. 143
Nelson Mandela Foundation 18–19, 20
neo-colonial intervention, state-led community development as 178–9
networks/networking 102–3, 114
no-advice 'rule' 129–30

non-governmental organizations (NGOs) 23–4, 66, 68–9, 80, 81–2
  see also civil society organizations
non-profit organizations (NPOs) 111–12, 116–17
Ntema, J. et al. 163–4, 165

observational skills 115–16
OLIVE 81–2
organic nature of community work 185

participation, protests concerning 144
participatory governance 98–9, 103, 146–7
participatory process, cooperatives and state-led community workers/practitioners 176–7
participatory urban renewal 162–3
Patton, M. 55, 56
People's Garden Centres 109, 112–13
people's movement stage of place-based practice 126
people's organizations stage of place-based practice 124–5
personal practice frameworks 88–9
perspectives 2–6, 29–36
  conflict transformation framework 39–41
  criteria for dialogical and relational inquiries 41
  positionality 41–3
  poverties 39
  re-orienting practice 36–9
  and responses 43–4
Peters, P. 95
phenomenological understanding of effectiveness 50–1
place-based development 23, 121
  stages 121–6
political practice *see* Southern Cape Land Committee (SCLC)
political trust and accountability, protests concerning 140–1
politics of evidence 9, 53–4
positionality 8, 41–3, 194
post-structural perspective 2–6, 29–31
Poteete, A. et al. 176, 177–8
poverties 39
poverty
  alleviation and food security 108, 110
  and inequality 18, 141–2
  urban 115, 116
  see also marginalized people
practical wisdom 88, 183, 190
practice frameworks 77–9
  assemblage of possibilities 81–5
  'big four' 79–81
  decolonizing practice 85–8
  personal practice 88–9
practices and practitioners 197–9
private-sector projects 23–4
professional development stages 77–8

professionalization 8, 24–5, 36
project stage of place-based practice 123–4
promissory reflections 193–200
Pyles, L. 36

qualitative questions 30
qualities of practitioners 197–9

Ramaphosa, C. 39, 136–7, 146
re-orienting practice 36–9
reconstructed community development 193–4
  and community protests 147–8
  and decolonial turn 195–6
  and effectiveness 196–7
  practitioners and practices 197–9
REFLECT approach 71
reflective practice 53, 56, 89
relational and dialogical inquiries, criteria for 41
relational work 37–9, 129
  '0-1-3' method of cooperative leadership 129–30
resilience, suffering and (double story) 17, 163
responsive local government 146–7
'right to the city' 153, 155, 165, 166
rights-based community development 80, 100
  see also informal housing and settlements
rural community organization and development 187
Rural Development Strategy 68

Schumacher, E.F. 63–4, 110
Scott, J. 170, 178
Second Barefoot Collective 69–70
'seeing like a state' 170–1
  see also cooperative development
seeing and making sense of community development 6–7
self-help
  and rights/advocacy approaches 189–90
  vs contractor-driven housing 164
service-delivery approaches
  co-creation 103–4
  vs community development approaches 37–8, 189–90
service-delivery protests 69, 108, 142–3, 144–5
shack dwellers
  social movement and protests 69–70, 139, 142–3, 146, 157
  see also informal housing and settlements
shallow vs deep normativity 61–2
Small Enterprise Development Agency (SEDA) 172
'social accounting'/'social auditing' 98
social enterprise-led projects 23–4
social guidance tradition 66, 67–9

social housing *see* informal housing and settlements
'social innovation' 55
social learning tradition 67, 70–1
social mobilization/movements
  Southern Cape Land Committee 100
  tradition 66, 69–70
social reconstruction tradition 71–3
  see also traditions
social-solidarity economy 109–11
South Africa
  approach to social change 20–1
  current policy context 22
  current programme context 22–3
  current state of play 21–2
  double story framework 17–20, 163
  location map of stories and case studies *92*
  training and professionalization context 24–5
South African Land Act (1913) 86
Southern Cape Land Committee (SCLC) 93–4
  aims 99–101
  democratizing local government 98–9
  democratizing project 96–8
  land issue 94–6
  practices 101–4
  summary and conclusion 104
'start anywhere, go everywhere' 130–1
state capture/captured state 39
  vs development state 136, 146
state-employed community workers *see* cooperative development
state-led community development 22–3, 68, 144, 189–90
  social guidance traditions 66, 67–9
  see also cooperative development; informal housing and settlements
statecraft dilemma and cooperatives 174–5
structuring the work 102–3
Stubbs, A. 73
suffering and resilience (double story) 17, 163
Sustainable Development Goals 110, 154, 163
sustainable livelihoods approach (SLA) 81, 84–5
'systems change' 55
systems thinking 56

technical/institutionalist approaches 38, 53, 121
  social guidance tradition 66, 67–9

statecraft dilemma 174–5
theories *see* perspectives
time element in decolonizing work 128–9
Timmel, S. 70–1, 83–4
traditions
  essentializing vs 62
  gifts of 63–5
  intellectually rooted 65–7
  shallow vs deep normativity 61–2
  types 66–71
  social reconstruction 71–3
training *see* education/training
Training for Transformation (TfT): critical framework 83–4
Tuck, E. and Yang, K.W. 3, 7–8, 35–6
Turner, J. 153, 154, 155

unemployment 18, 108, 143–4
urban community organization and development 186–7
urban farming 109, 112–13, 116–17
urban poverty 115, 116
urban slums *see* informal housing and settlements

van der Watt, P. 7, 19, 50, 87–8
violent protests 99, 139, 147–8
vision 4–5, 20–1
  and energy 184, 185, 186
  and possibilities 5–6

Watson, L. 36
Westoby, P.
  and Botes, L. 148
  and Ingamells, A. 88, 89
  and Kaplan, A. 38, 89, 186
  Kelly, A. and 5, 176, 185, 186
  and Lyons, K. 126
Wheatley, M. and Freize, D. 131, 185
women
  farmers/gardeners 109, 111–13
  female-headed households 110
  Hantam Community Education Trust 120, 126
  right to housing 162
'wounded societies in transition' 87–8

Žižek, S. 147–8
Zuma, J. 68, 136, 146